Literacy and Society

Center for Research in the Humanities

Copenhagen University

Literacy and Society

Edited by
Karen Schousboe and Mogens Trolle Larsen

Akademisk Forlag
1989

Literacy and Society

Edited by Karen Schousboe and Mogens Trolle Larsen

Akademisk Forlag
POB 54
1002 Copenhagen K
Denmark

Cover illustration by Erik Thorsen
Cover layout: Uffe Rosenfeldt and Bente Sivertsen
Printed by AiO Tryk, Odense

Acknowledgement: Jonathan Parry's article *The Brahminical Tradition and the Technology of the Intellect* (pp. 39-71) has previously been published as *The Text in Context* in: *Reason and Morality*, edited by J. Overing, Tavistock Publications.

ISBN 87-500-2784-0

Center for Research in the Humanities
Copenhagen University
Njalsgade 80
DK 2300 Copenhagen S
Denmark

Printed in Denmark 1989

Contents

Introduction

Mogens Trolle Larsen

Three names reappear in several of the papers in this volume: Jack Goody, Eric A. Havelock and Walter J. Ong, prolific writers who in a series of books and articles have expressed radical and highly influential opinions on the question of the importance of the shifts and changes in communication technology in world history. Although they come to these problems from different disciplines and cannot be said to represent any kind of united front, they do agree on the crucial point that "the technology of the intellect" explains or even causes fundamental historical transformations. Most of the contributors to this book are highly critical of at least the larger claims put forward by these authors; in fact, the conferences which formed the background for this book were convened by the Centre for Comparative Cultural Studies at Copenhagen university, precisely with the aim of contributing to a critical and searching appraisal of what may be called a technological explanatory model based on communication systems. The present book must therefore be seen as an attempt to introduce new and relevant arguments and empirical study into the on-going debate.

It is surely easily understandable that the question of the effects of changes in communication technologies should be of such burning interest in the age which is itself in the throes of a major "information revolution". In a situation where the general feeling seems to be that technological "progress" or "development" is rushing ahead like an express train into the night, propelled by its own internal logic and changing the world and our way of perceiving the world with irresistible force, it is obviously of vital interest to study other similar or parallel historical moments when new techniques for storing and disseminating knowledge, ideas and information were introduced; the most important of these moments appear to be marked by the invention of writing in ancient societies such as Mesopotamia and Egypt, the introduction of the full alphabet in Greece, and the invention of

7

the printing press in Europe. An understanding of the dynamics in these situations may give us a better point of departure for making decisions about our own complex world.

Each of these technological breakthroughs have been linked to major changes in a whole range of fundamental intellectual, socio-economic and political structures: "major steps" in the development of what we call science "followed" the introduction of writing in Babylonia, the alphabet in Greece, and printing in Western Europe according to Goody (1977: 51); the introduction of writing is "the single firm criterion for distinguishing the city, the nucleus of civilization, from other types of early settlements" (Sjoberg 1960, 33), just as it distinguishes history from prehistory and for some scholars civilized from non-civilized (Gelb 1963, 222); Lévi-Strauss has suggested that we should speak of people "without writing" rather than of "primitive" societies, thus introducing literacy as the meaningful distinction (1979, 15-16; see Ong 1982, 174-175); finally, to illustrate the essential role given to communication technology as an historical factor, Ong's evaluation of how diversified and vast the particular effects of the introduction of the printing press in Europe have been (in reference to Eisenstein 1979):

> Eisenstein spells out in detail how print made the Italian Renaissance a permanent European Renaissance, how it implemented the Protestant Reformation and reoriented Catholic religious practice, how it affected the development of modern capitalism, implemented western European exploration of the globe, changed family life and politics, diffused knowledge as never before, made universal literacy a serious objective, made possible the rise of modern sciences, and otherwise altered social and intellectual life (Ong 1982, 117-118).

Even though it must be accepted that Ong certainly does not wish to make writing or print the sole cause of all changes such as these, it is hard to avoid the conclusion that the terminology often tends towards the slippery, with words and phrases such as "followed", "implemented", "made possible", "conditioned" or even "caused", "altered" or "made".

A large part of the discussion has accordingly been oriented towards an evaluation of the question whether communication technology should be viewed as a "prime mover" or "sufficient cause" in historical developments, but it seems in fact that the discussion could meaningfully move on to more subtly defined problems. The seminal books by MacLuhan overstated positions which might have been more profitably formulated, and many of the other early statements, for instance by Goody, have been revised and reformulated by their authors, so that there is a real danger that the discussion now concerns views which are upheld by nobody - or at least no longer by their first authors. Eisenstein has tried to distance herself from a clearly technological mode of explanation and has pointed out that the title of her book describes printing as "an" agent rather than "the" agent, but on the other hand

> one cannot treat printing as just one among many elements in a complex causal nexus, for the communications shift transformed the nature of the causal nexus itself. It is of special historical significance because it produced fundamental alterations in prevailing patterns of continuity and change (Eisenstein 1983: 273).

As pointed out by Maurice Bloch later in this volume (9), when Goody edited a group of papers (Goody 1968) by anthropologists dealing with the role of literacy in traditional societies and prefaced it with his joint article with Ian Watt entitled "The consequences of literacy", it was remarkable that practically all the other contributions distanced themselves from the main conclusions drawn by Goody and Watt. Goody himself has since then suggested that a more correct title for the paper in question would have been "the *implications* of literacy" (1986, 12).[1]

Eric Havelock, on the other hand, remains convinced that such differences as may be described by contrasting Greece with Near Eastern societies are to be explained to a large extent as due to "a fact of technology", namely the invention of the Greek alphabet (cf. discussion in chapter 5).

In a recent discussion the British Anthropologist Brian Street attempts to draw up a characterization of two opposing models which in his view operate as the basis for much of this debate. The technological one, called "the autonomous model" of literacy

---

[1]See Goody 1986, 184where he speaks of the "effects" of the written tradition "as trends rather than as necessities".

assumes a single direction in which literacy development can be traced, and associates it with 'progress', 'civilisation', individual liberty and social mobility. It attempts to distinguish literacy from schooling. It isolates literacy as an independent variable and then claims to be able to study its consequences. These consequences are classically represented in terms of economic 'take off' or in terms of cognitive skills (Street 1984, 2).

To this he opposes an "ideological model" which is characterised by the basic assumption that "the meaning of literacy depends upon the social institutions in which it is embedded", that literacy cannot be treated separate from the forms in which it is known to us and which already have political and ideological significance, that the teaching of reading and writing depends upon a whole set of socio-economic and political structures etc. (Ibid., 8; see also Street 1987).

These models represent a special reading of the discussion which has been conducted by several scholars, who may not in fact feel at home in any of them. Brian Street has attacked especially Goody and claimed his right to deal with all his many statements, even though he recognizes that the development of Goody's thought on the subject has led to certain changes in the basic claims; however, this has been done without Goody making his changed position explicit, says Street, and he has not confronted basic contradictions in his own work (Street 1984, 9).

Street's ideological model is also open to criticism, however; Masao Miyoshi has pointed out that "the recognition of the co-existence of orality and literacy in a given society does not mean that oral and literate activities are identical either in operation or in consequence", and that by denying or underplaying the distinction between orality and literacy, Street "collapses the social variables into a single model of oral and literate mix, thereby licensing clearly against his intent the universalist reading of cultures and societies" (Miyoshi 1988, 17).

The proper balance in our evaluation of such high-level questions must be based on a series of informed analyses which scrutinize the empirical evidence in the light of the theoretical discussion. The present book provides a number of such investigations.

Goody's ideas, presented in detail in *The Domestication of the Savage Mind* from 1977, which suggested links between literacy and cognitive structures, referring to the "liberating effects" of writing, is analysed by Maurice Bloch on the basis of material from Madagascar and from modern Japan; a basic critique arising from this is that Goody's model is, if not outright Eurocentric, then at least "culturally specific" and accordingly cannot be accepted as a universalist thesis. Knowledge, speech and writing are patterned differently in the three cognitive systems dealt with by Bloch: Europe, Madagascar and Japan, and this leads to the conclusion that we simply do not have the ground rules laid for the kind of analysis attempted by Goody.

The detailed discussion of Indian literacy and religion provided by Parry relates specifically to the claim that literacy (or, in the similar argument developed by Eisenstein: printing) "enabled" or "led to" a transformation from what Parry refers to as "cognitive traditionalism" to "cognitive modernism"; if the point is that literacy *must* have the "liberating effects" suggested *unless* socio-economic conditions inhibit such a development, then the argument must be rejected: literacy may, according to Parry, be seen as no more than a passive prerequisite for such a transformation.

The claim that Goody's thesis is "culture specific" obviously connects it with the traditional historical view of Greece as the birthplace of western rationality, so it is interesting that Øivind Andersen's analysis of the early Greek material leads to the conclusion that "the liberating effects of writing have been rather overrated". He emphasizes the importance of the interrelationship between oral and written.

Eyre and Baines conclude after their detailed investigation of ancient Egyptian schooling and reading traditions that there are no easy or neat answers to be drawn from their analysis; on the other hand, the immensely rich Egyptian literary material provides theoretically relevant exemplifications of the complexities in the relationship between speech and writing, oral and literate traditions, over a long span of time. The three-thousand-year cuneiform tradition from Mesopotamia points to the same type of conclusion. Parry's rejection of the idea that the contrast between literate and oral should explain the transformation from traditionalism to modernism is paralleled by the refutation of the argument suggested by Havelock that the difference between Greece and the ancient Near East may be explained by the contrast between alphabet and a mixed logographic/syllabic system of writing. Neither literacy as such nor alphabetic literacy specifically can be seen as full or adequate explanatory frameworks.

Schousboe, in her analysis of the shifting literate practices in daily life in medieval Denmark, links these to socio-economic changes in demographic and landholding patterns, a historical development where writing clearly played a significant, although not a determining part.

Clanchy, finally, presents an eloquent argument in support of locating medieval writing practices in their religious and social context, rather than imposing on them our own ideas of the role and function of literacy. Such a procedure will allow us to understand the changes and the development involved in the adoption of literate practices, and in the relationship between a manuscript tradition and one based on print.

These papers, then, are concerned with our understanding of the use of literacy in other cultural and historical settings, whereas the three last papers have different foci. Holbek lets us take the viewpoint of the illiterate who knew about writing "from the outside" so to speak, and who regarded it as a magical mystery giving unknown powers. Harbsmeier provides another perspective by concentrating on the way in which writing has affected the western view of "the others". The change from "restricted" to "full" literacy in Europe of the 18th century reinforced the discrimination and exploitation already established by colonialism, leading to the discovery of "orality" as the absence of literacy, and literacy itself became power and repression, "a substitute for the sword".

Finally, and leading us to yet another avenue towards a better understanding of literacy, Jesper Svenbro guides us through the very different mental universe of early Greece to illuminate the "local" interpretation of the meaning of writing by way of a detailed analysis of the funerary statue of a young girl, Phrasikleia, and the inscription which belongs together with it. Svenbro's analysis shows how inscription and statue, in conjunction with the meaning of the girl's name, provide a kind of writing which lets the stone speak for ever a message which miraculously can still be understood in all its subtlety.

Bibliography

Eisenstein, Elizabeth 1979   *The Printing Press as an Agent of Change: Communications and Cultural Transformations in Early-Modern Europe*, vols 1-2. New York
Eisenstein, Elizabeth 1983   *The Printing Revolution in Early-Modern Europe*. Cambridge
Gelb, I.J. 1963   *A Study of Writing*. Chicago
Goody, Jack (ed.) 1968   *Literacy in Traditional Societies*. Cambridge
Goody, Jack 1977   *The Domestication of the Savage Mind*. Cambridge
Goody, Jack 1986   *The Logic of Writing and the Organization of Society*. Cambridge
Lévi-Strauss, C. 1979   *Myth and Meaning*. New York
Miyoshi, Masao 1988   The "Great Divide" Once Again: Problematics of the Novel and the Third World. *Culture & History* 3, Copenhagen, 7-22
Ong, Walter J. 1982   *Orality and Literacy. The Technologizing of the Word*. London and New York
Sjoberg, Gideon 1960   *The Preindustrial City. Past and Present*. New York
Street, Brian 1984   *Literacy in Theory and Practice* . Cambridge
Street, Brian 1987   Orality and Literacy as Ideological Constructions: some problems in cross-cultural studies. *Culture & History* 2, Copenhagen, 7-30

Literacy and Enlightenment

Maurice Bloch

In 1968 J. Goody edited a book, which has justly continued to exercise a strong influence on anthropological thought, called *Literacy and Traditional Society*. (Goody 1968). Its first chapter was a republication of a joint article by J. Goody and I. Watt on the implication of literacy. With some modification the argument of this article was reproduced in a later book which ranged much more widely, *The Domestication of the Savage Mind* (Goody 1977).

The original book was itself rather problematic. The problem was that apart from the Goody and Watt chapter all the articles in the book presented evidence which contradicted the central thesis of Goody and Watt, that literacy had brought about a sharp divide in the nature of knowledge in society. The problem was partly acknowledged by Goody who in his introduction elaborated the notion of 'restricted literacy' in order to explain cases of cultures which possessed writing but had not been transformed in the way predicted by Goody. However, as pointed out by Parry in this volume, the significance of limited literacy had largely disappeared by the time the publication of *The Domestication of the Savage Mind*.

Goody's argument seems to me in retrospect to have been extremely valuable in that it raised much useful discussion. Goody was voicing in a particular way a theory which is accepted implicitly by many social thinkers and which therefore needs examining critically.

I want to argue here, however, that Goody is not justified in the theory he puts forward. This not only because the historical evidence does not bear him out, as a variety of recent studies suggest, but because buried in his argument is an unacceptable view of knowledge and communication. This limitation has great significance in that it reveals some of the intellectual roots of anthropology which explain why an anthropologist such as Goody might look at the matter in the way Goody has done.

If we strip Goody's argument to its bare minimum it goes something like the following:

In pre-literate societies knowledge is buried in social relations. The value of what is said is not evaluated in terms of its truth but in terms of who says it. As a result criticism on the basis of reason or information is impossible without there being an attempt at revolt. Even when a revolt occurs criticism does not lead to an advance in knowledge but it leads simply to a change in political personnel. For example, knowledge about genealogies is endlessly moulded by the requirements of the changing present. Here Goody turns for support to classical functionalist studies of folk history. (Bohannan 1952, Cunnison 1959). Without genuine criticism the basis of authority can not be challenged, time can not be appreciated as lineal and above all science, separate from the web of social relations in which it was produced, cannot emerge and develop.

Once literacy is introduced everything changes dramatically. It is then possible to challenge authorised knowledge by using documents from the past. Under literacy in the Tiv lineage, so well observed by Laura Bohannan, at the moment when the Tiv elder began to recite an altered genealogy because of different politico economic circumstances, a voice from the back of the crowd would be heard saying "Wait a minute. This is quite inaccurate. What you said seven years ago was quite different. It is all written here in my notes." All at once the idea of scientific criticism would be there and also as a result of this challenge to obscurantist authority, democracy would be on its way. This is because in Goody's argument democracy is also seen as a result of writing. Literacy enables knowledge to be politically liberating. Indeed according to Goody it was as a result of their alphabet that the Greeks discovered democratic government.

Having reached this point in his argument Goody introduces a qualification to the effect literacy is said to have on the political. The reason why literate peoples, other than the Greeks, had not become true democrats was due to the fact that these people were unfortunately stuck with inferior types of writing. A prime example of these insufficient writing systems was ideograms. This limitation of ideograms, according to Goody, explained why democracy did not develop in countries such as China and Japan, though Gough in *Literacy and Traditional Society* casts doubt on Goody's interpretation of what happened in China.

The contrast which Goody draws sharply on either side of the "great divide" brought about by literacy echoes the theoretical changes which occurred in British anthropology at the time when structural functionalism was coming under attack. One central tenet of this is that knowledge is moulded by social conditions. This view, however, was being challenged from two different directions. On the one hand, the structuralism of Levi-Strauss stressed how the intellectual character of knowledge gave it a specificity which meant that it could not be reduced to the mirroring of the politico-economic. On the other hand, the growing concern in anthropology with complex, large-scale, literate societies made the view that knowledge could be explained purely in terms of the social structure of the unit studied by one fieldworker, clearly implausible. For example, how could one account for Hinduism in central India purely in terms of what was happening in that particular village?

Goody's work on literacy was principally a response to this second challenge from someone who had, up to then, been fairly closely associated with structural functionalism. Goody's solution to the problem posed by complex societies is simple. He argues that for pre-literate society knowledge is indeed moulded by the politico-economic context while this was not any more so for the more complex societies towards which his colleagues and himself were turning their attention. As a result it had to follow that some magic ingredient had brought about a change in the two different kinds of societies. A change so fundamental that different types of theories were appropriate for the two types. This magic factor was literacy.

In other words the general argument seems to be this: before literacy functionalist constraints explain knowledge but afterwards it is something which looks like logical positivism. The Chinese and Japanese were partly caught in the traps of functionalism by their unsatisfactory writing system.

In order to argue against Goody's thesis I turn in this chapter to two illustrative examples. One is from Madagascar and shows that literacy of itself does not free knowledge from the kind of politico-economic constraints which the structural functionalists had shown existed. The other is from Japan and it serves to show that the way Goody conceptualises the relationship between knowledge and writing is both ethnocentric and misleading. Implicitly I contrast these two examples with what I believe is the situation in Modern Europe.

Madagascar

In 1984, I attended an international colloquium on the history of the East coast of Madagascar which took place in Tamatave or Taomasina to give it its Malagasy name. The participants consisted for the most part of Malagasy historians and students mainly from the excellent history faculty of Tananarive. There were also a number of foreign scholars, including myself. Apart from these standard attenders of academic gatherings there were a few less predictable contributors. These were people who are best described as local worthies. They included local administrators, from the town, the police and the army, the heads of large business or development agencies who were appropriately given a rough ride when they described their various activities, and most prominently of all a local intellectual and politician, Arthur Besy.

Besy has had a significant role in the history of Madagascar this century. He was prominent in the resistance to the French occupation of the country and had been imprisoned a number of times. Since independence he has represented his country abroad notably as ambassador in Algiers, where he was able to re-form his earlier contacts with anti-colonial movements from the whole world and to recollect his hectic life in relative tranquillity. As a result his ever present scholarly bent developed and he became engaged in writing history, especially the history of his natal region of Tamatave. At the conference he presented the University of Tananarive with a typescript which must have been approaching a thousand pages dealing with the history of the area. His contribution to the conference also dealt with this subject. More specifically with the origin of the name Taomasina or Tamatave.

This presentation contrasted sharply with that of the professional historians. We had all been allocated 15 minutes to talk to our paper, although nearly everybody exceeded their time. Besy, however, went on for nearly two hours. While all the historical papers were delivered in French, as is usually done in Malagasy universities, and as was done in this case partly out of politeness to the non-Malagasy speakers present, Besy insisted in speaking in a most eloquent and traditional Malagasy. Totally wedded to this use of Malagasy was his style, that of traditional Malagasy oratory: following its formal structure, which has been discussed by a number of writers, stuffed full of proverbs and scriptural illustrations, redolent with repetitions, certain passages recurring again and again rather like the chorus in a popular song. As a result, if the content of his paper had been presented in a more Cartesian manner it would probably have not taken 15 minutes to speak. As academic history its content was unconvincing to Besy's university compatriots, whose work resembles the proverbial tiny stream flowing between mountainous banks of footnotes.

Yet, these academic historians listened respectfully, if not perhaps very attentively, to this grand oratorical performance. They recognised that this was a different kind of thing to what they did themselves and, that its value too, was to be respected.

Most interestingly Besy was also aware of this difference and commented on it at various points of the conference. He clearly felt that in spite of his polite reception, the whole of the proceeding were an attack on the kind of literary activity which had occupied his life in recent years, and so he defended himself. His justifications were basically in terms of who he was. His heroic and courageous life, his age, the patience with which he had learned from elders long ago, the long years of study, of reading, of writing his manuscripts, the famous people he had known, the honour and respect he had been shown as a diplomat around the world, at the United Nations and elsewhere, all these validated his historical contribution. Indeed he delicately implied that young upstarts like the people from the university or myself, although we were doing something which he could understand had its own rationale and rigour, and which had a place within its own limited and rather unimportant context, was not really history. Our futile lives, our age and our limited experience meant that we did not have the right to speak or *write* history.

Besy was using a distinction between two kind of language uses which is fundamental to Merina culture. On the one hand there is ordinary talk which is marked by an informal style and on the other there is the formal style of oratory, which is used for important matters especially history (Keenan 1975). The style of oratory, *kabary* is the mark of a person in authority, typically an elder. Besy saw his contribution to the conference in these terms.

The two kinds of language which the Merina distinguish reflects two aspects of the person. At birth a person is believed to consist entirely of wet perishable elements which are linked to individuality. However, as a person grows older a dry element begins to develop in them. This dry element is the ancestral element which will gradually take over, so that ultimately, some time after death, the person will have lost all wet individuality and will be entirely dry ancestor. Indeed I now look on Merina descent very much as a form of possession, (Bloch 1985: 73) in which the ancestral gradually colonises internally the living, the ancestral is a kind of dry coral which in the end will be all that remains of people when they are finally placed in the ancestral tomb. This process of possession is evidenced in elders in part by their ability to speak in a formal oratorical manner, it shows that they have the ancestral inside them since this type of oratory is considered the words of the ancestors. Ordinary talk is merely the wet speaking, the perishable individual which there is no point in preserving.

The process of internal drying is not merely the product of maturation, for the Merina it is the product of blessing. Blessing, for the Merina, occurs when the elders who are by definition close to the ancestors transmit their contact in a number of ways. This contact through blessing therefore makes you become an ancestor and so the descent group persists. Blessing creates descendants. Now, *Kabary* is seen as a form of blessing. As a result hearing such speech, like receiving other forms of blessing, transforms you permanently, it is what causes the ancestral coral to grow inside the descendants/hearers, thus it makes of the hearers descendants of the speakers.

For Besy writing or speaking history was the sign that he was close to the ancestors that he was speaking for them. He had the right to use this style and to represent them because in the past and throughout his life he had received the blessing of the ancestors in a number of forms, prominent among which would be hearing *Kabary* from elders. This had made him to grow inwardly into a more ancestral being, and soon he would be all ancestor, all dry. Of course this role was also due to his achievements and the two aspects of being an ancestor cannot be kept apart. This role comes from the light of experience. It is the culmination of a multitude of activities, of successes, of sorrows and hardships. This kind of authoritative authorship requires a very fixed and traditional oratorical form because that is the way of the ancestors and elders. Its rhytms and form make you hear the ancestors beyond the actual speaker. Such speech is the beginning of the organisation of society which time and ultimately death will fix in an ordered eternal pattern. As a result the slow formalisation matters as much as the content. (Bloch 1975)

If Besy felt that it was wrong and impossible to speak *Kabary* in French he had no such inhibitions about writing. Clearly what he had to say followed the traditional form of oratory characteristic of an elder. This, however, was not essentially oral, as he was speaking he was following a written text in French, and the great manuscript he presented to the university was in identical formal ancestral style. This manuscript was clearly for Besy the highest fruition of his historical scholarship as an elder, the highest stage of oratory. Besy's thought of himself first and foremost as a senior elder and a most important aspect of this was manifested in that he was a historical writer and a great orator, for him two activities were similar. This was because they were both marked by the style of *Kabary*, something which can persist even in translation in the written form, and which remains quite distinct from ordinary talk.

The case of Besy is significant in that it shows the irrelevance of literacy as an ideological transforming agent in such a case. His written work both in Malagasy and in French fulfils Goody's prescription for what is typical of pre-literate culture and the characteristics of his written work are with slight modifications those given by E. Keenan and myself for Malagasy oratory. (Bloch 1975; Keenan 1975)

The reason is that the relation which binds the rhetoric with the social which Keenan and I discussed for oral performances holds in just the same way for literate Besy as for non literate Malagasy elders. As would be the case for any elder it was his social position which validated his knowledge and criticisms from people without his standing were irrelevant.

This apparent continuity between the written and the oral could be attributed perhaps to the fact that writing is new in Madagascar and that as a result its social effects have not yet been felt. This would be completely wrong as the history of Madagascar shows. In fact Besy is the heir of an old literate tradition which grew up in the 19th century. He is typical of a whole class of Malagasy authors.[1]

---

[1]Although what is said in the following sections of this paper concerns the Merina it should be remembered that Besy was a Betsimisaraka. This however has little significance for my argument since the Betsimisaraka have very

Maurice Bloch

In 1968, in the book edited by Goody, I discussed the early history of Malagasy literacy. Since that time a great deal of excellent research has been carried out especially by Munthe on Malagasy manuscripts written in Arabic script (Munthe 1982) and by Ayache on the works of Raombana (Ayache 1976) by Raison-Jourde on missionary activity (Raison-Jourde 1977) and above all on the work of the many anonymous Malagasy writers whose work was compiled by Callet in the 19th c. in the book entitled *Tantaran ny Andriana* (Delivre 1974). On the whole, however, the general picture has remained unchanged. We do, however, know very much more now about what was being written especially by Malagasy historians, in the 19th century.

From approximately 1820 on, the Arabic script which had been used for astrological and later administrative purposes had been entirely replaced by Roman script. This was partly due to the influence of the London Missionary Society which not only encouraged the use of Roman script but spread literacy and even printing. (Munthe 1969; Raison-Jourde 1977). By 1829 there were in Imerina almost 1,500 pupils in school who were taught to read and write (Gow 1979: 7), and since there was a yearly intake the numbers of literate Malagasy must have numbered by then several thousands. The literary activity of the Merina during the period 1820 to 1835 was principally administrative.

From approximately 1835 on, the relation of the Merina to the London Missionary Society, and for that matter to all representatives of foreign countries, changed dramatically. The missionaries were expelled, the spread of literacy was seriously restricted and the schools closed. This is the period, not discussed in my earlier article, to which I briefly turn now.

What happened to Christianity during the period of isolation from 1835 to 1862 is well known and fascinating. Christianity, which was banned and brutally persecuted, flourished and developed in a way that was far more rapid and meaningful than when it had been tolerated and when missionaries had been present organising and building a number of churches. The reason for this development has been discussed and variously interpreted. What has been rarely explicitly noted is that during this period the same sort of thing happened for literacy. It too was

---

similar notions of ancestorhood and blessing. Also such members of the elite as Besy have been since the 19th.century merged with the Merina.

severely restricted, if not banned, but this was when Malagasy letters flourished.

During this period the administrative uses of literacy continued unabated, but a new phenomenon arose. A number of Merina began to produce manuscripts of a historical and ethnographic nature. Not many of these manuscripts survived though more are emerging all the time. The reasons for the disappearance of these manuscripts were many. They were destroyed during the period of Christian persecution. They were destroyed during the period of French repression when anything written in Malagasy was suspicious. They were bought by French "collectors" who usually then lost what they had obtained etc. However, enough of these are accessible to let us know what these written documents were like and why they were written in the first place. Indeed several have been published.

The missionaries from the first had introduced the Bible and devoted a large part of their efforts to establishing a written form of Malagasy into which it could be translated. (Munthe 1969). The significance of the Bible is that, in a way, it is the first book in Imerina. It was enthusiastically pushed by the missionaries. Its impact cannot be exaggerated and we also know something of the reaction to it and how it was seen during the period when the missionaries were expelled and when the manuscripts were written. This can best be understood in the way the Queen viewed Christianity. For her Christianity was an attempt "to make the Malagasy worship the ancestors of the Europeans: Moses and Jesus Christ in order that they stopped worshipping my ancestors: Andriananpoinimerina and Radama". In other words Christianity and the Bible was political subversion, an attempt to make the Malagasy subjects or descendants of the whites. (In Malagasy the same word can be used for subjects and children.)

For the Malagasy the Bible was seen as part of that knowledge which not only legitimates the existence of descent groups and the authority of their elders but also, as noted above, materially transforms people into descendants of those who disseminate it. This knowledge is carefully preserved and passed on from generation to generation by elders addressing their juniors. The display and the implicit teaching and transmission of such knowledge through oratory implies political authority whether of elders or kings who were represented as super elders. The receiving of such knowledge in the form of *Kabary* causes the ancestral coral, which ultimately takes you over, to grow inside you.[2]

Of course the display of such knowledge is not sufficient in itself, it is only powerful when it is part of the multi-faceted status of being an elder. If it is not part of such a multi-faceted status it is irrelevant or ridiculous (Bloch 1971). (This was how Besy viewed the display of knowledge of the historians.) However, when it is accompanied by sufficient power as was the case for the missionaries, it is a claim to power. When such people base themselves on a different genealogy, as did the missionaries, the propagation of such knowledge is a challenge to the incumbents. This is how the Bible was seen.

What marked out the Bible as the type of powerful transformative knowledge which was previously represented by the oratory of elders was its formal authoritative style, which the translators of the Bible naturally adopted. It was written *Kabary*. The fact that it was written and printed was significant, not because this marked a different kind of knowledge to the oral knowledge of elders, but because it represented a more powerful, impressive, efficient form of the same kind of knowledge. A new technology had been harnessed for an old purpose to make a competing claim. It was rather as if the orator was using a loud-hailer.

The response to the political challenge posed by the distribution of the Bible was that the Merina who wanted to resist this spiritual colonisation wrote their own 'Bibles'. These gave their histories, their genealogies and accounts of important status legitimating events. These 'Bibles' also gave accounts of traditional practices accompanied by their 'origins' which validated them. This was the traditional subject matter of the knowledge and oratory of elders as it is the subject matter of the Bible itself. The Merina, like their queens, were fighting back against the subversive implications of Christianity and its amplified oratory, by reaffirming their traditions and customs and using the same tool. It is therefore not a paradox but a totally understandable fact that these manuscripts should date from the period when the missionaries were out of the country because of the anti-European and anti-Christian reaction.

---

[2]It is interesting to note in this respect that nothing marks out a king as much as his right to make formal speeches.

This reaction to the Bible was exactly like the reaction of the Merina to all aspects of European culture during that period: highly pragmatic. It was a rejection of the subversive and political implication of things European, but a retention, indeed often a development, of European technology under the control of the Merina for their own ends. This is what the Merina did for metal working, and especially military technology, but also for a whole range of other techniques. They used writing in this way, principally for administrative purposes, but also for ideological purposes. They therefore used writing in their reassertion of their history and customs against the political threat of outside predators. They were using the technology of the Bible to fight it. This is what produced the manuscripts under discussion.

The written word was, and by and large still is, seen as a form of ancestral oratory. As a result it is largely treated in similar ways as oral *Kabary*. People without authority have no right to use it, and if they do they are ridiculous. What has been written once should be repeated in further writings and publications. It should be carefully transmitted from authoritative person to authoritative person. Written documents are not, any more than the words of a respected elder who uses the style of ancestral oratory, open to critical examination and evaluation. Reading written documents is exactly like listening to traditional Merina orators and what is written is by and large identical to what would have been said.

In other words Besy's writing and attitude was not a left over from an earlier preliterate age, he was not a kind of oral man who had learned to write but had not fully realised the implications of the tool he was using. In fact Besy was the heir of a century old literary tradition. He was using writing in the Malagasy way where it is a development of oratory. It is therefore not surprising that this use of literacy should share all the characteristics which Goody attributes to the oral.

This tradition is central and indeed typical of the Merina who are not only one of the most literate people I know but also one of the most literary. The number of Merina authors is quite bewildering. First of all they write little histories of their own descent groups which they have printed or typed and duplicated in the capital, then they write stories, ethnographies, novels and poems of varying quality but all of which clearly derive and are still very close to the oratorical forms which also continue to flourish. Indeed it is no accident that Malagasy authors, especially poets, have been major contributors to the French literary scene for at least the last fifty years. The Merina are certainly more literate than the English middle classes yet most of their work is like that produced by Besy, though usually shorter. Literacy has not transformed the nature of Merina knowledge - it has confirmed it.

What this Malagasy example shows is that the idea that literacy, of itself, has a liberating effect, or even leads to critical evaluative knowledge concerning the political situation, is quite wrong. What the Malagasy did in 19th century Madagascar with literacy was to use it as a tool for the kind of ideological practice which had before been oral. With writing they simply transmitted their ideology rather more efficiently. Literary knowledge did not act on its own, rather people used literacy for their own purposes. The people who were using literacy were part of a system of social relations and therefore it was in terms of that system of social relations that literacy was significant and its relation to knowledge was in terms of these uses. Literacy did not desocialize knowledge as is implied by Goody and it therefore had no political significance as a democratizing agent.

The modern situation of the history colloquium was of course not identical with that of the 19th century. When we consider the relation of Arthur Besy to the modern historians we do see different types of knowledge associated with different politico-social existences (the two types are only indirectly linked with literacy) occur side by side. This situation, however, is not one where genuine non-social knowledge confronts tainted social knowledge, where inevitably the former must defeat the latter. Rather the two types of knowledge are irrelevant to each other so long as there is no meaningful social relation between the people who are concerned with it. Besy was as irrelevant to the historians as the hypothetical man with the notebook in the back of the Tiv assembly. Similarly on his side Besy felt that the historians were complete irrelevancies and he ignored what they were saying, and indeed, as far as most Merina are concerned he is probably right.

The Enlightenment

In many ways it is strange that an anthropologist such as Goody should have made the mistake about the nature of knowledge in literate societies which is revealed by this Malagasy example.

After all anthropologists are probably the social scientists who have most emphatically stressed the social constraints on knowledge. The cause of the mistake seems to lie very much in the history of ideas of the subject as was already suggested above. It is thus worth tracing this history further back, not only to put Goody's position in context, but also because it enables us to identify the second problem in Goody's formulation which will be considered in this chapter.

When Firth, in a celebrated phrase, denied that Anthropology was the bastard of colonialism but rather that it was the legitimate child of the Enlightenment, he was claiming a genealogy which was not necessarily as unproblematic as he seemed to imply. First of all when we look at the Enlightenment it appears much more as a wonderful cacophony rather than an organised intellectual mass movement. Secondly, of course, the intellectual positions taken at that time have subsequently been heavily criticised.

There was, however, one moment in the French Enlightenment when mystical, anti-rationalist Rousseau, vitalist Buffon, humanist Diderot, empiricist Voltaire, rationalist D'Alembert got together and this was when they collaborated in the writing of the Encyclopedie. Although originally intended to be merely a translation of Chambers encyclopedia the editors agreed on a much bolder enterprise outlined in the entry "Encyclopedie" of the Encyclopedie. The idea was to make all knowledge available simply and clearly to the ordinary man in one illuminating book. Furthermore, the availability of this knowledge in a fairly easily accessible book was also to be politically liberating.

This was to happen when the obscurantism of priests and politicians supporting despotic and unjust governments had been dispersed by the clear light of knowledge emanating from their publication. This is one of the main themes of the whole book, revealed in the continual metaphorical use of the contrast between darkness and light (hence the "enlightenment", a metaphor which the contributors used themselves). The image of the opposite of enlightenment: theological and political obscurantism is also well developed as might be expected in such entries as 'Copernicus' but nowhere more so than in the myriad of ethnographic entries about such primitive peoples as Hindus (see the article on Brahmins) which shows how such peoples were enslaved by obscurantism by being denied access to science and knowledge. The way these ethnographic articles were written also made clear the irony of the inevitable concluding remarks, which always added how 'lucky' the Christian French were not to be so subject to such mystification. The book was, therefore, intended and was seen to be revolutionary, and its purpose was to be achieved through freely available knowledge which was to clear the hazes and curtains obscuring the light for illiterate primitives and orientals. In this general aim all the encyclopedists were agreed. It was only when they began to discuss what the light behind the veils might be that they fell out and were never able to get together again.

It is striking how the thinking of the encyclopedists seems to be repeated in the thinking of Goody and Watt. They seem to be all agreed that primitives and orientals have no access to socially free knowledge and are therefore at the mercy of obscurantist dominators. They also seem to agree with the encyclopedists that once knowledge is made freely available, preferably in book form, this will enable the oppressed to throw off their chains. Yet the history of ideas since the Enlightenment has been marked by the harsh realisation that things are not so simple.

This realisation came early, especially in the work of Rousseau, but most clearly at the end of the nineteenth century, by which time the apparent failure of such political events as the American and French revolutions to turn citizens into limpid rationalists led to the rethinking of the whole problem in a variety of ways. Much of this rethinking has been the source of modern social science theories. If we look at the three acknowledged founders of sociological thinking Marx, Weber and Durkheim, we see all three of them struggling in different ways this fact.

Marx in his early works is fascinated by the religiosity of the U.S. in spite of its "democracy". Durkheim points out the insufficiency of theories of religion which view the phenomenon as merely poor science, because if it was merely that it would have disappeared with the rationalist Enlightenment of the revolution. Weber argues, most radically of all that not only did liberalism not lead to a pure non social, non religious knowledge but that it itself had a religious, i. e. social, origin. Thus he seeks to argue that our scientific and political notions, especially the cardinal one of rationality are the product of non rational premises.

In a variety of ways all these authors are therefore reacting to the enlightenment view of knowledge; that once the power of priests and despots have been removed pure knowledge will shine forth. They say that there is no such thing as the pure light which the encyclopedists sought to reveal outside a social construction. For Durkheim knowledge is made possible by the totality of the pattern of social interaction in society. For Marx, and to a certain extent for Weber, knowledge varies in terms of the nature of different groups or interests in society. For all, however, the answer to the question of why liberating science does not shine forth irresistibly after the apparatuses of mystification engineered by rulers and priests have been swept away, is that the nature of knowledge is inseparable from social relations.

It was as a result of the theoretical positions of such writers as these that the functionalist theory of knowledge was formed, a theory against which Goody was later to react. It is therefore not really all that surprising that he should simply have moved back to the earlier position which Weber, Durkheim and Marx were criticising, on the well-known principle that the enemies of our enemies are our friends. Unfortunately such a reversal has taken us back to where we were and has reintroduced all the old problems. Knowledge cannot be separated from the social.

There is another fallacy which Goody has inherited from the Enlightenment. The metaphor of light standing for knowledge and of the obscuration of light standing for the lack of a suitable medium for the transfer of knowledge is also present in the work of Goody. This leads him to thinking of systems of communication purely as transmitters of something else, knowledge, from which they are totally independent. Thus for him systems of communication whether they are written, spoken, or otherwise, are merely ways of transmitting knowledge, they are quite separate from, not part of, knowledge itself. Systems of communication are therefore to be judged in terms of their transparency. This is particularly obvious in the way Goody treats different types of script. For him the less a script gets in the way the better it is. The less a script is thought about for itself the more efficient it is for communication. Hence Goody's low opinion of ideograms in China and Japan.

Japan

And here we must look at our second case: Japan. The facts about Japan immediately cast doubt on the reasons for Goody's low opinion of ideograms. The first fact is that the Japanese, unlike the Chinese, have had for centuries, side by side with ideograms of Chinese origins, two perfectly efficient phonetic writing systems available to them which they use in a number of ways and contexts. One would have thought that if ideograms were as cumbersome as Goody assumes they would have disappeared long ago and have been replaced by the phonetic systems. The second fact is that most studies of Japanese society make it clear that the Japanese have now, and have had for several centuries, a much higher level of literacy than was achieved in Europe with its purely alphabetic system. (Dore 1965). Thirdly, there is the fact that numerous reformers inspired by various waves of Westernisation have repeatedly attempted to replace ideograms by phonetic systems, yet these attempts at reform have always failed as ordinary Japanese have felt that the abandonment of ideograms would in many ways harm them. This is exactly the opposite to what the Goody thesis would lead us to expect, i. e. that such attempts at reform would be welcomed especially by ordinary people. Even the less ambitious attempts to merely reduce the number of ideograms in common use have only had very limited success and at the present time the number of ideograms used is, in spite of several Governmental attempts to stem the flow, growing at a healthy rate.

The reason for these facts, is that the Japanese attitude to the relationship between writing and knowledge is quite different to the western one. Our folk theory of this relationship goes something like this: Writing is a way of making the spoken permanent so that the spoken can be transmitted beyond the limits of hearing and so that the ephemeral spoken can endure. This is also how Goody views writing. The purpose of writing is to make us "read" the spoken behind it. The writing itself contains no information it merely transmits information which is elsewhere.

For the Japanese, however, almost the reverse is true in so far as writing with Chinese characters is concerned. The spoken is seen as one way of communicating knowledge whose form is in the characters, and it is a rather poor and inefficient way at that. To properly understand a spoken statement of import it should be written first. The Japanese are endlessly commenting on the inadequacies of their spoken language to express deep knowledge and they often gleefully point out how it is unfortunately full of homonyms. The significance of such remarks is that for them the characters are the base of knowledge and the spoken is a poor refraction of this base.

For the Japanese the characters themselves are the information. Thus, you will often see Japanese in serious discussion who feel that to make quite clear what one means to the other they either have to write the ideograms which correspond to what they are saying, or at least pretend to do so on their hands.

The specific nature of the reaction to the numerous attempts at simplification and diminution of the number of characters is highly revealing in this respect. The first and most furious response to the most recent attempt came from people who felt that their names were being abolished by the reform because the characters with which they were being written would not be acceptable any more. The Japanese did not think that a change in the characters being used, which would have produced exactly the same sound, would have merely been a change in the way their names were being written. The characters were the name, while the sound was merely the way the names were spoken. Hence abolishing the characters was abolishing the name. Once again the perceived relation between the spoken and the written is reversed between Japanese and European culture.

Perhaps the intrinsic value of the characters for themselves can be seen in two aspects of modern Japanese education which appear particularly strange to Europeans. The first is that the different stages of learning which a school child is achieving is typified by the number of characters he or she has learnt. The reason for this is not simply that there are a lot of characters to learn but that the characters contain inside them the knowledge which has to be assimilated. The child is not merely taught how to recognise and reproduce the character but above all to understand the knowledge they constitute. The closest parallel in Europe is the way having a wide vocabulary is thought in folk psychology to be a sign of wisdom. It is not the fact of knowing many words for themselves which is thought to be important rather it is that the mastery of the words is believed to indicate a mastery of the concepts.

The second insight which Japanese education gives into the nature of characters shows how they can convey meaning without in any way having to correspond to speech. Japanese schoolchildren are taught to "read" Chinese classics through the ideograms employed. But they have no idea nor any curiosity as to how to pronounce the text. They are not merely substituting Japanese sounds for Chinese sounds since, because Chinese syntax could not be more different from Japanese, the words occur in a totally different order. They read without having to attempt to reconstruct what the authors might have said. This is only possible because of the nature of ideograms not as units of sound but as units of knowledge.

Good literary style in Japanese is not judged by what the writing would say, were it read, but by the choice of characters with which the text is written. This means that authors choose with great care between a number of characters which when read are pronounced identically. This may lead to great obscurity as novelists for instance may choose for the sake of style little known characters which are not understood by the ordinary reader. The problem is overcome by the characters being paraphrased by others or by phonetic writing in the margin of the book. Again we can see it is not the sound which the writing produces which matters since the sound produced by reading the character and the marginal footnotes are identical.

The very Japanese word which is normally translated by the English word culture: bunka, is in Japanese made up of two characters which can be glossed 'to take the form of writing'. This is not only revealing in itself but it also illustrates how characters contain information and interpretation of knowledge which have the role of etymologies in folk learning. They reveal the true fundamental meaning of a spoken expression both in their shape as a whole and in the combination of the elements of which they may consist.

Most revealing however is the nature of Japanese calligraphy. The word calligraphy suggests to a European a careful exercise of decoration. European illuminated manuscripts were the decoration, the beautiful encasing of the word of God or of the fathers of the church with painstaking lengthy care. Indeed medieval books in their bindings resemble closely reliquaries which made their contents imperishable.

Japanese calligraphy is completely different, both in intent and in execution. First of all it should be the action of a moment on the part of the calligrapher. Random elements such as the marks left by stray hairs of the brush are particularly valued. They are the trace of the speed and the lack of retouching of the writing. For the same reason, the most valued paper for calligraphy is very much like blotting paper. It is impossible to write on it slowly without making a mess. The significance of this is that the speed required bears witness to the internalisation by long practice of the particular characters. The speed of the execution demonstrates how truly the knowledge that is the character has been learnt. It is the outward reflection of inner wisdom. What is inside one is the character, not the words, and the calligraphy is the fleeting material manifestation of this inner state. The Japanese view is that the characters in one self are the knowledge and that these can be manifested very poorly by speech and a little better by writing. While the western view is that what is in one self are thoughts which are believed to be necessarily in the form of words and that these words may take on a superior form when they are expressed through writing which is what gives them permanence and ultimate value.

For that reason the wisdom of famous men of the past, Buddhist saints for example, is not preserved by endlessly writing in ever more beautiful ways what they said, but rather in preserving their calligraphy which shows their wisdom even if what the calligraphies express are not their own writings but almost any sacred phrase. Indeed in a number of famous cases the calligraphy is of only one character.

A learned Japanese man is therefore one who has so internalised the knowledge of previous generations, that is characters, that he can produce it by semi-instinctive movement of a large part of his body without having to divert the transmission by the disruptive intermediacy of sound. The character is seen as a repository of knowledge in itself whether traditional or modern. It does not refer to information it is information.

The nature of ideograms is extremely complex but enough has been said to show that for the Japanese the relationship between the written and the oral and between the written and knowledge is completely different for the European way of looking at these things. A way which Goody assumes is universally the case. The idea that the ideograms might obscure the dissemination of meaning is absurd in the Japanese way of looking at things. It is viewed in just the same way as an attempt to enforce a reduction in the vocabulary would be viewed in Europe.[3] Any reduction in the number of ideograms is a reduction in knowledge. If the ideograms were simplified this would simply enslave in ignorance those who used such an easier script. Indeed this was very much the way that the Japanese viewed the syllabic scripts which were associated with women and which were seen both as the proof and the cause of their inferiority.

---

[3]This comparison was suggested to me by Professor W. Goodenough.

With such a view of writing as the Japanese the notion that the task of writing is to be transparent so that it does not hide knowledge becomes quite incomprehensible.[4]

Conclusion

This brief excursion into Japanese ethnography has fundamental significance for the Goody argument. It shows how culturally specific his view of writing actually is and how careful we must be when we use it for what it is intended to be: a universalist thesis.

The fact that the Japanese view the relationship between knowledge, writing and speech differently to the Europeans is not a reason why we should accept their folk view any more than we should, like Goody, accept the European folk view. Rather it should make us reconsider the theory critically, especially the relationship that we see between knowledge and the potentially material phenomena that is writing.

In this chapter we have seen three possible patterns associated with Europe, Madagascar and Japan. These three can be represented in the diagrammatical form which concludes this chapter. They reveal variation on a number of levels but there are probably many more possibilities that could be found in cultures not discussed here.

First we have the European pattern. There thought and knowledge is believed to be primarily a matter of language. These linguistic thoughts are visualised as individual creations of the moment. They are transitory, always changing and flowing, and because of this, valuable thoughts are always in danger of being lost. These thoughts/words may emerge from the individual in the form of spoken language. This is again visualised as a fluid individual phenomenon. However, thanks to writing, it is possible to fix and make permanent individual thought or language and so valuable knowledge is not lost. Written language is therefore immobile and this permanence should be marked by the care and deliberate way in which it is made. Also because writing is permanent it is not so individual as the spoken word, this is be-

---

[4]Basil Hall Chamberlain writing in the late nineteenth century makes exactly the same point. "We mean that the writing here does not merely serve to transcribe words...the slave in fact becoming the master" and he goes on to explain why as a result there can be no question of the attempts at Romanisation succeeding. (Chamberlain 1971 p. 520).

cause the individual is itself perceived as fleeting and when his or her language is fossilised it becomes a common possession to be stored in libraries. The European view of writing thus ultimately rests on a European view of the person as a unique individual and his or her place in society.

Secondly we have the Malagasy pattern and this again requires an understanding of the notion of the person in cultural terms. There again thought and word are associated, but as every thing that pertains to the individual and his body these are of two radically different kinds. On the one hand there are the fluid individual thoughts linked to the wet side of the body. Like that side of the body these should have no permanence and should not be fixed, either by oratory or by that extension of oratory, writing. On the other hand there are those thoughts/words which are the manifestation of the ancestral in the self and which gain prominence as one gets older and approaches the ancestors. These have permanence because the ancestors are permanent and everlasting. They manifest themselves in a form of speech, formal oratory, which is non individual and immobilised and this may be further immobilised by writing.

Finally we have the Japanese. There what should be permanent is the ideal concept which should have been put in the head of a person by long education and practice. This ideal character is very reminiscent of a Platonic form. The outward manifestation of the learnt forms are visualised as fleeting shadows and indeed should be so. These outward manifestations are of two kinds. One, speech, is a low form and it is continually denigrated. The other is more noble, it is the material writing which, although also an outward shadow of its source, is closer to it than speech. However, it would be wrong if the outward manifestation was confused with its permanent origin and so the best writing is that which flaunts its fleetingness.

Until such ground rules of the relationship between thought, knowledge, speech and writing have been established the kind of ambitious task attempted by Goody cannot begin.

Bibliography

Note: I wish to acknowledge the help I received from the National Museum of Ethnology of Japan for the short research I carried out in that country. I am particularly endeted to Dr. S. Tanabe for his help when discussing this subject.

Ayache, Simon (1976) *Raombana l'historien. (1809-1855) Introduction a l'edition critique de son oeuvre.* Ambozontany, Fianarantsoa.

Bloch, Maurice (1968) Astrology and Writing. In Jack Goody (ed.) *Literacy in Traditional Societies.* Cambridge University Press, Cambridge.

Bloch, Maurice (1971) Decision Making in Councils among the Merina of Madagascar. In *Councils in Action.* Cambridge papers in Social Anthropology 6, Cambridge University Press, Cambrige.

Bloch, Maurice (1975) Introduction. In *Political Language and Oratory in Traditional Society.* Academic Press, London and New York.

Bloch, Maurice (1985) *From Blessing to Violence, History and Ideology in the circumcision ritual of the Merina of Madagascar.* Cambridge University Press, Cambridge.

Bohannan, Laura (1952) A Genealogical Charter, *Africa* Vol XXII no. 4.

Callet, R. P. (1908) *Tantaran ny Andriana eto Madagascar.* Academie Malgache, Tananarive.

Chamberlain, Basil Hall (1971) *Japanese Things, Being Notes on Various Subjects connected with Japan,* reprint of 1904 original. Tuttle, Rutland and Tokio.

Cunnison, Ian (1959) *The Luapula peoples of Northern Rhodesia, Custom and History in Tribal Politics.* Manchester University Press, Manchester.

Delivre, Alain (1974) *L'Histoire des Rois D'Imerina, Interpretation d'une Tradition Orale.* Klincjsiek, Paris.

Dore, Ronald P. (1965) The Legacy of Tokugawa Education. In Marius T. Jansen (ed.), *Changing Japanese attitudes towards Modernisation.* Princeton University Press, Princeton.

Goody, J. (1968) *Literacy in Traditional Societies.* Cambridge University Press, Cambridge.

Goody, J. (1977) *The domestication of the Savage Mind.* Cambridge University Press, Cambridge.

Gough, Kathleen (1968) Implications of Literacy in Traditional China and India, in Goody 1968.

Gow, Bonar A. (1979) *Madagascar and the Protestant Impact.* Longman and Dalhousie Press, London.

Keenan, Elinor (1974) Norm makers, Norm Breakers: Men and Women in a Malagasy Village. In R. Bauman and J. Sherzer (editors), *Explorations in the Ethnography of Speaking..* Cambridge University Press, Cambridge.

Keenan, Elinor (1975) A sliding Sence of Obligatoriness, in Bloch 1975.

Munthe, Ludvig (1969) *La Bible a Madagascar, Les Deux Premieres Traductions du Nouveau Testament Malgache.* Forlaget Land og Kirke, Oslo.

Munthe, Ludvig (1982) *La Tradition Arabico-Malgache vue a travers le Manuscrit A-6 d'Oslo et d'autres Manuscrits Disponibles.* T.P.F.L.M. Antanarivo.

Raison-Jourde, Françoise (1977) L'Echange Inegal de la Langue: L'Introduction des Techniques Linguistiques dans une civilisation de l'Oral. (Imerina au XIX siècle) *Annales E.S.C. ,* Paris

Europe

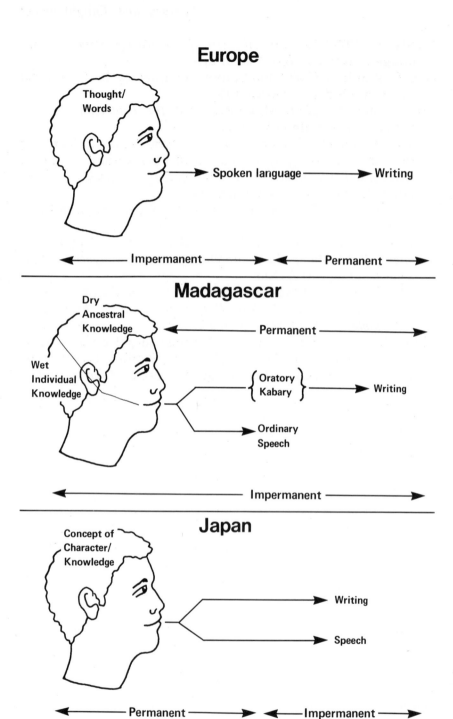

Thought/Words

Spoken language ⟶ Writing

← Impermanent ⟶ ← Permanent ⟶

Madagascar

Dry Ancestral Knowledge

Wet Individual Knowledge

← Permanent ⟶

{ Oratory Kabary } ⟶ Writing

Ordinary Speech

← Impermanent ⟶

Japan

Concept of Character/ Knowledge

Writing

Speech

← Permanent ⟶ ← Impermanent ⟶

The Brahmanical Tradition and the Technology of the Intellect[1]

J. P. Parry

The Technology of the Intellect

In *The Domestication of the Savage Mind* (1977), Goody takes up and develops a thesis which he had originally outlined in a joint article with Watt (1953), and which was further elaborated in his edited collection *Literacy in Traditional Societies* (1958a). *The Domestication* was published in the year after Goody's *Production and Reproduction*, and although the two volumes deal with quite different topics, their general inspiration is extremely close. In its barest outline the argument of the latter is that there is a causal relationship between the kind of agricultural technology (plough versus hoe) and the kind of inheritance rules present in a particular society, and between these inheritance rules and the forms of kinship and marriage. *The Domestication of the Savage Mind* assigns an equally prominent place to technology - "the technology of the intellect". It offers a view of human development in which literacy is the crucial variable with the potential for transforming social and mental life. The present paper provides a commentary on this view in the light of material on traditional Hindu India.

Many writers have discerned a radical contrast between the modes of thought characteristic of traditional and modern society. Though Goody speaks of a continuum rather than a di-

[1]An earlier draft of this paper was presented to "The Patterns of History" seminar at the London School of Economics, the South Asian Anthropologists Group and at the University of Sussex. I gratefully acknowledge the helpful comments received on these occasions. Thanks are especially due to André Béteille, Maurice Bloch, Mary Searle-Chatterjee, Chris Fuller and Mick Mann for their critical scrutiny of a previous version of the text.

chotomy, he does not deny that this fundamental difference exists but seeks to explain it in terms of literacy. For Horton (1970) a critical distinction between traditional and scientific thought is the essential scepticism of the latter. But Africans, says Goody, are no more credulous than people in the industrial West. The real contrast is rather that in the absence of literacy they cannot accumulate or reproduce scepticism. With writing a closer scrutiny becomes possible, and hence the perception of contradictions not immediately apparent in oral discourse. Writing is also a pre-condition of syllogistic reasoning, and of logic as a formalized set of analytic procedures (1977: 11). By contrast, pre-literate societies "are marked not so much by the absence of reflective thinking as by the proper tools for constructive rumination" (1977: 44). With the heightening of critical activity made possible by literacy goes a movement from magic to science and from myth to history (which obviously depends on written records). Historical thinking in turn favours a stress on linear as opposed to cyclical conceptions of time; while scepticism promotes science, which encourages a process of secularization (1977: 150). Literacy further permits an enlargement of political scale and more depersonalized systems of government, lends itself to more anonymous modes of transmission of knowledge, and - by recording individual innovation - promotes the growth of individualism and stimulates creativity.

Book learning, however, has its costs. It leads to a "restriction of spontaneity" (1977: 144). For Goody knowledge in pre-literate societies seems to be an almost infinitely plastic resource. As in the Malinowskian view of myth, it is continually manipulated to serve as a charter for current social alignments. But "ideas communicated by literary means can never be totally absorbed like those passed on orally, because the book always remains there as a check upon the transformations that have taken place" (1958b: 216). A second cost of literacy is structural analysis which is merely an artefact of literate modes of thought and literate representations, and which therefore grossly distorts the thought processes of oral cultures. The irony, of course, is that Goody's real target here has taken precisely the opposite view: for Lévi-Strauss the structural method is only appropriately applied to *oral* myths, since in a literate culture the text is "no longer the unadulterated product of the structure of the mind but deformed by the constraints of social life during the epoches of its reinterpretation" (Pitt-Rivers 1977: 130).

To my mind the striking thing about this catalogue of corollaries which Goody derives from literacy is that - as I endeavour to document below - almost none of his predictions hold unambiguously good for traditional India. In part perhaps the problem derives from the fact that while he clearly recognizes the wide differences between literate traditions, at times he nevertheless seems to slip into an unconscious equation between literate societies and 'cognitive modernism', and between pre-literate societies and 'cognitive traditionalism'. Horton (1932) - from whom I borrow these terms - falls into the same trap when taking stock of, and refining, his earlier argument in the light of Goody and others. By revealing differences between past and present, he argues, literacy weakens the belief that existing knowledge is legitimated by an unbroken tradition stretching back to the time of the first ancestors, and encourages a theoretical pluralism which is likely to give rise to an "inter-theoretic competition" which is one of the critical characteristics of cognitive modernism. At its most obvious level, however, the kind of data discussed below clearly suggest that literacy is quite as compatible with a thoroughgoing cognitive conservatism as with its converse, and that this cognitive orientation displays a remarkable tenacity in a context from which inter-theoretic competition has for many centuries been by no means absent.

But Goody is not, of course, unaware of the kind of situation I describe; and he himself draws explicit attention to cases of "restricted literacy" where writing is largely confined to religious uses and where "the Book becomes less a means to further enquiry, a step in the accumulation of knowledge, than an end in itself, the timeless depository of all knowledge" (1968b: 237). So literacy may encourage 'criticism and commentary on the one hand and the orthodoxy of the book on the other" (1977: 37).

Given this second possibility, in what sense can literacy be seen as a critical causal factor in the emergence of the syndrome of mental attributes supposedly characteristic of modern society? It is, we are told, an enabling rather than a sufficient condition. In the sense of a general precondition for - as the Neolithic Revolution was a pre-condition for the Age of Steam - his argument would surely be as unexceptionable as it would be vacuous. But it is clear that Goody intends something far stronger. What I take him to mean is that the "liberating effects" of literacy will almost inexorably lead in the direction I have outlined *unless* a powerful set of socio-cultural conditions inhibit this development. Exactly

what these conditions would be is, however, left largely unspecified although attention is drawn to the restrictive practices
of a religious literati anxious to preserve their monopoly over
the sources of mystical power.

Adopting such a focus we might ask why literacy failed to
promote "cognitive modernism" in the kind of context I describe.
By formulating the issue in these terms, however, we immediately concede to literacy a causal role in the transformation
of mental life. In the concluding paragraphs of this paper I by
contrast suggest that its significance as a dynamic force is questionable. Rather than providing a positive thrust towards the
kind of rationality characteristic of modern science, all we can
confidently endorse is the truism that it is a necessary prerequisite for such a development.

It is perhaps only natural that academies should have a
propensity to exaggerate the unique significance of book learning,
and Goody is by no means the only one who is prone to do so. In
their manifesto "For a Sociology of India", Dumont and Pocock
(1957) insist on the postulate that sociologically India is one. "The
very existence, and influence", they claim, "of the traditional
higher, Sanskritic, civilization demonstrates without question
the unity of India. One might think that it does not only demonstrate, but actually constitutes it" (p. 9). What is implied here,
then, is that the unity of India is - in part at least - a consequence
of the fact that all Hindus acknowledge the authority of the same
set of texts and thus subscribe to the same set of fundamental
ideas and values. We are therefore dealing "not merely with a
cultural unity" as among neighbouring African tribes (1957: 10).
This last proposition - that in the pre-literate world continuities
between neighbouring societies do not concern fundamental
values but are "merely cultural" - is I would argue a kind of opti-
cal illusion created by the tradition of functionalist anthropology
and would not be borne out by systematic regional comparisons
of the sort being undertaken by Andrew Strathern for Highland
New Guinea (e. g. Strathern 1982), or Adam Kuper for parts of
Bantu Africa (e. g. Kuper 1982). More pertinent here, however, is
that a textual tradition can surely only "constitute" an ideological
unity *if* one assumes that the texts themselves display a unity of
ideas and values, and that all Hindus derive the same message
from the same text. But when the scriptures themselves differ on
such fundamental matters as monism, theism, vegetarianism
and caste (Singer 1972: 43), and when Tilak and Aurobindo Ghose

invoke the *Bhagavad-Gita* as justification for violence in the cause of nationalism while Gandhi makes it the corner-stone of his doctrine of non-violence (Cohn 1971: 55), there is surely good reason to doubt whether either of these assumptions is valid.

In line with their stress on the unity between text and the religion as it is actually practiced, Dumont and Pocock reject the Great tradition/Little tradition dichotomy, and represent the relationship between textual and popular 'levels' as one of homologous structures and the local working out of a general idea. For the villagers themselves, they say in criticism of Marriott (1955) who implies otherwise, there are not two traditions but simply one. Hinduism on the ground is not conceptually separable into different elements (cf. Tambiah 1970: 369). For reasons I take up in the section after next, however, my own ethnographic experience leads me to believe that the facts are on Marriott's side.

The Ethnographic Context

The ethnographic experience referred to, and most of the observations reported here, derive from fieldwork in the city of Benares.[2] Benares is one of the most important centres of pilgrimage in India, and is inextricably associated in the Hindu mind with death and the transcendence of death. Each year scores of old and terminally sick people come to the city in order that they may die there; thousands of corpses are brought for cremation on one of the two principal burning *ghats*, and hundreds of thousands of pilgrims bring the ashes of a deceased relative to immerse in the Ganges or make offerings to their ancestors there. But what is also central to the identity of Benares is its ancient tradition of Sanskritic learning. A number of distinct theological traditions have at one time or another been influential in the city's religious history; though it is orthodox Brahmanism which remains the dominant influence.

With a population of little over half a million, and with an adult literacy rate of around fifty per cent (India Year Book 1974),

---

[2] Fieldwork in Benares was carried out between September 1975 and November 1977 (supported by the Social Science Research Council) and in August 1978, August-September 1981 and March-April 1983 (supported by the London School of Economics and Political Science). I am deeply obligated to Virendra Singh for his language instruction, and to him and Om Prakash Sharma for their research assistance.

the city now supports three independent universities, all of which pride themselves on a strength in Sanskrit studies and Hindu philosophy. The Sanskrit University, founded in 1792 "with the object of preserving and cultivating the literature, laws and religion of the Hindus" (Smith 1963: 336), is almost exclusively concerned with these subjects. Kashi Vidyapith was established in 1921 and has direct roots in the Nationalist Movement and Gandhian ideology; while Benares Hindu University was established in1916 "to impart instruction in Hinduism to Hindu students" (Altekar 1937: 286). More directly relevant to the present discussion are the now dwindling number of traditional *pathasalas* (or schools), devoted to transmitting under the tutelage of a Brahman *guru* a knowledge of the sacred scriptures and an ability to recite the Vedic *mantras*. For Benares and its immediate environs I have a list of 142 of these, though the total number of students receiving this type of education is probably less than the two thousand estimated by Saraswati (1975: 19).[3]

Numerically far more significant than the small, though highly prestigious, class of Sanskrit pedagogues attached to such institutions are the vast array of different kinds of Brahman sacred specialist who cater to the religious needs of the pilgrims, mourners and inhabitants of the city: Vedic chanters, Funeral Priests, Temple-priests, Pilgrimage-priests and so on. This sacerdotal class provides the ritual technicians of Sanskritic Hinduism rather than its theoreticians. It is they who actually conduct the rituals prescribed by the texts, who expound their meaning, and who in this sense mediate between the textual tradition and the theologically untutored. Not that they could (by their own criteria) be appropriately described as prodigies of learning. Indeed their reputation for avarice is at least as great as their reputation for scholarship. Though all of them are literate in the vernacular, only a small minority have any real command of Sanskrit. Though they learn to read, they do not on the whole learn by

---

[3] While the prestige and influence of these institutions is now much diminished, it is not clear that they catered for much larger student numbers in the pre-British period. Bernier observed that in the mid-seventeenth century "the town contains no colleges or regular classes, as in our universities, but resembles rather the schools of the ancients, the masters being dispersed over different parts of the town in private houses.... Some of these masters have four disciples, others six or seven, and the most eminent have twelve or fifteen; but this is the largest number" (Bernier 1968: 334; originally 1670). From a much earlier date, however, we learn of an establishment with five hundred students (Basham 1971: 165).

reading. The majority rely principally for their religious knowledge on the oral tradition of their communities, and secondarily on the religious pamphlets and digests in Hindi which are sold throughout the city. The Sanskrit *mantras* they recite have been learned by rote; they have little idea of their "real" meaning, and are often reduced to inaudible mumbling or brazening it out with gobbledy-gook in the confident expectation that their patrons will never know the difference. Though my most intimate contacts in Benares are with priests rather than with scholars or laymen, I would claim that the attitudes towards scriptural learning which I describe in what follows are common to an extremely wide segment of the population.

The Literate Tradition of the Benarasi Brahman

For all my informants - whether priests, ascetics or ordinary householders - there is a sharp distinction, which brings me back to the Dumont-Pocock criticism of Marriott, between the *shastrik* (or scriptural) and the *laukik* (or popular). Belief and practice are visualized as a composite of both. The *shastrik* elements are *pramanik* ('proven'), eternally valid and binding on all Hindus, and in their interpretation the Brahman is pre-eminent. By contrast, the *laukik* is ephemeral, a mere matter of local usage to be discarded if it offends against contemporary canons of good sense, and here it is often the women who are regarded as the repositories of tradition. Admittedly this *shastrik/laukik* division is itself derived from the *shastrik* domain; but the fact remains that it is internalized by many illiterate Hindus who clearly represent their religious universe as composed of elements taken from two conceptually separable traditions.

Debate on theological issues, or on correct ritual practice, always starts from this distinction. If it can be established that a particular item is *shastrik*, then there's an end of the matter, it is unquestionably authoritative. In 1981, for example, a bitter controversy developed over whether to continue the custom of cremating the corpses of the affluent next to the footprints left by lord Vishnu as he sat performing the austerities by which he created the world at the beginning of time (cf. Parry 1981). Considerable financial interests were generally held to be at the root of the matter. The debate - to which many column inches of the local press were devoted - was however couched entirely in terms of whether the practice was textually sanctioned.

While everybody agrees that the *laukik/shastrik* distinction is of fundamental significance, there is - as this last example shows - no general consensus on what belongs to which category. Moreover some practices which in fact have no backing at all in the ancient texts (for example, the fifty mile circumambulatory pilgrimage of the city) are almost universally believed to be scriptural and are rated as *shastrik*, while others (like animal sacrifice) which do indeed have a respectable textual pedigree are generally regarded as merely *laukik*. The central point that I want to stress, however, is that that which is *believed* to be textual is - at least in principle - beyond debate, while that which belongs to the oral tradition is not. At the risk of labouring the point, the *textual* tradition is here accorded an ideological immunity to sceptical scrutiny, while the oral tradition is the focus of continual critical evaluation.

The equation I imply between the *shastrik* and the literate, and between the *laukik* and the oral is however only a first approximation. More precisely, the *shastrik* is that which is sanctioned - or held to be sanctioned - by the ancient Sanskrit texts[4] (a category which will itself require qualification in due course). Both their age and their language are crucial aspects of their authority.

Sanskrit is *deva-vani*, "the speech of the gods". Since many of the sacred texts purport to be a transcription of divine conversation or instruction, their original and most authoritative form is clearly Sanskrit. Sanskrit is far more than a language. It is a badge of civilization. Indeed the word itself means "cultured" or "refined". When my Benares friends say - as they often do - that Europeans have no *sanskriti*, they are not merely referring to a linguistic deficiency; but to the well-known fact that Europeans fornicate like dogs, never know who their fathers are, and have no religion and philosophy to speak of. In short, they are without culture - Sanskrit merely being the vehicle for *sanskriti*. It is only in this light that one can begin to appreciate the cultural appositeness of M. N. Srinivas's choice of the label "sanskritization" for the process by which the lower castes come to take over the customs and style of life of their superiors. Sanskritization is something far more than is suggested by the dry sociological jargon "reference group behaviour". It took a Brahman anthropolo-

---

4 Technically the *shastras* are the "law books" and compilations of the post-Vedic period. In everyday speech, however, the term *shastrik* is used indiscriminately to cover beliefs and practices validated by the whole range of sacred texts from the Vedas to the Puranas and Dharmasastras.

gist to coin a term which so perfectly captures the idea that it is above all a process of refinement and civilization (cf. van Buitenen 1966: 34).

The *shastras*, then, are written in the language of the gods and even at their dictation. Consistent with this they are the repositories of all authentic knowledge. Knowledge, then, is not something to be *discovered*, as in the western scientific tradition, but something to be *recovered* from the texts (van Buitenen 1966: 35). The absolute truth has already been revealed and is there for man to appropriate if only he can penetrate their meaning. Sanskrit thus provides an essential handle on eternally valid knowledge.

But what kind of knowledge is that? The first thing to be said is that not all knowledge is equally worthwhile. One *aspect* of my informants attitudes - which is strongly marked in the tradition at large - is a comparative devaluation of knowledge of the empirical world, which is after all the product of illusion (*maya*) and created by the divine play of the gods (*lila*). During my Benares fieldwork I was continually being upbraided for wasting my time with meaningless enquiries of a sociological character. I have no doubt that such admonishment was generally prompted by a certain uneasiness about what I might discover; but the reproach reflected and appealed to a deeply rooted cultural value that nothing of lasting worth is to be learnt from such matters. Real knowledge is knowledge of a metaphysical truth which liberates the soul from the endless cycle of existence - a knowledge which is revealed in the texts but which is generally thought to be obtained only by years of submission to a rigorous ascetic discipline. The theological premise which underlines such attitudes is that suffering and evil are not - as in mainstream Christianity - the consequence of original sin, but rather of ignorance of this truth. The obvious parallel is with the Christianity of the Gnostic Gospels (Pagels 1979). In both cases not only is man's problem located in ignorance, but the answer is to be found *within* the individual, who having found it becomes one with God - himself a Christ or a Siva.

But this is only one side of the picture. While what is of permanent value is knowledge which leads out of the world, the scriptures also provide the keys to an understanding by which it may be mastered while in it. They contain, that is, instructions of a pre-eminently practical kind which, properly understood, are the source of a fabulous power - a power which is conferred on those who travel the path which leads to liberation, but which must be renounced if liberation is to be obtained (though it is hard to suppress the suspicion that for a majority the real attraction is the journey rather than the destination). Continual play is made between the term *shastra* (i. e. the texts) and *shastr* (a weapon) - the *shastras* being the most powerful weapons at man's command. In Benares I have often been told - and I have heard variants of the same story elsewhere - that Max Muller stole chunks of the *Sama-veda* from India, and it was by studying these that German scientists were able to develop the Atom bomb. The *rishis,* or ancient sages, not only knew all about nuclear fission, but as (what we would call) mythology testifies, they also had supersonic aeroplanes and guided missiles. Of a piece with such claims is the commonly made assertion that every ritual detail prescribed by the texts has some justification or other in terms of modern science, and if this scientific rationality remains obscure that is only because of the rudimentary state of our present knowledge. In reality, then, the *shastras* are a highly developed science which the *rishis* presented as religion (*dharma*) since they knew full well that in the degenerate times to come the wisdom they embodied would not be properly understood and could only survive as blind faith.

It is of course tempting to see in all this a kind of defensive reaction to the encounter with cosmopolitan science and British imperialism. Indeed my example of the stolen fragments of the *Sama-veda* immediately recalls the widespread Melanesian belief that the Europeans had excised various pages from the Bible in order to prevent them from obtaining cargo. I do not doubt that there is an element of this kind in what I have described, though it seems to me that there is more to it than that, and that the interpretation of religious texts as technical know-how is not the departure it might at first sight appear. The essential point is that in traditional Indian thought there is no conceptual divide between "religious" and "scientific" knowledge. Without any sense of incongruity the texts known as Puranas contain terrifying accounts of the fate of the souls of sinners, sandwiched between sections on - say - mineralogy and medicine. Again, in modern Hindi the term *shastra* elides what we would separate. The *shastras* are the sacred texts, but sociology is *samaj-shastra* - where the word has become a suffix which is used very much like the suffix "-ology" in our language, and conveys the idea of a theoretical discipline. A standard Hindi-English dictionary lists the following equivalents: "scripture(s), a religious or scientific treatise, a composition of divine or secular authority, science....".[5] The term thus broadly corresponds to the original meaning of the English word 'science' as knowledge in general.

While everything that I have said so far might seem to imply that the written is always privileged over the oral, it is important to stress that this written tradition is itself held to be based (at least in the case of certain texts) on an originally *spoken* revelation made by the gods, and to be preserved largely by oral transmission; and further that the most ancient and authoritative texts - the Vedas - are conventionally classified as *sruti*, that which is 'heard' (as opposed to *smriti* which is 'remembered'). Indeed Brahman culture is very much a culture of the spoken word, and a desire to dominate verbally, to render others speechless by the force of one's own speech and erudition, is a striking aspect of the ethos of the Benarasi Brahman, and is institutionalized in the *shastrarth* - a kind of formalized verbal battle over the interpretation of the texts.

Given this premium on the spoken word my earlier emphasis on the prestige of the written text may seem paradoxical. This apparent contradiction, I would argue, is more properly seen as a disjunction between principle and practice. While in theory it is oral transmission which has ideological pre-eminence, in fact such knowledge may be suspect for its authority rests on that of its repositories. In these debased times human memory has supposedly become so fallible, and the pedagogical tradition of the Brahmans so enfeebled and corrupted, that the authenticity of knowledge transmitted by purely oral means can no longer be automatically accepted as axiomatic. Instead of a mere prop to memory, a supplement to the instruction of a teacher, the written text may now be regarded as a more reliable guide to an ancient wisdom once more fully apprehended through personalised transmission.

While Goody is clearly correct to note that literacy provides the potential for more anonymous modes of communicating knowledge, the Brahmanical tradition has gone as far as it possibly can to evade this possibility. It is uncertain when the Vedas were actually composed, or even when they were first written down. But what is generally agreed by Indologists (e.g. Winternitz 1927: 36;

---

[5] For a body of scientific theory to rate as a *shastra* presupposes its unquestioned authority. Since it remains contentious, Darwin's theory of evolution would not be described as a *shastra*, but rather as a *siddhant* or 'doctrine'.

Staal 1961: 15) is that many centuries separated the two things, and that it was not for want of literacy that they were not written down earlier. Though Goody (in press) has recently challenged this claim in proposing that "the role of writing in the composition or transcription of the Vedas must remain a serious possibility from the historical point of view", there can be no question about the consistent hostility of Brahmanical thought to the graphic reproduction of the Veda. Indeed some of the later texts condemn to hell those who reduce the Veda to writing (Kane 1976: 2: 349). It should be (and still is) preserved by direct transmission from teacher to pupil, a process involving the endless repetition of each verse until it has been completely mastered and an elaborate system of mnemonic checks and phonetic rules (*vyasa siksa*) designed to ensure the exact replication of the proper sound.

Rather than the essential character of oral discourse being modified by intellectual procedures inseparable from literacy, as Goody predicts for literate cultures, it would be nearer the mark to say that in traditional India it was literary expression which was subordinated to the demands of oral transmission, for much of the sacred literature was composed in a form and with a redundancy which was clearly intended to facilitate memorisation and faithful replication.

A very high proportion of the Sanskrit corpus is written in verse rather than prose, and this applies to the texts on medicine, astronomy and architecture, and to historical and biographical works, as much as to those which deal with such purely 'ritualistic' topics as sacrifice (Winternitz 1927: 3). Goody passes over the possible relevance of the distinction between prose and verse for his argument about the association between literacy and cognitive modernism. Its significance is, however, suggested by Merton's (1978: 19) observation that in seventeenth century England the revolution in science went along with a marked shift of interest from poetry to prose - both developments revealing an increasing preoccupation with the exposition and description of empirical phenomena.

If verse is better suited than prose to the faithful memorisation of the text and its exact verbal replication, then one might perhaps see these preoccupations as being in turn the typical product of a scribal (as opposed to a print) technology. In a scribal culture, the argument would go, much knowledge continually sinks into the sand as manuscripts disappear and as texts progressively 'drift' away from their original, and the over-riding preoccupation tends therefore to be with the retention of what is already known. Books are scarce, their contents imparted to most only because they are read aloud, and memorisation retains a significance it does not possess in a print culture where books are readily available (c.f. Ong 1982: 119; Hirst and Woolley 1932: 36-8).

In India however - as in many other traditional cultures - this emphasis on the precise reproduction of the text has been motivated more by a concern with the precise reproduction of sound than by a concern with the retention of the meaning it conveys. The words in themselves have power once they are vocalised. For this power to become manifest they must be pronounced with precision and exactly the right inflection. Wrongly accentuated they may have an effect opposite to the one intended (cf. Kane 1976: 2: 347). I can best illustrate the importance of pronunciation by the case of a south Indian Brahman I know who earns his living performing mortuary rituals on Benares's principal cremation ground. He claims to have memorised three of the Vedas and to have learned to recite them with complete accuracy. Since Presidents Nixon and Ford short-sightedly overlooked his letters offering to put this remarkable skill at their disposal, he wishes me to make it known that he would be prepared to consider a post in the University of London, and that his appointment should be treated as a matter of urgency since it is only a question of time before he loses the full set of teeth essential for a flawless recitation. Seen in the light of all this, it is clearly irrelevant whether the written word exists in printed or manuscript form. In either case the memorisation of its proper verbal manifestation remains an equally insistent need; and one which cannot therefore be wholly accounted for by the technical deficiencies of a scribal mode of communication.

The most powerful words of all are those of the Vedic *mantras* which are recited as an indispensable part of every major ritual and are what makes it efficacious. The *mantra* is not a prayer but a kind of sound form of the deity it embodies. More than a supplication it is a means of coercion.[6] By *japa* - the repeated muttering of Vedic passages - the Brahman chanter may achieve for his client success in litigation, the restoration of good health or the

---

[6] In the tradition at large the matter is not wholly unambiguous however; and even amongst my own informants there would be some who would stress an aspect of entreaty.

indefinite postponement of death - the more ambitious the project the larger the number of repetitions required.[7] The content of these passages is not, however, understood. Those ritual specialists who are competent in classical Sanskrit are quite unable to comprehend the archaic language of the Veda. Even amongst the traditional *scholarly* community of the city, and despite persistent enquiry, I experienced enormous difficulty in finding a Pandit who could confidently render any of the Vedic *mantras* used in the mortuary rituals into Hindi.

While all twice-born castes have in theory the right to study the Veda, it is only the Brahmans who are authorized to teach it. The stress on oral transmission and correct pronunciation clearly ensures that their indispensability in this role remains unthreatened by the potential literacy provides for circumventing pedagogical control by private study. Without the guidance of a *guru* book learning is said to be without value and even an obstacle to the acquisition of knowledge (cf. Kane 1976: 2: 322, 349).

Power is with the word, and the word is with the Brahman; or - as my informants endlessly quoted - "the gods control the world; *mantras* control the gods and the Brahmans control the *mantras* ". It was after all the Brahman who at the beginning of time emerged from the *mouth* of the sacrificial body of primeval man, while the progenitors of successively lower *varnas* emerged from successively lower parts of his body. It is they who are descended from the ancient *rishis* who originally received the divine revelation and expounded it for posterity. But above all it is the Brahman's purity that qualifies him for Vedic study - which must be suspended if either teacher or pupil is afflicted by the pollution of birth or death,[8] or if the place of study is in any way rendered impure.

Even in the modern educational institutions of Benares the Brahmans' monopoly over Sanskrit education remains jealously

---

[7] Not only the Veda but also the recitation of sacred texts of lesser prestige confers untold benefits. For the birth of a son the household priest will be asked to read the *Harivamsa Purana*; for the liberation of a soul who got stuck as a marginal ghost (*preta*) the *Shrimat Bhagavata Purana*. Though it is often said that it is necessary to listen to the text carefully if the desired result is to be obtained, and though the Sanskrit verses are accompanied by a Hindi commentary, attention tends to be rather fitful.

[8] According to the ritual experts, Vedic *mantras* cannot in theory be chanted as part of the mortuary rituals of the first ten days after death which is the period of most intense pollution (though in practice this is not invariably true).

guarded, and I was told with much circumstantial detail of a well-respected Sanskrit scholar who has been repeatedly denied tenure at Benares Hindu University because he is of a Brahman subcaste traditionally disqualified from teaching the Veda. When the Sanskrit University (as it continues to be known) was officially re-named after Sampurnanand, the non-Brahman Chief Minister of the State, the Brahman-dominated student body staged a series of strikes and demonstrations.

Ideologically, Brahmanical pre-eminence is inseparable from their learning. The respectable Brahman is a scholar and a teacher rather than a priest. The priesthood is, as I have discussed at length elsewhere, regarded with equivocation since priests must necessarily accept the gifts (*dana*) of their patrons if the ritual is to work, but these gifts embody the sins of the donor (Parry 1980). Though in practice seen as an impossible ideal, the theory is that they can 'digest' these sins by the meticulous performance of certain rites and by passing on the gifts they have received, with increment, to a number of other Brahmans. The relevance of this here is that the transactional code it implies also obtains for learning. Indeed Mrs. Stevenson (1920: 228) reports that the Brahman's teaching is assimilated to the category of gift (*dana*), and it is therefore not surprising that it should be governed by the same rules. These state that what the Brahman takes in, he must at all costs disgorge again, for if he fails to keep in circulation what he has received he will be required to pay the direst penalties in this and future lives. Here we are clearly in a quite different universe from those ideologies - like that of the Hindu Tantric or the New Guinea Baktaman (Barth 1975) - where the most powerful knowledge is the most highly secret and where access to it is as narrowly restricted as possible. Barring the Shudra - whose ears are to be filled with mercury if he hears the Veda - the Brahman's knowledge is theoretically something to be disseminated.

The specialists generally assert that over the centuries which separated their original composition from their commitment to writing, the Vedas were transmitted without significant alteration; and clearly this claim does not altogether square with Goody's characterisation of oral knowledge as a highly volatile and malleable resource. The supposition of faithful oral transmission has recently - though in my view unconvincingly - been contested by Goody (in press) and Ong (1982: 65-6).[9] In any event the Veda must in certain respects be regarded as a special case. But attention has also often been drawn (e.g. Shulman 1980: 11) to the remarkable continuity between many classical myths and those of the contemporary village, where the presumption is that their transmission has been almost exclusively oral. Again, Wadley (1975) remarks on the lack of variation in the (unwritten) non-Sanskritic dialect "*mantras*" employed by the exorcists of Karimpur over the forty year period since the Wisers' fieldwork; and Smith (1977) persuasively argues that the Pabuji epic of Rajasthan does not conform to Lord's findings for Yugoslavia, but is an example of an oral "text" performed without improvisation or significant deviation from an original composition. The difference between the two traditions, he suggests, is related to the liturgical role of the Rajasthani epic; a suggestion which would receive support from Wadley's evidence (1978) that while in the

---

[9] There is no way, they point out, that such stability could possibly be demonstrated in the absence of writing; and while it is certainly the case that Brahmanical dogma insists on the meticulous accuracy of oral transmission, this is no reason for accepting their testimony uncritically - a point which is brought home by Lord's (1960) work on Yugoslav bards, whose claims for the perfect repetition of their performance from one occasion to the next are both sincere and demonstrably false. The case of the Veda invites reassessment in the light of such findings. Ong (1982: 62-3) nevertheless cites some impressive evidence of stability in cases of purely oral transmission, and plausibly suggests that ritual recitations and those constrained by music and/or rigid metrical forms are least susceptible to distortion and drift. Why these considerations should be ignored in the case of the Vedas is left unclear.

What is incontrovertibly established is that the highly formalised, disciplined and rigorous methods developed for teaching the Veda do result in a remarkably accurate reproduction of what has been taught by purely oral transmission. Goody suggests that what makes this possible is the application of mnemonic techniques that depend on the reduction of language to a visual form and therefore presuppose a literate culture - the implication being that verbatim reproduction of such accuracy could not be matched in a pre-literate one. This seems questionable. Is it really obvious that verbatim memorisation *is* dependent on the visual representation of language, or that visual representation necessarily implies writing? Would not the commonplace observation that writing is destructive of memory suggest that oral knowledge is more likely to be faithfully reproduced in a pre-literate culture? While it is certainly the case that the elaborate theory of phonetics laid down in the Sanskrit texts which deal with the pronunciation and transmission of the Veda (e.g. Pattubhiram Sastri 1976) is inconceivable without literacy, is it equally clear that the actual teaching methods employed were wholly dependent on this theoretical apparatus and are unimaginable without it?

case of those religious stories classed as *kissa* there is legitimate scope for a personal rendering, in the case of those which are classed as *katha* and which are distinguished by being recited within a *ritual* frame, the emphasis is on the careful reproduction of a set text. What seems clear at any rate is that oral knowledge of this kind may display a surprising resilience to change over long periods of time (cf. Ong 1982: 62-3).

Of more immediate interest here, however, is the other side of Goody's contrast - the relative immutability of knowledge which he associates with a literate tradition by contrast with an oral one, and which he sees as imposing a "restriction on spontaneity". On the contrary, I would like to emphasize its mutability, and its malleability to the requirements of practical life.

The Vedas, for example, as commonly cited as being the ultimate authority on matters of moral and religious duty (*dharma*). Yet the paradox is that these ritualistic texts do not contain any "positive injunctions that could be used directly as rules of conduct" (Heesterman 1978: 81). In fact, to follow Heesterman's argument, their lack of any real bearing on the practical world is essential to their inviolability. Since they are not bound to the social world they are immune to the corrosive effects of the changes it undergoes. Given that the Vedas are the ultimate authority on matters they do not pronounce upon, the common recourse is to the "transcendent vision", as Heesterman puts it, "of a human authority" - a sage or a *guru*. But how is one to judge *his* credentials? The conventional answer is in terms of his knowledge of the scriptural revelation. It is his knowledge of texts that have nothing to say about *dharma* that authorises him to rule on it. The way would seem to be open for him to say what he likes.

The content of the Veda is fixed; but its direct application to practical life is minimal. I now turn to a much later text where this situation is reversed. The *Garuda Purana* is one of the eighteen so-called *Mahapuranas*, or Great *Puranas*, which were all supposedly composed by the legendary sage Vyasa at the beginning of the *Kali Yuga*,[10] the Black Age of historical time in which we actually live and which is the last and most degenerate of the four epochs of the world cycle. The text is one to which my informants continually refer; is regarded as the final word on mat-

---

[10] There are actually two slightly different traditions: the first that there is one *Purana* in heaven which Vyasa divided into eighteen on earth; the second that Vyasa transmitted only one *samhita* ("compilation") to his disciples, and it was subsequently subdivided.

ters relating to death, mourning and the conduct of the mortuary rituals; and it is with these matters that their version is exclusively concerned. During mourning it is read daily in the house of the deceased by a Brahman priest who is called in specially for this purpose.

An English translation of the *Garuda Purana* by an eminent Brahman Pandit has also been published from Benares. What is striking, however, is that virtually the only thing that the two versions have in common is the claim that unsurpassable benefits accrue to those who hear them, and the exhortation to give liberally to the Brahman who recites them. While the one deals only with matters related to death, the other has little to say on this topic, but ranges over a diffuse set of other subjects from aphrodisiacs to the medical treatment of horses. The translator of this version (1968: iii-iv) acknowledges the existence of the first as one of the parts, or *khandas,* of which the work has often been held to consist. But he goes on to say that "it requires nothing more than average intellect to detect that (it)...is manifestly an interpolation......bad in reason and rhetoric." This "spurious portion" has therefore been expunged in an attempt to restore the text to its original form. We therefore have at least two entirely different versions of the same work. According to a recent scholarly study, however, it is very doubtful whether either of them bears much relationship to the ancient texts of the same name since the contents of none of the existing versions conform to what is said about the *Garuda Purana* in other better authenticated *Puranas* (Gangadharan 1971: 120, 124). It is, then, almost as if the *Garuda Purana* is an empty box into which an enormous range of possible contents might be poured by selecting from a vast array of manuscript sources of greater or lesser antiquity and authenticity.

A critical edition of the *Garuda Purana* is about to be prepared by the Kashi Raj Trust, a scholarly foundation set up and funded by the Maharaja of Benares to promote and disseminate knowledge of the Hindu texts. Amongst its most important projects is the publication of "authorized" versions of each of the *Puranas,* restored as nearly as possible to their original form by "scientific" principles of textual scholarship imported from the West. Manuscripts of the *Purana* in hand are collected from all over India, and are collated verse by verse. In the case of the *Garuda Purana,* for example, manuscripts have been obtained from as far afield as Kathmandu and Tamilnadu, Jammu and Calcutta. The oldest of these is probably no earlier than the beginning of the seventeenth century, and not one of them contains all of the three *khandas* (parts) of which the work is traditionally supposed to comprise. Variation within each *khanda* is itself enormous; and there are three quite different versions of the *preta-kalpa* - the part which relates to death and which my priestly informants unsuspectingly believe to be the complete and invariant work. In order to arrive at an authoritative text, the Trust's Pandits select the 'best' version of each passage, so that the new edition is a composite put together from quite different sources. In choosing between variants one of the rules applied is that the more impenetrable the verse the more authentic it is likely to be - clarity suggesting the intrusive hand and crude mind of later copyists. I need hardly say that the result of this procedure is likely to be an obscurity that lends itself to rival interpretations and requires a Brahman scholar for its elucidation.

Following Biardeau (1968), the more interesting point however is that what has been borrowed is a method which was developed in order to reconstruct, out of relatively minor variations between texts, the original written text of the author. But in the case of the *Puranas* it is very doubtful that there ever was a single original written text - the probability being that we are dealing with a number of quite different recensions which evolved out of the oral traditions of the regions from which each comes. What we have, then, is an attempt to restore something which probably never existed. Yet for the Brahman Pandits it is a matter of faith that it did exist, and that it was actually composed by Vyasa whom they regard as an historical individual rather than as a generalised symbol of tradition. In other words, the whole apparatus of the critical edition is directed - as Biardeau notes - to the essentially religious purpose of recovering as nearly as possible the divine inspiration of a purely mythical character. The objective result, however, is a completely new recension of the work.

As the Pandits are apt to see it, authentic fragments of Vyasa's revelation may have been preserved in the oral tradition of Vyasa's revelation may have been preserved in the oral tradition as well as in the manuscript sources, and they therefore regard it as perfectly legitimate to supplement the latter from their own knowledge of the tradition as it was handed down to them. Here we can recall the experience of the great Sanskritist, Georg Buhler, who was presented with a copy of the *Nilamatapurana* by the

Maharaja of Kashmir. When Buhler later visited Kashmir and checked the originals he discovered that the beginning of his text was the copyist's own insertion. Yet all the Pandits with whom he spoke rated his version as the best (Rocher 1983). Today, one of the most renowned Puranic scholars in Benares is quite forthright in the view that a new edition or translation of a text should be an original work incorporating details known to the Pandit but somehow missing from his sources. The implication here is clearly that the 'text' is not conceptualised as a purely literary document. Its "authentic version" is rather an original and sacred revelation, the recovery of which may require recourse to *both* written and oral sources (the authenticity of the latter - if not also of the former - being validated only by the prestige and authority of its Brahman repositories).

Although everybody is aware that there are eighteen 'Great' *Puranas*, even amongst scholars there is no complete unanimity on which they are. Dozens of other works are also rated as *Puranas*, though not in the major league. More generally, the canon of sacred literature is by no means closed. Shulman (1980: 37-9) refers to a fascinating account written by a disciple of the nineteenth century Tamil scholar Minatcicuntaram Pillai, who ran what Shulman appositely describes as a 'Purana-industry'. Commissioned by a wealthy patron, he would search out old manuscripts on the deity or shrine for whose glorification he was asked to work, make prose versions of any relevant mythology and visit the temple itself. He then composed orally and at great speed while one of his pupils recorded his words. On one occasion he is reported as having reeled off fifty verses without preparation or hesitation. Clearly the style of composition was highly formulaic - and in this respect at least invites comparison with the bardic tradition which produced the *Odyssey* and *Iliad*. The obvious but significant difference, however, is that while Homer belonged to a pre-literate culture, not only did Minacicuntaram Pillai belong to a literate one, but he was also himself a man of letters. Once more, then, a pattern purportedly characteristic of oral cultures is seen to persist in a highly literate one. More germane to my present point, however, is that while the precise provenance of these particular texts is known, it is not hard to imagine that similar compositions of fairly recent date have in a relatively short space of time acquired an antiquity which links them with the direct inspiration of Vyasa at the beginning of the present world epoch.

Although in principle superior authority always resides with the most ancient texts, and although this might seem to promote an extreme religious conservatism, the notion of time as progressive degeneration in fact allows considerable scope for manoeuvre.

Practices - like animal sacrifice and asceticism - which were appropriate in the Age of Truth at the beginning of time are no longer suitable to man's degraded nature in the Black Age. It is in precisely these terms that the Puranic texts often claim their equality with, or sometimes even their superiority to, the Veda (Kane 1977: 5: II: 914; Bonazzoli 1983). On the one hand they go out of their way to borrow its authority by presenting themselves as a kind of primer on the original revelation which the gods have provided out of compassion for the impoverished intellect of modern man. But they may on the other hand claim a pre-eminence in the degraded conditions of the present, and can justify quite radical innovation by reference to the exigencies of the Age (cf. Srinivasen 1980). The authority of the Veda is acknowledged as supreme, though Vedic precepts must perforce be modified in an epoch so debased.

One device by which the Puranic texts may be assimilated to Vedic revelation is by collapsing their mythological composers into one. The *Kashi Khanda*, which is a eulogy of Benares (and which probably dates from around the fourteenth century A.D.), opens with an account of how it came down to us from the gods. It is told here by Vyasa to the reciter (Sut) as it was told by the god Kartik to the sage Agastya, as Kartik himself heard it recounted to the goddess Parvati by his father Siva. What is obvious is that this elaborate pedigree is intended to establish a direct line of oral transmission from Siva to the reciter. But what is also happening here is that the *Kashi Khanda* is being equated with the *Rg-Veda*, the oldest of the Vedic texts. Agastya and his wife (Lopamudra) were the first human beings to hear it, just as in an earlier incarnation they are sometimes said to have been the first to receive the revelation of the *Rg-Veda*. In relation to Goody the more general point, however, is that the individuality of those who actually did compose these works must at all costs be suppressed since the authority of the text relies on establishing its direct transmission from the gods to a mythical sage who is credited with its preservation for posterity. So far from perpetuating individual achievement, the object here is to efface it. It is clearly not only oral communication which has a propensity to "swallow up" the creative product of the individual "in a body of transmitted custom" (Goody 1977:27).

What this example might also alert us to is that the texts not only purvey a vision of time as progressive degeneration, but also as endlessly repeating itself. If it moves downwards it does so in spirals regularly returning to the same point, only lower down. In Puranic mythology, for example, the same characters keep reappearing in different incarnations, and re-enacting more or less the same events. Indeed, as my informants would appear to see it, these events continue to recur in the present. For example, the English - as I am ceaselessly reminded - are the descendants of Ravana, one of the main protagonists in the epic *Ramayana*. Ravana was the demon king of Lanka, the lustful abductor of the goddess Sita and a fallen Brahman whose knowledge gave him fantastic power. His wife, Mandodari, bore him a son at an astrologically disastrous moment. The boy was set to drift on the sea and was carried by the current to England, which is now populated by his descendants. In her next incarnation Mandodari, the mother, crops up again as Queen Victoria. In a similar vein I have several times been told that Mrs. Gandhi has a reincarnation of the regenerate demonness Trijata, who befriended Sita in Lanka; and that the Americans are the descendants of Raja Bali - the explanation for which is perhaps provided by the fact his mythological come-uppance was the consequence of his interested and vain-glorious donations. I cite all this not so much for its perspicacity about international relations, but to establish the point that the sacred texts purvey a model of time which is directly carried over into perceptions of present-day reality. There is, it seems to me, at least as good a case to be made for the argument that in traditional India literacy has promoted a cyclical conception of time, as for Goody's claim that it encourages a durational notion.

More generally, modern communications are - in the medium term at least - just as likely to reinforce "traditional" religious values, to lend a helping hand to the 'civilizing' process of Sanskritization, as to contribute to a process of secularisation. With the coming of the railways one of the most likely long distance journeys for many a rural peasant is a pilgrimage; and with literacy and printing in the vernacular he is as likely to pick up a book or a pamphlet on a religious theme as one which promotes a secular 'disenchantment' of the world. Wadley (1978) reports, for example, that apart from school-books, the only books which find their way to Karimpur are religious works published in the vernacular.

Another angle on the extent to which the literate tradition moulds, or constrains, knowledge would be to look at the way in which some of its key concepts are actually interpreted by the actors. The terms *moksha* and *mukti* mean 'liberation', which is conventionally described as the highest goal of human existence. The religious pre-eminence of Benares is associated with the fact that all who die there are held to achieve this goal. But the paradox is that nobody seems to be agreed on what exactly it is. The commonest view is that it is a "cessation of coming and going" - that is, of rebirth. You no longer "have to bear the pain of the womb", or have "to wander between the 840,000 kinds of life form". But some informants interpreted this as an extinction of the individual soul, which "is absorbed into the universal Spirit as water mixes with water", while others took it to imply a perpetual and sybaritic residence in heaven. While either of these psssibilities might find textual sanction, many people take the definitely unscriptural line that "liberation" is here to be understood as the promise of a happy and prosperous rebirth (cf. Parry 1981).

Now it may at first sight appear tempting to see this as part of the process of "parochialisation" whereby "the essentially unlearned and non-literate nature of the little tradition obstructs the direct transmission or spread of elements downward from great (tradition) to little" (Marriott 1961:204). As the thoughts of the literati filter through to the masses their original meaning is diluted and transformed. The problem, however, is that those informants who interpreted the doctrine that 'death in Benares is liberation' in terms of a privileged rebirth included a number of sacred specialists, and I was as likely to get the doctrinally orthodox view from an illiterate pilgrim as from a professional priest. While I do not wish to discount the very real possibility of sheer ignorance of the *Shastric* tradition amongst the priesthood, I am inclined to look for the explanation of such variation as much in the contradictions inherent within textual Hinduism as in the adulterating influence of the so-called "little tradition". That is, the reason why some informants flatly rejected the claim that all who die in Benares are released from the cycle of rebirths may stem in part from the perceived inconsistency between this doctrine and other scripturally sanctioned beliefs - from a belief, for example, that the only way to escape the world is to renounce it.

With regard to matters of belief the kind of variation I have described is characteristic. But with regard to ritual practice - even allowing for the self-acknowledged incompetence of many of the priests and the surreptitious editing in which they indulge if the rewards look unpromising - there is much greater standardisation. Unless he knows it by heart the priest more or less follows a printed manual (*paddhati*). But the manuals only tell him what to do and say, not what it means; and exegesis of the ritual is often highly discrepant. We are back, then, to my metaphor of the empty box into which quite different sets of contents can be put.

This contrast between the variability of belief and the constancy of ritual form is, however, far from absolute. For a start there are quite significant differences of form between, for example, the mortuary rituals laid down in the different manuals followed by the Maithila community of Benares, the South Indians and the indigenous population of the city. The latter generally follow a *paddhati* known as the *Preta Manjari*. Even here the printed editions vary considerably not only in the number of errors which have crept into the Sanskrit text but also in length - the most extensive containing many details omitted from the shortest.

Moreover at least some of the priests creatively elaborate on what is laid down in the standard manual. A South Indian funerary priest once told me that when a woman of one of his client families dies in childbirth her corpse must by purified by bathing it 108 times before it is fit to be cremated. Intrigued by this information, I asked a large number of north Indian priests what they would do in such circumstances, and was consistently assured that no special rituals were required. One of these was my friend Sita Maharaj, with whom I discussed the matter at length, and to whom I told what I had heard from my south Indian informant. On visiting the cremation ground some weeks later I was intrigued to find Sita Maharaj presiding over the 108 purificatory baths of a female corpse. He had eventually tracked it down in an old book, he claimed, and had decided to adopt it into his repertoire. Incidentally his brother, Ram Maharaj, has often groused to me about Sita's insistence on doing things according to his own interpretation of the Shastras, even if it annoys their clients. "But Ram Maharaj is not Sita. I do what they want. In my whole life I have only performed two or three *sraddhas* (mortuary rites) according to the *Shastras*. I emphasise *lokachar* (the popular tradition). What the women of the family say, that's the truth. Blowing our conch shells, we Brahmans throw dust in people's eyes."

I conclude, then, that the 'restriction on spontaneity' imposed by reducing knowledge to a written form is in fact rather minimal. I have also suggested that in the context I have been discussing the written form - so far from promoting scepticism - provides a certain immunity against it; that the potential which literacy provides for the anonymous transmission of knowledge and the recording of individual innovation is evaded, and that textual knowledge is intimately bound up with the magical power of words and the pursuit of a metaphysical truth which is likely to inhibit any trend towards a more "rational" scientific outlook. There is at least as much evidence to suggest that literacy promotes Sanskritisation as secularisation, and cyclical as against durational notions of time.

Literacy and "cognitive modernism"

If we start from the (questionable) promise that literacy plays a crucial causative role in the transformation from "cognitive traditionalism" to "modernism", then the next obvious step is to ask why in some cases this "take-off" apparently aborts. Why, in other words, do some literate societies (or part-societies) fail to realise its full potentialities?

One possible answer here would be in terms of the insufficient development of the technology of the intellect in the pre-print world, for in much of the recent literature it is the development of printing, rather than the development of literacy, which is seen as providing the crucial impetus for a revolution in human thought processes. Indeed it is striking that Eisenstein (1969, 1981, 1983), attributes to print almost exactly the same range of cognitive 'advances' as Goody attributes to literacy. Viewed from this perspective the crucial break is not that between pre-literate and literate, but that between scribal and print cultures.

In the former, texts not only have a tendency to 'drift' cumulatively away from their original source as they pass through the hands of generations of copyists, but many of them are lost or destroyed completely. Knowledge rests on a precarious foundation, and most of it is accessible only to the wandering scholar. In such a context the preoccupation is with retrieving what is already known; with recovering the wisdom of the ancients rather than with discovering something new. Before print it was in fact almost impossible to know whether a discovery was new. By vastly increasing the sheer quantity of knowledge available, print promoted a change in its qualitative character. Systematic cross-referencing became possible, thereby enhancing the likelihood of sceptical scrutiny and allowing for new intellectual combinations. What was known to the ancient world could now be established, could be found wanting and could provide the basis for a cumulative advance. In a scribal culture, by contrast, "there could be no systematic forward movement, no accumulation of stepping stones enabling a new generation to begin where the prior one had left off" (Eisenstein 1969: 65). Associated with the development of print goes the shift from magic to science, and the growth of individualism." It was print technology which gave birth to the notion of intellectual property rights ["an absurdity...where every book copied is a minor victory over ignorance and wastage" (Hirst and Wooley 1982:41)]; "which encouraged publishers to advertise authors and authors to advertise themselves" (Eisenstein 1969: 58), and which recorded individual achievement in a form and on a scale hitherto unknown. The transmission of knowledge became a more anonymous process, which allowed for the auto-didact. But in a scribal culture books remain relatively rare items, and most people are acquainted with their contents only by hearing them read aloud. As a result they tend to take the form of compendia covering a wide range of diffuse topics, and "oral performance sets its demands on composition" (Hirst and Woolley 1982: 36). It was, in short, "the shift from script to print (which) revolutionised Western culture", and which effected "a shift in human consciousness" (Eisenstein 1969: 19, 56). Before print literary products had a restricted circulation, and it is this simple fact that gave rise to the cognitive syndrome associated with "restricted literacy".

It might in other words be plausibly argued that many of the features I have described for traditional India are common to the pre-print world in general, and are a direct consequence of the technological deficiencies in a scribal mode of communication. Even such highly particularised cultural notions as the idea that knowledge is - (or is like) - a 'gift' which must be circulated if it is not to destroy its possessor, might be seen in terms of the necessary preoccupation of such a culture with the problem of preserving existing knowledge.

While the argument of the previous paragraph has a certain force, the causal proposition that printing promotes a spirit of sceptical scientific enquiry, a weakening of confidence in old theories and the development of new intellectual paradigms obviously presupposes a specific institutional context. If in early modern Europe access to the new means of communication had been monopolised by priests and rulers, and denied to "free-wheeling urban entrepreneurs", then - as Eisenstein (1983: 273) herself explicitly acknowledges - the picture would have been significantly different. Far from being an instrument of intellectual liberation, under such conditions the printing press is far more likely to be an instrument of domination used to entrench the ruling paradigms. Moreover, the process of feedback from readers to publishers and authors which - on Eisenstein's showing - provided an important source of new information and facilitated a cumulative advance of knowledge in the early era of print, is clearly only likely to occur in a context where the submissions of the lay public are considered worthy of serious attention, and where the empirical knowledge they supply is highly valued. In short, the "printing revolution" was revolutionary only because it was associated with a much wider "democratization of society and learning" that was already under way. In a different institutional context (as for example in China and Korea) the implications of print technology were quite different (cf. Eisenstein 1983: 273); and the development of this technology is therefore manifestly insufficient to account for the "great transformation" of mental life.

It has often been argued that the scientific revolution which took place in Western Europe in the sixteenth and seventeenth centuries was positively promoted by the religious climate created by the Reformation. All believers with the capacity to do so now had "the right, and even the duty...to study Scripture without depending on the authority of tradition and hierarchy, together with the right and duty to study the other book written by God, the book of nature, without regard to the authority of the fathers of natural philosophy" (Hooykaas 1977: 109). Literacy itself became a moral obligation required of the believer so that he could directly receive the word of God (cf. Strauss 1981; Lockridge 1981). Though Newton and others saw themselves as retrieving knowledge which had been lost rather discovering anything really new (Hall 1983: 14), the general expectation was that the wisdom of the ancients *would* be surpassed, for in science "truth is the daughter of time" (Hooykaas 1977: 113). No pope was recognised in either religion or philosophy; the domain of science was freed from both ecclesiastical authority and that of the ancients, and was increasingly allowed to proceed by reference to its own autonomous rules and procedures. Since the Protestant God was remote and mysterious, he could only be known through his works and the investigation of his creation (Merton 1978; Parsons 1968: 523). " The study of natural phenomena (was seen as) an effective means for promoting the glory of God" (Merton 1978: 71); empirical knowledge was highly valued and a premium placed on its practical utility - for what sweetens the lives of mortals is good in the sight of God (Merton 1978: 72). Painstaking observation and experiment became the scientific expression of the Puritan emphasis on labouring tirelessly in God's calling; and the relatively positive evaluation of both manual labour and artisan-type occupations favoured technological advance and the rise of experimental science. Made in the image of God, man moreover exercised dominion over nature and therefore had the right to master it by technological means.

The contrast between all this and the Brahmanical tradition I have described is radical. Far from a priesthood of all believers, the *shastras* are to be transmitted and interpreted only by those with the authority to do so, and literacy is not a requirement laid on the devout. Knowledge progressively dengerates with time, and is therefore something to be recovered from the sages of the past, whose wisdom cannot be surpassed in the present. Consistent with this is an emphasis on its faithful reproduction rather than on innovation and experiment; and on memorization over complete understanding. Since the *guru* provides a life-line to past tradition, his authority is paramount and a sceptical scrutiny of his teaching discountenanced. The *shastras* contain the last word on both science and salvation, and science does not constitute an autonomous domain apart from religion. Nor does the book of nature hold the keys to a transcendent truth. Knowledge of the empirical world is rather devalued - as is consistent with the notion that it is a world of illusion and an obstacle to salvation. "The gods love the mystic"; they "are fond of the obscure (and) detest direct knowledge", say the Satapatha Brahmana and the sage Yajnavalkya (quoted in Chattopadhyaya 1977: 272, 277). Real eternally valid knowledge is of a soteriological nature; and in so far as one incidentaly acquires a practical means of controlling the world by the acquisition of knowledge that leads out of it, this control is of an essentially magical nature associated above all with the power of the spoken word. The tradition moreover accords a relatively low status to manual labour and craft occupations, and offers little stimulus to experimentation and technological innovation.

I do not, of course, intend to claim that all this represents the *only* strand in traditional Hindu thought; or to suggest that all the divergent traditions of Hinduism were equally antipathetic to that "rational empiricism" which characterised the emergence of modern science in Western Europe. Nor is my objective to account for the failure of Indian science to sustain its early promise (though I do suggest that the authority of the particular tradition I describe would be *one* of the factors relevant for such an account). A proper exploration of these issues is both beyond the scope of this paper and the competence of its author; and would obviously demand a consideration of politico-economic constraints which have not been touched on here.

The point of juxtaposing the two situations is rather that it directs attention to the enormous disparity between the two cognitive worlds, and emphasizes the necessity of understanding the transformation of mental life to which Goody alludes in relation to the wider context in which it actually occurs. But once this wider context is brought into the picture, the assumption that literacy is an active agent in the process - an assumption which underlies the questions with which I opened this section - begins to look rather dubious. Literacy is certainly a general precondition for the transformation, but surely reveals as much about the specific conditions under which it is likely to occur as the Neolithic Revolution reveals about the conditions likely to produce Stevenson's "Rocket". Once we have recognized that it provides no more than a passive prerequisite for "cognitive modernism", it comes as no surprise that the "cognitive traditionalism" supposedly characteristic of preliterate societies is no less marked in most literate ones. In terms of types of rationality, any antithesis between oral and literate cultures is false.

Bibliography

Altekar, A. S. (1937) 'History of Benares' in *Journal of the Benares Hindu University*, Vol. XX, pp. 47-75, 243-86.

Barth, F. (1975) *Ritual and knowledge among the Baktaman of New Guinea*, New Haven: Yale University Press.

Basham, A. L. (1967) *The wonder that was India*, Fontana Ancient History.

Bernier, F. (1968) *Travels in the Mogul Empire*, Delhi: S. Chand & Co.

Biardeau, M. (1968) 'Some more considerations about textual criticism', *Purana*, Vol. 10, No. 2: 115-23.

Bonazzoli, G. (1933) 'Remarks on the nature of Puranas' in *Purana*, Vol. XXV, No. 1, pp. 77-113.

Chattopadhyaya, D. (1977) *Science and society in ancient India*, Calcutta: Research India Publications.

Cohn, B. S. (1971) *India: the social anthropology of a civilization*, New Jersey: Prentice-Hall Inc.

Dumont, L. & Pocock, D. F. (1957) 'For a sociology of India', *Contributions to Indian Sociology*, I: 7-22.

Eisenstein, E. L. (1969) 'The advent of printing and the problem of the Renaissance', *Past and Present* , Vol. 45: 19-89.

Eisenstein, E. L. (1981) 'Some conjectures about the impact of printing on western society and thought: a preliminary report', in H.J. Graff (ed.) *Literacy and social development in the West*, Cambridge: University Press.

Eisenstein, E. L. (1983) *The printing revolution in early modern Europe*, Cambridge: University Press.

Gangadharan, N., (1970-1) *Garuda-Purana- a study*. (Printed as a supplement to *Purana*, Vol. 13, 1: 1-112 & 2: 105-74).

Garuda Purana (n. d.), (Sanskrit with Hindi commentary by Sudama Misra Shastri). Varanasi: Bombay Pushtak Bhandar.

Garuda Puranam: A prose English translation by Manmatha Nath Dutt Shastri (1968 2nd Edition). Varanasi: Chowkhamba Sanskrit Series vol. LXVII.

Goody, J. & Watt, I., (1963) 'The consequences of literacy', *Comparative studies in society and history*, vol. 5, no. 3: 304-45.

Goody, J. (ed.) (1968a) *Literacy in traditional societies*, Cambridge: University Press.

Goody, J. (1968b) 'Restricted literacy in northern Ghana', in J. Goody (ed.) *Literacy in traditional societies*, Cambridge: University Press.

Goody, J. (1976) *Production and reproduction: a comparative study of the domestic domain*, Cambridge: University Press.

Goody, J. (1977) *The domestication of the savage mind*, Cambridge: University Press.

Goody, J. (in press) 'Oral composition and oral transmission: the case of the Vedas'.

Hall, A. R. (1983) *The revolution in science 1600-1750*, London: Longman.

Heesterman, J. C. (1978) 'Veda and dharma', in W. D. O'Flaherty & J. D. M. Derrett (eds.) *The Concept of Duty in South Asia*, pp. 80-95, New Delhi: Vikas Publishing House.

Hirst, P. & Woolley, P. (1982) *Social relations and human attributes*, London: Tavistock Publications.

Hooykaas, R. (1977) *Religion and the rise of modern science*, Edinburgh: Scottish Academic Press.

Horton, R. (1970) 'African traditional thought and Western science' in B. Wilson (ed.) *Rationality*, pp. 131-71, Oxford: Basil Blackwell.

Horton, R. (1982) 'Tradition and modernity revisited', in M. Hollis and S. Lukes (eds.) *Rationality and relativism*. Oxford, Basil Blackwell.

India Reference Annual (1974) Delhi: Ministry of Information.

Kane, P. L. (1976) & (1979) *History of Dharmasastra*, Vols. 2 & 5, Poona: Bhandarkar Oriental Research Institute.

Kuper, A. (1982) *Wives for cattle: bridewealth and marriage in Southern Africa*, London: Routledge and Kegan Paul.

Lockridge, K. A. (1981) 'Literacy in early America 1650-1800', in H. J. Graff (ed.) *Literacy and social development in the West*, pp. 183-200, Cambridge: University Press.

Lord, A. B. (1960) *The Singer of Tales*, Harvard Studies in Comparative Literature, 24, Cambridge, Mass: Harvard University Press.

Manusmriti (*The laws of Manu*). Translated by Georg Buhler. New York: Dover Publications, 1969.

Marriott, McKim (1961) 'Little communities in an indigeneous civilization', in M. Marriott (ed.), *Village India: studies in the little community*, pp. 175-227, Bombay: Asia Publishing House.

Merton, R. K. (1978) *Science, technology and society in seventeenth century England,* New Jersey: Humanities Press (originally published in 1938 as vol. IV, Part 2 of *Osiris: studies on the history and philosophy of science, and on the history of learning and culture*).

Ong, W. J. (1982) *Orality and literacy: the technologizing of the word,* London: Methuen.

Pagels, E. (1979) *The Gnostic Gospels,* London: Weidenfeld and Nicholson.

Parry, J. P. (1980) 'Ghosts, greed and sin: the occupational identity of the Benares funeral priests', *Man* (n. s.), 15 (1), 88-111.

Parry, J. P. (1981) 'Death and cosmogony in Kashi', *Contributions to Indian Sociology* (n. s.), 15 (1 & 2), 337-65.

Parsons, Talcott (1968) *The Structure of social action,* Vol. 2: Weber. New York: The Free Press.

Pattubhiram Sastri, P. N. (1976) *Vyasa siksha.* Varanasi: Veda Mimamsa Research Centre.

Pitt-Rivers, J. (1977) *The fate of Schechem, or the politics of sex: essays in the anthropology of the Mediterranean,* Cambridge: University Press.

Preta Manjari, (Samvat 2032. Compiled by Sudama Misra Shastri and revised by Mannalal Abhimanyu), Varanasi: Bombay Pushtak Bhandar.

Rocher, L. (1983) 'Reflections on one hundred and fifty years of Puranic studies', *Purana,* Vol. XXV, No. 1, pp. 64-76.

Saraswati, Baidyanath (1975) *Kashi: myth and reality of a classical cultural tradition,* Simla: Indian Institute of Advanced Study.

Shulman, D. (1980) *Tamil temple myths: sacrifice and divine marriage in the South Indian Saiva tradition,* Princeton: University Press.

Singer, M. (1972) *When a great tradition modernizes: an anthropological approach to Indian civilization,* London: Pall Mall Press.

Smith, D. E. (1963) *India as a secular state,* Princeton: University Press.

Smith, J. D. (1977) 'The Singer or the Song? A reassessment of Lord's oral theory'. *Man* (n.s.), 12 (1), 141-53.

Staal, J. F. (1961) *Nambudiri Veda recitation,* S'-Gravenhage: Mouton & Co.

Stevenson, S. (1920) *The rites of the twice-born.* London: Oxford University Press.

Strathern, A. (1982) 'Witchcraft, greed, cannibalism and death', in M. Bloch & J. Parry (eds.), *Death and the regeneration of life,* pp. 111-33, Cambridge: University Press.

Strauss, G. (1981) 'Techniques of indoctrination: the German Reformation', in H. J. Graff (ed.) *Literacy and social development in the West,* Cambridge: University Press.

Srinivasan, A. (1980) 'Order and event in Puranic myth: an analysis of four narratives from the Bhagavata Purana', in *Contributions to Indian Sociology* (n.s.), 14 (2): 195-212.

Tambiah, S. J. (1970) *Buddhism and the spirit cults in North-east Thailand,* Cambridge: University Press.

Van Buitenen, J. A. B. (1966) 'On the archaism of the *Bhagavata Purana*', in M. Singer (ed.) *Krishna: myths, rites and attitudes.* Chicago: University Press.

Wadley, S. S. (1975) 'Folk literature in Karimpur: a catalogue of types'. *Journal of South Asian Literature* 11: 7-17.

Wadley, S. S. (1978) 'Texts in contexts: oral traditions and the study of religion in Karimpur', in S. Vatuk (ed.) *American studies in the anthropology of India.* New Delhi: Manohar Books.

Winternitz, M. (1927) *A history of Indian literature,* Calcutta: University Press.

The Significance of Writing in Early Greece - a critical appraisal

Øivind Andersen

Introduction

In this paper, I am mainly concerned with the implications of literacy for some aspects of Greek literature, intellectual history and political development down to the fifth century B. C. Students of this phenomenon in Ancient Greece are much indebted to the paper on "The consequences of Literacy", first published by Jack Goody and Ian Watt in 1963, and particularly to Eric A. Havelock's *Preface to Plato* from the same year. Havelock has since developed his ideas in his monumental book *The Greek Concept of Justice* (1978) and in papers that are now conveniently collected in a volume called *The Literate Revolution in Greece and its Cultural Consequences* (1982), while Goody has given a fuller treatment of the effects of writing on "modes of thought" in his book *The Domestication of the Savage Mind* (1977).

While rejecting "any dichotomy based upon the assumption of radical differences between mental attributes of literate and non-literate peoples" (Goody and Watt 1963: 44) and while accepting that "even in our civilization writing is clearly an addition, not an alternative to oral transmission" (68), Goody and Watt "attempted to review the liberating effects of changes" in communication technology (Goody 1968: 4) and to "relate certain aspects of the Greek achievement to this breakthrough in technology" (3). More generally, Goody in his later book raises the problem "how and why domestication occurred" (Goody 1977, 16) and tries to disentangle "the particular features of "modes of thought" that appear to be affected by changes in the means of communication" (19). Havelock's is a quadruple concern: To explain the way orally-preserved communication was operating; to argue the perseverance of the oral tradition right down to the

73

time of Plato; to show how and why Plato destroys "the immemorial habit of self-identification with the oral tradition"
(Havelock 1963: 201) and to argue for the specific significance of
the invention of the alphabet and of alphabetic writing in Greece
as opposed to any previous writing system. For Havelock, the
Greek alphabet is "a piece of explosive technology, revolutionary
in its effects on human culture" (Havelock 1982: 6), while it was
only with Plato that it became established as a "new idiom ...
ushering in a completely new stage in the development, not only
of the Greek but of the European mind" (Havelock 1963: 267. See
also 1982: 71, 73, 87f.). Others before Plato had moved in the same
direction: There was a process of awakening. The fundamental
answer to the question: *how did the Greeks ever wake up?* must,
according to Havelock "lie in the changing technology of
communication" (Havelock 1963: 208).

More specifically then, I am concerned with the problems of
this awakening. I have no quarrel with those who maintain that
writing has affected *our* "modes of thought" and claim that
"more than any other single invention, writing has transformed
human consciousness" (Ong 1982: 78). What we must beware of,
however, is deducing from such global statements consequences
for the users of the written word in early Greece or for that matter
in any particular society or historical epoch. When we look more
closely at the first elements of literacy within a primary oral culture and not at a literate culture in contrast to an oral one -
examining not the realm of literacy as opposed to that of orality,
but the border area between them - it becomes difficult indeed to
talk confidently of the effects and implications of writing and to
pin down the significance of the new technology. Introducing
graphic symbols for speech is "a long and changing process"
(Goody 1977: 19), and the transition from orality to literacy is a
slow one, as Ong has pointed out (Ong 1982: 115f.).

Goody is "not trying to put forward a simple, technologically
determined, sequence of cause and effect" and sees no justification for "a monocausal explanation of a unilineal kind" (1977:
10). Others seem to remove literacy from the realm of causes altogether. In a recent book *On Literacy* (1982), Robert Pattison, with
seemingly due respect, but hardly quite fairly, places strictures on
what he calls "the excesses of Goody and Watt" (221) and the
"naïve belief" of Havelock (224). The argument that "the superior
technology fundamentally alters the mental and social organization of these written cultures just as the application of iron or

steam revolutionizes human ideology and social structure ... cannot survive exposure to common sense. All cultures are by definition oral cultures. When men learn to write they do not then forget how to speak" (24). For Pattison, whose concept of literacy is not tied up with letters, but relates to "individual and cultural awareness of language" (7), it is even possible to state that "a highly developed literacy existed in Greece before the advent of reading and writing" (46). "Writing did not make the Greek mind sceptical, logical, historical, or democratic. Instead it furnished an opportunity for these predispositions to flourish" (45). In my opinion, Pattison's book has its merits, but it loses some of its value when it throws us back on factors like the "predispositions" of the Greeks. However, he has an important point to make in stressing that "no two societies will have the same literacy" (VIII). The conditions of literacy must be investigated specifically and individually for each society. It is difficult to isolate writing and, if I may say so, it is important not to see writing in isolation as a causal factor when trying to explain cultural change.

Let me make sense out of this truism with regard to the situation in early Greece. After some 400 years of non-literacy, writing was re-introduced into Greece during the eighth century B. C. Moreover, it was alphabetic writing that was introduced this time, accentuating the Greek achievement from any earlier writing system. But how far are we justified in making writing, or the alphabet, a motive force in Archaic Greece? It was not only writing that was introduced, but a whole host of cultural elements from the neighbours of the Greeks in the Eastern Mediterranean, be they material, social, political, religious, mythological, mathematical. Writing was only one among many things that the Greeks adapted from the East. The Greeks are innovators in alphabetic writing, but they stand in a stream of cultural diffusion as well. What people may or may not make out of a writing system, even a phonemic one, may perhaps be suggested by the runes in Central and Northern Europe, which were introduced to peoples who were not exposed in the same way to the overall cultural impact of more advanced neighbours. That witty philologist, H. D. F. Kitto, comparing the Greek Archipelago and the Hebrides, once remarked that the sea-ways from the latter islands did not lead "to a Phoenicia or Egypt, but either to a mainland which was but little different, or into the North Atlantic, where a man would either drown, or come back no wiser than he had set out" (Kitto 1957: 31). Even if the Greeks first invented the alphabet, any account of the Archaic age must pay due attention to all the circumstances and not talk as if the Greeks were left in a vacuum with their script.

We must be careful then, when proclaiming "the rise of Greek Civilization" as "the prime historical example of the transition to a really literate society" (Goody and Watt 1968: 42), that we do not rashly *first*, equate the rise of Greek civilization with the transition to a really literate society, and *second*, explain the rise of Greek civilization by the transition to a really literate society. And what are we to understand by the term "a really literate society"? In this field terminology is often too loose and concepts too little refined that they can function as useful tools in an historical analysis.

A "literate" society?

The earliest Greek inscriptions range round the middle of the eight century (Jefferey 1976: 26). In a certain sense, literacy was widespread from the end of that century. Short inscriptions are found on vessels and stone in many parts of the Greek world. Literacy was never restricted in the sense that it was reserved for a particular class or group. But certainly the alphabet had a restricted use, in reading and particularly in writing. Papyrus was hardly in common use in the Greek world until the sixth century. There was a variety of local scripts. The copying of manuscripts was time-consuming and slow. The continuous nature of Greek writing did not make for easy reading. Even in the sixth and fifth centuries it seems to me misleading to talk about "popular literacy, or the use of writing as an autonomous mode of communication by the majority of the members of society" and about the city states of Greece and Ionia as societies "which as a whole could justly be characterized as literate" (Goody and Watt 1963: 40). With Finley, I do not share "historians' enthusiasm whenever they find examples of the ability of illiterates to scrawl a signature on a document they could not read" (Finley 1983: 30) or, say, on a vessel or a potsherd.

One of the few recent books on Greek history to take explicit note of the problem of literacy, is Oswyn Murray's *Early Greece* (1980). I am astonished at his statement that Archaic Greece was "a literate society in the modern sense, indeed the first literate society of which we have reasonably detailed knowledge" (96).

This statement is based on a very liberal definition of literacy. When it comes to fluency in reading or understanding long literary texts or complex arguments, Murray rightly insists: "At this higher level Greece in many respects long remained an oral culture... and writing was seldom a normal or preferred mode of communication if speech was possible. The cultural historian will regard Greece as an oral or a literate culture according to the areas he is investigating" (96f). When Goody (1977: 42) states with regard to Thales' speculative thinking, that "it is significant that this kind of critical discourse is seen as emerging in one of the first widely literate societies", this, to my mind, is to beg the question, quite apart from the problem of significance.

Of Greek literature down well into classical times, it may be said that it was not written for readers. In Athens in the middle of the fifth century, it may perhaps be said that "books had a wide circulation", but only if we do not forget that "public oral communication was still the essence of communal life" (Humphreys 1978: 228). To delimit that "wide circulation" even more and to relate literacy - "Literary literacy" that is, not the ability to scratch down a name or to read a short message - to the social dimension, one may say, with Finley (30) that "The plain fact is that never in antiquity did any but the élite (or their direct agents) consult documents and books." The "truly" and "really" literate society of Classical Greece seems to me to be a fiction and consequently cannot serve as a factor in a causal explanation.

Poetry

Still, it may be that writing in itself made thoughts possible for a Thales or things possible for a poet in early Greece that were not feasible in a totally oral community. Let us therefore consider the poets and their works. For works *were* written down.

Turning first to Homer and the *Iliad:* There on the one hand you have the oral-epic tradition, while on the other hand you have the text of the *Iliad* amounting to some 16 000 lines of hexameter verse. Somewhere in between you have the poet, someone whom one may name Homer and call a "monumental composer", or at least you have the occasion and process of writing down the poem. In assessing the significance of writing in the creative process, one has to have an idea of what poetry in the oral tradition was like. I will only stress a couple of features that tend presently to be underrated.

Doubtless the epic bard generally identifies himself with the values of the aristocracy, which are the dominating values of the society; no doubt he has to adapt to circumstances and fulfil the expectations of the local big men in the audience for whom he sings and from whom he expects remuneration. But one should not overstress the weight of the tradition and the amount of social control. Quite rightly, it has been said that "Even in non-literate societies there is no evidence that individuals were prisoners of preordained schemes, of primitive classifications, of the structures of myth. Constrained, yes; imprisoned, no" (Goody 1977: 33). Oral traditions seem to me often to have been considered in a too "collectivistic" way. For Havelock, Homer can serve as a paradigm and as "tribal encyclopedia" because he makes a sharp distinction between the story on the one hand and the "content of the code" on the other (cf. especially Havelock 1982: 122ff). In the collective representation of the society's values and aspirations, the story in this view is instrumental, but not essential. I wonder, however, whether we must not, to a higher degree than Havelock seems to allow for, reckon with the story and the characters conveying a moral. On certain occasions in the epic, one person will seek to influence another by way of telling a mythological story to be taken as warning or model. May we not be justified in believing that the Homeric bard uses his material in much the same way? Certainly, the way he explicitly and implicitly exposes the heroes to criticism and comment should warn us against seeing heroic poetry as too conforming and conformist.

When it comes to the technicalities of composition, the idea that Homer was illiterate (and blind, for that matter) has long since served as an explanation and excuse for all kinds of inconsistencies and shortcomings in his poems. Sometimes one comes across apodictic statements like the following one, made by a scholar who nevertheless hails the poet of the *Odyssey* as "a supreme master of the art of story-telling": "Delicate and subtle preparations *now* for what will follow in five hundred lines' time, veiled and indirect allusions *now* to what happened five hundred lines ago - such artifice lies beyond his power, even supposing that it lay within the bounds of his imagination" (Page 1955: 142). From certain presuppositions about the limits of the art of the oral poet, Page denies the existence of certain things in the poem and even places them outside the range of possibility. Others, having demonstrated the artifice of the poet, may feel compelled to deny the hypothesis that the poem was orally composed. Widely different as these positions are, they have as their common tenet certain ideas about what the oral poet can or cannot do. The point that I want to make against this kind of argument is not the material one, viz. that foreshadowing, echoing and allusions are basic to the art of the oral poet, but one of method: We simply cannot know what the poet could do. Analogies from other traditions can only help us part of the way, I am afraid. We do not know what a Greek bard could manage without an alphabet.

On the other hand, what could the alphabet possibly mean to the oral poet of about 700 B. C.? There are two positive ways of answering this question, both to my mind equally misguided. One takes the poetic genius for granted and suggests that the alphabet may have been developed with a view to serving the needs of a monumental poet whose aspirations would make him want to transcend the limits of the oral tradition. "What the poet needed (and what the Muse gave him) was an alphabet" (Wade-Gery 1952: 14). Or one takes the potentialities of the medium for granted in practice and looks upon the new medium as epoch-making in that it made it possible to compose in a new and more refined way, by re-reading and correcting the work.

To me, it seems more likely that the effects of writing would be detrimental to the art of the "oral poet" absorbed in the tremendous work of elaborating a text of several thousand hexameter verses. Surely he would have lost speed and confidence and got confused. Of course, the first written texts will be characterized by an oral, formulaic style. But then, what does the art of writing contribute? And what does the concept of "literacy" contribute to our understanding if "orality is not despicable. It can produce creations beyond the reach of literates, for example, the *Odyssey*" (Ong 1982: 175)?

Psychologically as well as materially, writing must be considered incidental to the Homeric poems.

This applies also to the peasant-poet Hesiod about 700 B. C., author of the *Theogony* and the *Works and Days*. Havelock (1963: 63) calls him an oral poet because of his "obvious proximity to the non-literate condition of Greek culture and claims that "the Muses of Hesiod are the Muses of all epic poets" (95), while on the other hand Hesiod initiated "the revolution in the technology of preserved speech" (295). Hesiod's *Theogony* is "on the borderline between oral performance and written composition" (Ong 1982: 143), leaning heavily on Peabody 1975) - "he makes three tries at the same material to get going". So one may really ask what exactly the art of writing meant to Hesiod. The emergence of "a general world view... in isolated or "abstracted" form" violating the canons of easy oral memorization makes Havelock assume that "Hesiod is operating with the help of the written word" (296). But thorough study of the language of Hesiod has shown that nothing should compel us to believe that writing must have played a part in the composition of the Hesiodic poems (Edwards 1971). It may well be that the poetry of Hesiod constitutes "a mental leap forward" (Havelock 1982: 213). But I cannot see any justification for postulating writing as an enabling factor. Hesiod, like Homer, composed "in his mind".

That Hesiod actually wrote down his poems, is hardly proved, as some will have it, by the fact that Hesiod in the *Works and Days* develops the concept of the double Strife (v. 11ff) in a way different from the *Theogony* (225f). He may not be correcting a written text, but rather his own mind as of earlier, when it seemed to him to be otherwise. But the poems of Hesiod consist partly of very personal utterances, referring to family circumstances and to his encounter with the Muses, and such information would not presumably have been passed on and preserved except in the words of Hesiod. "The individual poet", however, is not a *product* of personal literacy. Hesiod's self-consciousness was socially conditioned. He was a sturdy peasant, who greatly valued independence, and who was basically independent. He was a peasant who wanted to be a poet as well. Here, and not in the mastery of writing or in any literate consciousness, lies his individual character.

I now turn briefly to the lyric poetry of the 7th and 6th century B. C. Of this poetry it has been said that "with the introduction of the alphabet writing became available as an aid to composition. This does not mean that a new art of written composition was grafted on to the traditional technique of oral epic. On the contrary, written verse differed as much from oral verse as did verse from prose. The poet who used writing could select each word with care. The first such poets in Greece abandoned the hexameter, the meter of oral epic, and developed new meters, namely, elegiacs, iambics and lyric meters. Moreover, where oral epic had kept to customary ideas, the new poets could express their individuality; they could challenge convention and voice their own loves and hates" (Sealey 1976: 27f). Two questionable assumptions are made here. First, that written verse (necessarily?) differs from oral verse and that the metres of lyric poetry developed only with the help of writing. What writing made possible, however, was the preservation of a kind of verse that is not in itself the product of writing. Second, that writing was an aid to composition. This only holds true to a certain extent - and we should not be carried away by the idea of poets with a pencil and plenty of paper and Indian rubber. To see the writing system as encouraging "the development of forms of patterning that possess a visuo-spatial component" (Goody 1977: 159) is hardly possible in the case of early Greece. If anything can explain the visuo-spatial structure of lyric verse - that is: as it is represented in modern, metrical editions - it is the musical or rather the instrumental and choric elements that belong to this kind of poetry, and which are now irrevocably lost to us. These elements flourished and died with the performance, making the text alone a rudimentary monument of the poetic achievement. There can be no denying that writing has played some part in composition, but its significance is difficult to assess. And where do sweeping statements like: "Of course by Sappho's time (fl. c. 600 B. C.) writing was already structuring the Greek psyche" (Ong 1982: 147) take us?

Essentially, early Greek poetry - choric and monodic, religious and secular - was created in response to a personal situation or to serve a public occasion. However, "the lyric poets of the 7th century, although still composing in the first instance for oral performance, are conscious that their words will travel and last" (Humphreys 1978: 218). "The poet speaks to posterity as well as to his immediate audience" (220) and "the new hope of immortality or of rapidly spreading fame" was brought about "by the introduction of writing" (219). Yes and no. Such statements may lead some to think that after an oral performance for immediate audiences, the poem would start on a "literary" career and, as a piece of "literature" secure the poet's fame amongst the readership. This kind of idea seems to lie behind also the claim that "the rise of written literature marks an enormous change in popular taste" (Sealey 1957: 318). Even granted some sort of change in preferences away from epic towards other forms of poetry, what are we to make of the "popular taste" for reading poetry in early and classical Greece? Certainly, both the circulation within the city and the wider circulation within the Greek world would mainly be oral. Not the text, but the song and the message is the vehicle of the poet's fame. And would the commitment of verse to a scroll of papyrus imply better hopes for future fame than would oral transmission, granted the prevailing material and social conditions and granted the fact that the concept of a readership, let alone a "literary heritage" was not yet conceived of?

Philosophy

I must refrain here from going too far into the problem of the significance writing has in the history of Greek philosophy. Traditional accounts hardly address themselves to the problem at all. In his *The Origins of Greek Thought* (1982 [1962]), Jean-Pierre Vernant has brilliantly sketched the spiritual universe of the city-state and firmly embedded Greek philosophy in society. Less convincingly, to my mind, he argues that "writing became the medium of a common culture and permitted the complete dissemination of knowledge previously restricted or forbidden" (52). Knowledge was made public in books "such as those that Anaximander and Pherecydes are said to have been the first to write, or those that Heraclitus deposited in the temple of Artemis at Ephesus" (53). In being committed to writing, the truth of the sage "was wrenched from the closed circle of the cults and displayed in broad daylight before the gaze of the whole city" (53).

But if one accepts the publication of a "book" *es to xynon* or *es meson* by Pherecydes, mentioned in the spurious letter of Thales to Pherecydes (Diogenes Laertius I, 43f, cited by Vernant 54), one must also take into consideration that Thales in that very letter reckons himself amongst those "who never write anything." And Heraclitus, according to Diogenes (IX, 6) placed his book "in the temple of Artemis, as some day, having purposely written it rather obscurely so that only those of rank and influence should have access to it, and it should not be easily despised by the populace...". Indeed, one has seen this act of Heraclitus as a deliberate protest against the idea of serving the public (Harder 1963: 78). Briefly, I think it is important to keep in mind that much of what we call Greek philosophy was expounded in verse and has other characteristics which imply that it relied mainly on oral communication, as has been well shown by Havelock (1982: 220-260); that the "successions" of Greek philosophers speak for oral transmission from teacher to pupil; and that such writings as there were basically served as points of departure for discussion within a circle of friends or pupils. Even if it may be said that Anaximander was the writer of the first Greek prose book, it may not be wise to deduce from this fact "that he was therefore the first philosopher who addressed a general public" (Greene 1951: 39). What is a general public?

I would also question the validity of the assumption so often made, that the many inconsistencies in the beliefs and categories which were exposed to *readers* when Homer and Hesiod were available as written records, were so important for the formation of a comparative and critical attitude to the accepted world picture. When Xenophanes takes exception to Homer's gods, it is not because he has been able to scrutinize a copy of the *Iliad* and the *Odyssey*. When Hecataeus announces that "What I write is the account I believe to be true. For the stories the Greeks tell are many and in my opinion ridiculous", he has been working on oral traditions.

Politics and Law

A few words must suffice on the significance of literacy for politics and especially for the development of political democracy. Democracy, as we know it, "is from the beginning associated with widespread literacy", and "the ease of alphabetic reading and writing was probably an important consideration in the development of political democracy" (Goody and Watt 1968: 55). In general, I think one should be careful in not overstressing the written basis of Athenian democracy and the relevance of literacy for an explanation of the political development. For the relative equality of political rights for the citizens of classical Athens and for the widespread participation in public affairs I would look first, say, to the technology of warfare, especially with a view to the implications of the hoplite phalanx and later of the use of common men as oarsmen in the fleet.

Even in the fifth century, we must keep in mind the extent to which matters were handled orally. Ostracism of course could not function without writing. But misspellings abound; we are told that Aristides was asked by somebody to write down the name "Aristides" on a sherd; ready-made potsherds in some quantity have been found, obviously for distribution. In fact, the institution of exile for a period of several years, which was the result of ostracism, in itself testifies to the oral and face-to-face nature of politics in the polis. "The most effective way to eliminate undesirable ideas - and undesirable individuals, political opponents - was by exile or capital punishment. That prevented oral communication, and nothing else mattered significantly". (Finley 1983: 29).

It may also be that we tend to make too much of the fact that Solon had the laws set up in public for everybody to read. Something undoubtedly was achieved by the publication of laws in this way. But one should note that even by the middle of the 5th century "nomos might or might not refer to written legislation; in other words, the question of writing is immaterial to the definition of a political nomos" (Ostwald 1969: 44). The wording of some inscriptions from that time seems to justify the conclusion that "the problem whether or not a given regulation existed in writing was of less importance to those who regarded themselves bound by *nomos* than it is to us. Writing or its absence did not apparently make a *nomos* any less binding... What did matter was that it was a practice or regulation regarded as binding within a given community" (44f). There is also the point that the laws themselves are open to and in need of interpretation. "Unless the right of interpretation is 'democratized', the mere existence of written laws changes little" (Finley 1983: 30). It is the use and abuse of laws that count. Isocrates, the rhetor, a contemporary of Plato, while hailing the few and orderly laws of the forefathers, is unhappy with the laws that are established in his own time and which are full of so much confusion and of so many contradictions that no one can distinguish between the useful and the useless (cf. *Panathenaicus* 144). "Now everyone would admit, I think, that our laws have been the source of very many and very great benefits to the life of humanity... Wise men ought to appreciate the fact that while any number of men both among the Hellenes and among the barbarians have been able to lay down laws, there are not many who can discourse upon questions of public welfare in a spirit worthy both of Athens and of Hellas" (Antidosis 79f; Loeb transl.). So, those who invent such discourses should be held in higher esteem than those who propose and write down laws, inasmuch as they are rarer, have the more difficult task, and must demonstrate superior qualities of mind. Especially now, as the laws which have been laid down are innumerable, the task of the rhetor becomes ever more difficult (summary of 81-83). This kind of thinking takes account of the fact that written laws are only the rudiments of the political order. To Isocrates, the fact that written laws may be easily borrowed from one state to another, proves that they are not significant for the establishment of a good society. For "virtue is not advanced by written laws but by the habits of everyday life" (*Areopagiticus* 39f).

Plato and Isocrates on writing

This has now brought us to some further remarks on how some Greek intellectuals valued writing. It is well known that Plato rated the spoken word higher than the written. The dialogue *Phaedrus* deals mainly with oratory. There Socrates tells how the Egyptian king Thamus rebuked the god Theuth for claiming that his invention of writing would provide a "recipe for memory and wisdom": "If men learn this, it will implant forgetfulness in their souls; they will cease to exercise memory because they rely on that which is written, calling things to remembrance no longer from within themselves, but by means of external marks; what you have discovered is a recipe not for memory, but for reminder, And it is no true wisdom that you offer your disciples, but only its semblance; for by telling them of many things without teaching them you will make them seem to know much, while for the most part they know nothing; and as men filled, not with wisdom, but the conceit of wisdom, they will be a burden to their fellows" (275ab). The written word is dead, helpless and inert, to use characteristics suggested by Socrates at other places in the *Phaedrus*.

There is seemingly an emphasis here on memory as "the repository of the cultural tradition in oral society" (Goody and Watt 1968: 50). Some have even seen this as a reassertion of the claims and powers of oral memory, now put into philosophic use (Notopoulos 1938: 482). But this at least is not Plato's main concern in defending the spoken word. He is concerned about the dialectical process and the pursuit of true knowledge. In his *Seventh letter* (341cd) he says: "I have composed no work about these matters, and shall never do so; for this subject cannot be expressed in words like other subjects of study, but only after long association and close companionship with the subject itself is a sudden sight born in the soul, like a blaze kindled by a leaping spark, and at once becomes self-sustaining." Truth is obtained in a face-to-face situation, in dialogue. In *Protagoras* (329a) Socrates complains that books cannot answer questions. Written words "seem to talk to you as though they were intelligent, but if you ask them anything about what they say, from a desire to be instructed, they go on telling you just the same thing for ever",

Socrates says (*Phaedrus* 275d). The spoken word is appropriate to the occasion and to the person addressed, so that "anyone who leaves behind him a written manual, and likewise anyone who takes it over from him, on the supposition that such writing will provide something reliable and permanent (!), must be exceedingly simple-minded" (277c).

One finds a similar concern with the spoken word with the rhetors. Alcidamas wrote a treatise on *Those who Compose Written Speeches*, where he defends the superiority of spoken and extemporary discourse and calls the written speech a mere phantom or imitation of it. One of those who come under attack, is Isocrates, who composed "speeches" that were never meant for oral delivery at all, but served as pamphlets. Isocrates, however, developed his own theory of the right word at the right time and attacked those who "do not know that the art of using letters remains fixed and unchanged, so that we continually and invariably use the same letters for the same purposes, while exactly the reverse is true of the art of discourse. For what has been said by one speaker is not equally useful for the speaker who comes after him... Oratory is good only if it has the qualities of fitness for the occasion (*kairos*), propriety of style, and originality of treatment" (*Against the Sophists* 12f). Isocrates repeatedly comes back to "what the occasion demands". It is also part of Isocrates' rhetorical theory that a rhetor will write discourses which are worthy of praise and honour. "It is inconceivable that he will support causes which are unjust or petty or devoted to private quarrels, and not rather those which are great and honourable, devoted to the welfare of man and our common good" (*Antidosis* 277).

Just at the time when classical Greek prose reaches it highest peak, and just in the two authors that have created the most accomplished works of classical prose literature, we find a clear consciousness of the difference between the spoken and the written word and a very high appreciation of the spoken word. As Greek literature becomes conscious of itself as *literae*, it harks back to the ideal of a living, oral tradition.

Conclusion

The time has come to summarize. I have stressed the strength of the oral tradition in early Greece and warned against explanations that take for granted that we are dealing with a "literate society" or that writing and writings had any great role to play.

Thus, I have questioned and qualified some statements of modern scholars and some current opinions on the significance of literacy in Early Greece. I think it may be said that the liberating effects of writing have been rather overrated for the period that concerns us here. It is hard to see that it was writing that released the genius of a Homer or sparked off the originality of an Hesiod or created the self-consciousness of the lyric and elegiac poets. Writing seems not to have been a motive force in the rise of philosophical speculation and literacy can hardly be said to be essential to the rise of Democracy.

Those, I think, are the aspects that need presently to be stressed.

Illustration 1

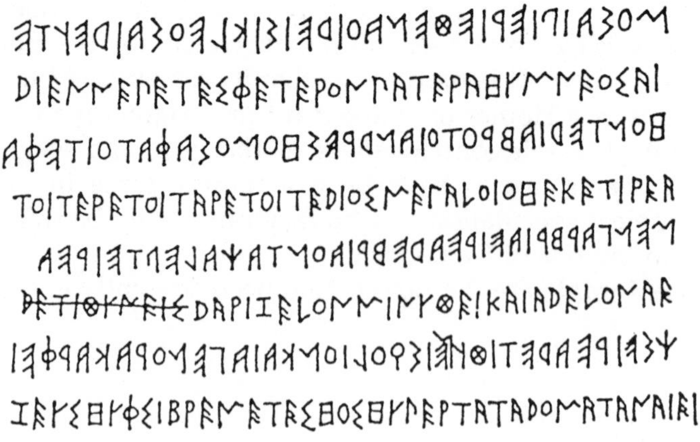

ƎTYƎQIAƷOƎↃᛉƷIƎQIOAMƎⵙƎIᛑƎIⵒIAƷOᛐ
DIℲᛐᛐℲᒋℲTℲƧⵖℲTℲPOᛐⵒATℲPAᛈᛉᛐᛐℲOƧAI
AⵖƎTIOTAⵖAƷOᛐOᛈƷAᛑᛐAIOTOᛑᛈAIↃƎTᛐOᛈ
TOITℲPℲTOITAPℲTOITℲDIOƧᛐℲⵒALOIOᛈℲKℲTIPℲA
ᛑƎᛑIℲTↃℲᒋAᛌATᛐOAIᛑᛑƷↃAℲᛑᛑIℲAIᛑᛑᛑAᛐƎᛐ
ᛈℲTⵙOᛉᛐℲᛁↃDAPIIℲLOᛐᛐIᛐᛌᛙℲᛁKAIADℲLOᛐAℲ
IℲⵖᛑAᛌAᛑᛑOᛐℲᛑAIAᛌᛐOIↃOᛈↃↄℲᛑᛙITℲᛑAℲᛑᛑᛌᛌ
IℲᛌↃℲᛈᛁⵖƧIBPℲᛐℲTℲƧᛈOƧᛈᛌᛑℲPTATADOᛐATAᛐAIℲI

The first text of Hesiod's *Works and Days* probably looked something like the above, according to its latest editor. The text was
written *boustrophedon* ("as the ox turns" in ploughing), starting
top right and continuing left-right-left throughout.
From: *Hesiod. Works and Days, Edited with Prolegomena and
Commentary* by M.L. West, Oxford 1978, p. 60.

Illustration 2

Specimen of an *ostrakon* or a potsherd, in this case the bottom of
an Athenian vase. The inscription reads THEMISTHOKLES
NEOKLEOS ("Themistocles, son of Neocles").
From about 480 B. C.

Bibliography

Edwards, G. P. (1971) *The Language of Hesiod in its Traditional Context*, Oxford.

Finley, M. I. (1983) *Politics in the Ancient World*, Cambridge.

Goody, J. (ed.) (1968) *Literacy in Traditional Societies*, Cambridge.

Goody, J. (1977) *The Domestication of the Savage Mind*, Cambridge.

Goody, J. and Watt, I. (1963) *The Consequences of Literacy*; first published 1963, reprinted in Goody (1968) 27-68.

Green, W. C. (1951) The Spoken and the Written Word, *Harvard Studies in Classical Philology* 60, 23-59.

Harder, R. (1943) Bemerkungen zur griechischen Schriftlichkeit; first published 1943, reprinted in *Kleine Schriften*, hrsg. von W. Marg, Munich 1960.

Havelock, E. A. (1963) *Preface to Plato*, Oxford.

Havelock, E. A. (1978) *The Greek Concept of Justice: From Its Shadow in Homer to Its Substance in Plato*, Cambridge, Mas./ London.

Havelock, E. A. (1982) *The Literate Revolution in Greece and Its Cultural Consequences*, Princeton.

Humphreys, S. (1978) 'Transcendence' and intellectual roles: the ancient Greek case, *Anthropology and the Greeks*, London.

Jeffery, L. H. (1976) *Archaic Greece. The City-States c. 700-500 B. C.* London.

Kitto, H. D. F. (1957) *The Greeks*, Pelican books.

Murray, O. (1980) *Early Greece*, Fontana Paperbacks.

Notopoulos, J. A. (1938) Mnemosyne in Oral Literature, *Transactions and Proceedings of the American Philological Association* 69, 465-493.

Ong, W. J. (1982) *Orality and Literacy. The Technologizing of the Word*, London.

Ostwald, M. (1969) *Nomos and the Beginnings of the Athenian Democracy*, Oxford.

Page, D. L. (1955) *The Homeric Odyssey*, Oxford.

Pattison, R. (1982) *On Literacy. The Politics of the Word from Homer to the Age of Rock*, Oxford/ New York.

Peabody, B. (1975) *The Winged Word. A Study in the Technique of Ancient Greek Oral Composition as Seen Principally through Hesiod's Works and Days*, Albany, New York.

Sealey, R. (1957) From Phemios to Ion, *Revue des Études Grecques* 70, 312-355.

Sealey, R. (1976) *A History of the Greek City States 700-338 B. C.*, Berkeley/Los Angeles/ London.

Vernant, J.-P. (1982) *The Origins of Greek Thought*, London.

Wade-Gery, H. T. (1952) *The Poet of the Iliad*, Cambridge.

Interactions between Orality and Literacy in Ancient Egypt[1]

Christopher Eyre
John Baines

1. The Egyptian writing system

One approach to the reality of literacy lies in relating the working of a script to the way it is learnt, and to how it is read. Its origins and history are also relevant, because they may set preconditions for the context and manner of its use (Schenkel 1983). It is not clear whether writing was invented independently in Egypt, but there is no direct systematic dependence on another script. The earliest and the latest hieroglyphic texts work on the same basic principles, although there is constant development. There are historical variations (and indeed variations according to text genre), in the sophistication with which those principles are applied, and in the explicitness with which the script encodes the phonemic and semantic levels of the language.

The pictorial signs of the hieroglyphic script (Gardiner 1957; Schenkel 1976; 1984) fall into two categories - 'semograms' that indicate meaning, and 'phonograms' that encode phonetic information. For practical purposes they may be subdivided into four groups. Pictorial signs that may stand alone for a word (picture of a man, read 'man'), the 'logograms', are relatively rare. They were more common in earlier periods, when written vocabulary, and so the danger of ambiguity was smaller. A set of

[1]This is a revised version of a paper given in November 1985 at the conference 'From Orality to Literacy and Back', under the sponsorship of the Center for Sammenlignende Kulturforskning of Copenhagen University. We would like to express our thanks to the organisers, Mogens Trolle Larsen and Michael Harbsmeier, for their kind invitation to participate, and for a valuable, informative and enjoyable weekend.

uniliteral, or rather 'uniconsonantal' signs represents the consonantal phonemes of the language (vowels are not specifically en-
coded). A few dozen multiconsonantal signs represent series of
two or three consonants. These are not syllabic signs, and do not
carry implications of vowel quality. The consonantal structure of
a word is usually written by a combination of uni- and multiconsonantal signs complementing each other. Finally there are taxographic signs: pictorial signs used at the end of words to point to
the general sense or the specific meaning of the word (so-called
'determinatives').

Egyptian texts read from right to left

shtp = s + htp + t + p + taxogram.

Hieratic

Demotic

Phonemic signs may have variant readings. Some signs are used
as semograms in one context and phonograms in another, and
the boundaries between multiconsonantal signs, taxograms, and
true 'logograms' are shifting and hard to define. However, these
historically conditioned features do not cause real problems in
reading. The script seems to have developed from a prehistoric
(or rather pre-literate) use of pictures, through the addition of
other signs, which were devised originally on a rebus principle.
These operated firstly as aids to 'reading' the picture, but also as
ways of writing words not susceptible to representation simply as
pictures, so that a mixed system developed, capable of representing whole syntactic units of language, and not just single words
or ideas. To develop this capacity, the 'aids' became uni- or multiconsonantal signs, and eventually outweigh the truly pictorial
element that persists in the taxograms. The script becomes very
difficult to read if a balance between these sign classes is not
maintained, and Egyptian texts were never written by uniconsonantal signs alone in the fashion of an 'alphabet', although the
process of developing single signs to represent individual consonantal phonemes underlies that invention. The origin of the alphabet is disputed, but it probably derived from the development
of a script for a west Semitic language in the mid-2nd millenium,
consisting of a series of signs that used Egyptian hieroglyphs of

the 'uniconsonantal' type as model or inspiration (Gardiner 1942: 55-64; Millard 1986). Such an internal development never took place in the writing of Egyptian. The alphabet eventually adopted, in the early centuries A.D., was borrowed from Greece.

2. Elementary education

At latest by the early Twelfth Dynasty (c. 2000 BC), the classic period of the Middle Kingdom, a standard system of formal elementary education in literacy was established (Brunner 1957; Williams 1972). The main evidence for its conduct consists of numerous schoolboys' exercises from the New Kingdom village of Deir el-Medina (c. 1300-1100 BC), combined with direct and indirect references in literary texts. The general outlines of the system are not in doubt, although the picture is incomplete, its historical development is difficult to trace, and in important details it may have been different in the earliest periods.

From the Middle Kingdom on, and probably even earlier, hieroglyphs themselves were not the script of education, as they were not the script of literature or administration. Until the late period (c. 650 BC) the hieratic script was used. In principle this was a cursive version of the hieroglyphic script, with a direct relationship between each hieratic sign and its corresponding hieroglyph. In practice hieroglyphs, if learnt at all, were a secondary subject. Rare New Kingdom ostraca from Deir el-Medina preserve hieroglyphic versions of basic school texts that were normally written in hieratic, and this may imply that transcription formed an exercise in learning the pictorial script, but hieroglyphic writing exercises are generally rare. The clear distinction between hieratic and hieroglyphic as subjects for instruction could belong to the early Middle Kingdom, but it may be chance that the few Old Kingdom school exercises are hieroglyphic (Brunner 1957: 77 and fig.5; note also Scott n.d.: pl.3, and the traditional cursive, semi-hieroglyphic writing of texts of the Book of Kemyt, below p. 95). Cursive hieratic tended to draw gradually away from hieroglyphs. At the beginning of the New Kingdom it is possible to trace a renewal of sign forms that drew hieratic temporarily back towards its hieroglyphic originals (Megally 1971: 1-15), but by the end of the New Kingdom the normal tendency was leading in secular texts to the development of the distinct demotic script (c.700BC), which cannot be transcribed directly into hieroglyphs.

The language of the texts used for elementary instruction was classical literary Middle Egyptian, which was used for hieroglyphic texts down to the Roman period. It had ceased to be used for administrative, business, or even literary texts, in late New Kingdom hieratic, which used Late Egyptian for such texts. The vernacular of the New Kingdom differed considerably from Middle Egyptian, which itself had never been a 'true' vernacular. The term 'Late Egyptian' covers a variety of written styles, differing with date, place, and genre, but all substantially influenced in grammar and vocabulary by the vernacular. Written Late Egyptian seems to have been learnt after the basic Middle Egyptian texts, but in the same general way.

The method of instruction may usefully be compared with that of traditional Quranic or Rabbinic schools. It was based on the additive learning of set literary texts. Most of these were classic works of the early Middle Kingdom. 'Useful' textual material was only introduced at a later stage. Thus, in the teaching of Late Egyptian model letters rather than classical works were used as set texts. (For the teaching of demotic the situation was a little different) We cannot know how much ordinary schoolboys absorbed of Middle Egyptian literature, but the best scribes were familiar with the major works, quoting them, or rather echoing their phraseology in the composition of formal and official texts. For the less highly trained these texts may have been little more than reading and writing exercises, and eventual familiarity with them might not even have borne comparison with the ordinary Englishman's memory of the Chaucer or Shakespeare he read at school.

Elementary school exercises consisted of a single, simultaneous process of memorising standard set texts in both oral and written form. A passage of a few lines was copied out and worked over phrase by phrase. Each phrase was a unit of a few words, of convenient length for oral repetition and additive memorising. In schoolboys' copies these units are frequently marked by red pointing. The student presumably learnt each phrase aloud by oral repetition, wrote it, and then progressed to the next, until the whole exercise had been completed. The end of the exercise may be marked by a red 'period' sign, and sometimes by a date. The class then seem to have read and chanted the passage rhythmically in unison, learning the 'text' and its written appearance at the same time. Writing, reading, and reciting were thus closely connected from the beginning. Visual, oral and auditory aspects of reading were not separated, and all written texts were also heard. The schoolboy's understanding of the script was built up from whole phrases, through words, to individual sense units or morphological units (such as pronominal endings), sign groups, and only in the last resort to individual signs.

Analytical didactic works played no significant part in elementary education. The first work learnt was the Book of Kemyt. This was partly an exercise in pen use and sign formation, for it is almost always written in vertical columns, and an intermediate script of cursive semi-hieroglyphs, long after vertical columns had been abandoned in secular texts. The text is not so much literature as a ragbag of important phrases and formulae put together for teaching purposes, probably at the very beginning of the Middle Kingdom. Nevertheless its format and structure is that of a literary didactic text, and it was used in the way described above. An apparently more analytical category is the class of didactic text termed onomasticon (Gardiner 1947). Such texts purport to list everything in creation in thematic order; they are lists, not dictionaries. Some manuscripts are written as lists in columns; others in continuous lines of text. They are, however, entitled 'teachings' (**sb3yt**), like the classic 'wisdom texts' in the school syllabus, and their didactic use was evidently similar. Passages from them, written on writing boards and ostraca, have the appearance of schoolboys' exercises; one example even has the pointing that frequently marked divisions of school text. The inclusion of lists of rare or unusual and difficult words in texts used as advanced writing exercises is also well attested. The onomastica would thus have been learnt in schools like other literary texts, additively, by copying and chanting. The best pupils absorbed and learnt to recognise and reproduce the lists of titles, place-names, gods and their shrines, features of the material world, and objects that surrounded them in daily life, but they also learnt what the words looked like and how to reproduce them in writing.

The earliest literacy education may have used the 'informal' style typical of any craft apprenticeship, with the pupil copying and ultimately emulating 'father' or 'master' (cf. Scribner and Cole 1981: esp. 65-8), and the organised system developed for classroom use, as known from the New Kingdom, was perhaps a formalisation of this technique. However, as the hieroglyphic and hieratic scripts drew apart at the end of the New Kingdom, there may have developed a more analytical approach to teaching of the skilled at the secondary stage when hieroglyphs were learnt. This is suggested by the fact that hieroglyphs and hieratic ceased to be commensurable, so that hieroglyphic texts came to be drafted on papyrus in hieroglyphs (e.g. Winter 1967), and by the organisation of a Graeco-Roman period hieroglyphic 'dictionary' (1st-2nd Century AD; refs in Smith and Tait 1983: 209-13), which is analogous to that of the sign lists in modern grammars of Egyptian. The signs are ordered thematically, with transcription (that is, hieratic equivalent), and a reference name based on what is depicted or on the reading of the most common word in which it is used. (A possible fragment of an earlier New Kingdom sign list from Deir el-Medina has a different, less analytical(?) organisation; Pleyte and Rossi 1969-76: pl.144).

A similar impression of late period education is given by the number of preserved fragments of onomastica, 'lexical' texts, and learned listings. A partial organisation by sign category is also found in a hieratic onomasticon of the Graeco-Roman period, although this is composed in Middle Egyptian, and may be based on earlier originals. It would not be implausible to suggest that the onomasticon as such belongs to a very early class of literature, although as yet no very early examples have been found; a form of 'literature' based on the listing of information could potentially be traced back to earlier models than a genre requiring the used of connected sentences. In Egypt, narrative appears in texts at a relatively developed stage of script use (Baines 1983: 577-8). The early importance of lexical lists in Mesopotamia would support such a hypothesis. 'School' works in Demotic (Kaplony-Heckel 1974; Bresciani et al. 1983; Devauchelle 1984; Smith and Tait 1983: 198-213) begin to show alphabet-like ordering. The set texts were not all old classics (which did not exist in demotic as a new script); a higher proportion of everyday, 'useful' texts was added to the more typical wisdom texts and proverbs. Grammatical exercises and paradigms become common. Another practice attested after about 1000 BC is the use of stylistic/linguistic exercises involving composition of similar sentences in Middle and Late Egyptian (Caminos 1968). Such practice may have become increasingly important for advanced work after the New Kingdom.

Foreign educational practice (notably Greek, but also cuneiform and Aramaic) may have been influential, and offers valuable analogies for Egyptian. In cuneiform, sign or word lists appear among the earliest texts. The distinction between the two genres is blurred, for in the earliest script sign and word overlap to some extent. Such texts later diverged into lexical lists and sign lists. Developed Babylonian cuneiform was a syllabary enlarged by the use of Sumerian 'xenograms', and the initial learning of sign lists seems a natural elementary exercise in a way that it would not be for Egyptian hieratic. Both analytic organisation of cuneiform sign lists according to phoneme, and grammatical paradigms, are attested from Mesopotamia by the Old Babylonian period (c. 1800). Such approaches could not be normal to learning and reading habits for scripts such as New Kingdom hieratic or demotic, which were read by group and not by sign.

3. Orthographic conventions and reading method

Students of hieratic, or later of demotic, were not taught a basic 'alphabet' or sign list. For hieratic this would not necessarily have been an effective method of teaching, or, more accurately, if such a method had been used, the reading process and the consequent development of the script would presumably have followed different lines. The role of sign groups is fundamental to the development of hieratic and of demotic as scripts distinct from hieroglyphs. It can best be seen in the way the initial signs in a word retain distinct shapes, while subsequent signs tend to deteriorate into series of squiggles. Although this is found to some extent in all handwriting, such cursive forms tend in Egyptian script to become the standard writings of the word, and not merely abbreviations of forms that were sometimes written clearly and fully.

These tendencies are especially marked at the end of the New Kingdom and in the Third Intermediate Period (c. 1000-650 BC). At this period the phonetics and grammar of spoken Egyptian were far from those implied by the written language, although the hieroglyphic script and the language which it wrote had in principle remained stable. The pictorial value of taxograms (or 'determinatives') was to a degree lost to writers of hieratic, so that certain taxographic groups tended to become in effect conventionalised word endings that do not have a one-to-one correspondence with any contemporary hieroglyphic spelling. They tend to appear in words for which they were not historically correct or meaningful, although taxograms could properly be transferred from word to word as a normal procedure in hieroglyphic script. However, at this period signs that were in origin phonetic were sometimes transferred as parts of groups, along with the 'true' taxograms; here the scribe had lost sight of hieroglyphs.

For hieratic, 'error' is not really the right term for many such writings, for they constitute orthographic changes specific to the script, and irrelevant to hieroglyphs. In the hieroglyphic transcription of a hieratic text of this period the orthography can seem wildly eccentric, although even the most extreme examples have some internal logic and consistency (e.g. Volten 1937; Caminos 1977). This development is not simply the result of a decline in educational and scribal standards, and a less general understanding of the classic texts used in school, resulting in the incompetence of all but a few scribes in historically based orthography. It also reflects attempts to produce orthography that would represent better current pronunciation and the vernacular, and be more convenient for administrative purposes. This freer attitude to using sign groups that historically had true taxographic value as mere word endings coincides with a tendency towards 'phonetic' error in the orthographic use of phonograms. Such 'phonetic errors' and non-historical writings can be confusing (e.g. Ward 1981: 371-3) and make texts very difficult for the modern reader. At any rate, the eventual result was the Demotic script, the orthography of which is far from traditional hieroglyphic orthography.

The point of departure for analysing the reading process is the fact that instruction in writing was organised around units longer than the individual sign. Only in a few learned circles - notably the temples of the Graeco-Roman period - were the principles underlying the hieroglyphs exploited systematically to vary orthography. In such cases texts are written in non-standard, sometimes even cryptographic, spellings. The extreme example is a pair of texts in the temple of Esna, in which almost every hieroglyphic sign is in one case a crocodile and in the other a ram. For the modern student some analysis of individual sign usage is integral to learning and using hieroglyphs, and in general a deliberately analytical approach would seem more suitable for use with hieroglyphs than with the hieratic script. The great variety in the fullness of writings and the arrangement of signs in inscriptions of all dates shows that those regularly concerned with the script could analyse their usage. However, a truly analytical approach was not necessary for the ordinary reader in antiquity, once the script was moderately well developed and regularised (by about the 4th Dynasty, c. 2500 BC), and so long as transcription from hieratic was relatively straightforward. Most hieroglyphs, being used for formal display texts, were transcribed from hieratic originals on papyrus. Since those who read hieroglyphs also read hieratic, the normal reading processes were probably similar so long as both were living complementary scripts (that is, probably until the development of demotic).

In reading, the Egyptian probably began by pronouncing the words which his eye recognised as units, that is, as 'logographs' - groups perceived together as written words. Texts were apparently read by identifying groups of signs, not by spelling out and adding together the sounds of the individual signs as in a phonetic transcription or, in cases of uncertainty, an alphabetic script. After the earliest stages of learning the reader need seldom have had difficulty in word division, for most words end in taxograms. At the same time the regular differentiation of homophonic roots in writing, by the use of differing patterns of phonemic signs and different taxograms, helped the logo- or semographic reading of Egyptian. This is in many ways similar to the approach of an experienced modern reader of English, who recognises words and phrases visually as units rather than adding up their phonemes. Nor is it very different from reading a more 'logographic' script such as Chinese. A skilled reader may move quickly, glossing over signs or words not immediately deciphered, and filling in from the context. In a fully 'logographic' script the reader is in a hopeless position if the unknown words are too many. In a true alphabetic script he can slow down and spell out the words, and can to a degree pronounce without understanding, which may ultimately help him to identify meaning.

With a syllabary rather than an alphabet the practice is similar, but more demanding and often less efficient, especially where the syllabary uses multivalent signs. The reader has more signs to deal with, and often more complex problems in trying out the variant possibilities of unit division and word recognition (cf. Scribner and Cole 1981: 164-5). The regular notation of consonantal structure in the early Semitic consonantal 'alphabets' retains many of the characteristics of a syllabary, since signs may ultimately represent consonant + optional undefined vowel. If the word was not immediately recognisable, the reader would try a variety of vocalic patterns around the written consonantal structure.

Language type and structure, script adequacy, and ease of writing are often considered to be interrelated, but this is not necessarily so in the most direct sense, and as an approach to writing it can be over-deterministic. The lack of vowels in the writing of Semitic languages is not due simply to the importance of roots and the unimportance of vowels to their representation (cf. Ullendorff 1958: 69-72); it can be a serious inconvenience. Modern teaching of literacy in Arabic and Hebrew uses vowel markings far more than is normal for the scripts. In most contexts vowels are marked only where the full spelling out of unfamiliar words is felt necessary. It is rather that the Semitic consonantal 'alphabets' produced semantic units that for reading had each to be worked with as a unit - that is, as a logographic whole - and not simply as the sum of its parts. They do not produce the attempt at fuller phonemic representation that is a real alphabet. To some extent the regular patterning of tri-consonantal roots in the lexical and grammatical structure of Semitic languages may have allowed the balance in their 'alphabetic' writing to lie in the direction of such historically determined logographic features while allowing reasonable reading efficiency, whereas Indo-European languages may require more phonological information for effective reading, but this is an insufficient explanation in itself. It is more important that traditional habits die especially hard in the practice of literacy. The use of a true alphabet would have the same advantages and disadvantages for the representation of Semitic as for other languages, but historical and cultural factors are vital; orthographic reforms are rarely successful when a language's writing system is well established and widely used.

Word division and simple punctuation are common in the early Semitic consonantal scripts, in a way that is not normal earlier for non-alphabetic scripts or later for true alphabets (Millard 1970). Their reading by purely oral spelling out and trial of sound was presumably inefficient. A partly logographic technique was probably necessary (as with modern Arabic and Hebrew), and this will have been aided by the word division. The true alphabet favours an opposite approach, by reducing the logographic element in favour of greater phonemic representation. Lack of word division and punctuation make reading slower and more difficult. This is a serious obstacle to logographic reading in an alphabetic script, and is thus associated with a general style of oral reading through spelling out individual signs and syllables - the normal style of reading taught, for example in early mediaeval schools (cf. Saenger 1982).

The advantage of encoding vowels is paramount as the uses of writing become more complex. The fuller the writing, the easier it is to deal with the unfamiliar, and hence a larger written vocabulary. Literacy is then potentially less limited. Theoretically all technical restrictions on the size of written vocabulary should disappear for the user of an alphabetic script, although cultural factors provide other limitations, and for all but the most skilled this point will be of more significance for reading than writing the unfamiliar. The same is in principle true for a syllabary, although the extra inconvenience will be a real limitation. For an ordinary scribe using a truly logographic script there are definite limits to vocabulary in reading and writing; this will apply to Egyptian hieratic and demotic, in which unfamiliar spelling easily fails to be related to the normal writing of a word. Even Egyptian found it necessary to develop an apparently phonetic style of "syllabic orthography" for representing foreign words and names in hieroglyphs. The development of the more and more cursive hieratic and demotic scripts worked in the opposite direction to that of the alphabet, making the recognition of sign groups more important and analysis through the serial identification of individual signs more difficult. This trend was advantageous for scribes who dealt with a relatively limited range of texts. The mnemonic advantages of such logographic habits would help deal with familiar classes of text efficiently, although limiting literacy in other ways, and meaning that to reach higher levels of literacy required a very long training, considerable memorising, and constant practice. However, in the context of restricted literacy the general character of the text will mostly have been known in advance.

The issue of the balance of advantage between logographic and phonemic representation in writing is not dead. It is, for instance, at the centre of discussion about English spelling reform. It further involves evaluating how reading technique has altered with the change from script to print. For most of its history the alphabet, as written in script, was typically read by an oral technique involving phonemic recognition and the enunciation of individual signs and syllables, rather than initial concentration on sense units (Saenger 1982). One of the most significant changes associated with the spread of printing is an improvement of visual format; not just clarity of sign form, but also the universal adoption of word spacing, paragraphing, and punctuation (Ong 1982: 117-23). None are inventions of printing, which comes at a time when silent reading and related improvements in format were well established (Saenger 1982), but the achievement of consistency is crucial, and this was historically spurred by the mechanical and relatively impersonal process of producing the page of printed text. With this can come more effective silent reading; the possibility of scanning through text, of picking out by eye only specific features, and of improving the internal hearing inherent in silent reading. Historically the balance has thus swung back from a more 'phonetic' to a more 'logographic' style of reading, although this is now used in a much more powerful fashion than in the ancient Near East. For this reason logographic features in orthography can have advantages; much of the historical and 'irregular' orthography of English helps the efficient reader to get at meaning visually rather than aurally (e.g. Vachek 1973). In logographic terms this may seem similar to the way that historical non-phonetic orthography is the norm for Egyptian, and logographically central to the reading of hieroglyphs (Edgerton 1941), but the reading technique is qualitatively different.

Distinctions and graduations between silent reading and reading aloud are associated closely with the speed of reading. Short term memory seems to have limited capacity for the written or heard units it needs to store until an 'utterance' is complete (a sentence, clause, 'idea unit'). In principle writing allows such 'utterances' to be expanded in comparison to natural speech (cf. Chafe 1985), since it is possible to re-scan the individual section until understanding is registered, and since for a given span of time it is possible to assimilate more words visually than aurally, provided the format is sufficiently clear (cf. Saenger 1982: 373). Conversely, the slower a text is read the more we need to pronounce the words, aloud or in the head. Slow reading is associated with difficulty in obtaining sense, and with the acoustic search for a satisfactory reading, but it also fixes the provisional reading in the mind until the complete unit of sense has been deciphered. The echoes of an aural stimulus may be better retained than purely visual stimuli for the longer time spans of slower reading.

Silent reading existed in Egypt, as it did rather more commonly in the classical world (Knox 1968), but with limited efficiency and little scope for development. It was 'noiseless' rather than 'silent' reading, which requires sufficient speed to take in whole 'utterances' before the visual impression of their first elements is lost. This demands a high level of logographic efficiency in recognising the shapes of words and phrases without reading individual signs, and so increases the quantity of text that can be absorbed at one time. Silent reading becomes a process in which perception - or one should rather say performance - of language from text becomes heavily visual, and significantly less auditory, although in varying degrees all 'performance' of written texts is visual and 'logographic' as well as auditory.

4. Literacy and language: syntax and style

Too direct a relationship should never be presumed between spoken language and written text. However oral the reading technique in the ancient world, written language never simply represented, or had a direct relationship with vernacular spoken language, any more than is the case in the modern world (cf. e.g. Ong 1982: 75-7; 165-70). At the beginning writing provided a means of notation, not a representation of speech (Bottero 1982; Schenkel 1983; Cooper forthcoming), and the history of written language in the ancient Near East is that of a means of recording rather than of communication; parallel with spoken language in many respects, but different in its construction and use. In the modern context silent reading may be seen as helping to place written language on a non-oral plane, separate from spoken language. This does not apply to the distinction between written and spoken in the classical world, and still less to ancient Egypt. The importance of true silent reading is quantitive, since by intensifying efficient reading it means that more writing can be used. It is thus also qualitative, since written text becomes a more acceptable and independent means of communication as well as means of record and notation (cf. Clanchy 1979). This sort of silent reading requires a clarity of presentation that is only regularly attained with the wide dissemination of printed texts. In the ancient Near East, especially in the early stages of writing, tabular layout aided scanning and non-verbal assimilation of information, but this method of presentation was seldom used for continuous texts, and only partially offset the complexity of the scripts.

The average position of the readers and writers of a culture, on a scale from slow reading aloud to efficient silent reading, might be observable in written language. One feature by which 'literate' language may differ from oral language is in the length and complexity of its sentence or utterance structure, and in particular the use of more, and more diverse, embedded and subordinate clauses. In principle 'literate' language can develop greater range and complexity of prosodic patterns and types of subordinate clause. For written coomunication these need explicit grammatical or lexical marking and must follow set patterns if they are to form part of a clear sentence structure, since intonation and gesture cannot provide support. Spoken language is often a hotch potch of individual short utterances, fitted together as much by intonation and gesture as by grammatical or lexical means - the 'bricolage' of the 'savage mind' applied to linguistics and discourse analysis. Between the two poles, slow reading or slow identification of higher sense units ('utterance', clause, sentence) requires strong auditory stimulus: speaking or mouthing the script units (signs, syllables, words) as they are read, in order to assist memory in building up higher units. Thus it is advantageous for those units of 'utterance' to be short and independent. These points can be exemplified by Egyptian evidence.

Traditional grammars of classical Middle Egyptian (e.g. Gardiner 1957: 36; note Ullendorff 1958: 72-3 on Semitic in general) stress the unimportance of formal subordination, and the corresponding importance of parataxis to produce 'virtual' subordinate clauses - the placing of two formally independent 'main' clauses in juxtaposition where a language like English would mark one as subordinate to the other: "The king rages like a panther. His enemies flee". The extent and nature of subordination, and the definition of the basic prosodic unit (or 'sentence'), remain controversial for Middle Egyptian (e.g. Callender 1983), but overt marking of subordinate clauses (of time, circumstance, cause, result) analogous with that of modern European languages is limited in the early stages of Egyptian, and increases during its historical development. By Late Egyptian there is considerable growth in the use of prepositionally introduced clauses, of separate markers of grammatical subordination, and of the relative adjective to introduce relative clauses where earlier participles or 'relative forms' were used. Conversely, a passage of Middle Egyptian seems naturally to break up into short, discrete units - 'idea units'. These seem to interact, with little formal grammatical or lexical marking of relationship, to build up higher semantic units in a process where simple addition plays a leading part.

Such features of language change seem to be common, whether or not they are universal. They raise questions about the relationship between spoken and written language. It is a general assumption that language changes essentially in spoken rather than written forms, and that spoken grammar and syntax are broadly comparable at all levels of society, before mass literacy enables written language to interact widely with spoken norms, to the extent of influencing and even setting standards of spoken usage. Under such an assumption it is difficult to see how a society like ancient Egypt, with very low levels of literacy (Baines and Eyre 1983: 65-74), would generate 'literate' linguistic complexity. The issue of potential general patterns of syntactic development (e.g. Comrie 1981a), like that of potential universals of language change in general (cf. Comrie 1981b: 203- 18), is more complex than that of other, better investigated universals, such as colour terminology (for Egypt see Baines 1985). It is not easy to see precisely how the development and use of writing as such (rather than its external imposition from a dominant culture; cf. Comrie 1981b: 196-7; Kalmar 1985) might directly influence the development of language, and specifically of syntax, nor how such influences might relate to social and cognitive change in a society with very restricted uses of writing. The point of departure for written language is in semi-linguistic notation and formalised speech. For literacy to influence syntactic development would seem to require that written language stand apart and move further away from spoken language; that contrary to normal opinion it develop actively and to some extent independently, and then influence spoken language. This seems possible only in a highly literate society (e.g. Householder 1971). It is to be presumed that non-grammatical factors - both social and cognitive - are involved, and a complex mixture of cultural and linguistic influences must be taken into account. It is apparent in Egyptian material that textual style may be historically conditioned by what had previously been written down, and by the historical development of genres of written text (cf. Helck 1972; Assmann 1983). Conversely, especially tortuous constructions may to be found in argument, dictated letters, and reported speech; such texts are difficult for the modern reader because they are poorly attested and essentially spoken styles.

5. Literacy and literature: 'metrics' and style

This area of interaction between syntax and writing seems to be little explored in terms that are helpful here. For present purposes it may be better to consider the structure and style of literary composition. (For Egyptian literature in relation to writing, Helck 1972; Baines 1983: 577-8; Assmann 1983; Schenkel 1983.) The first cycle of love songs from Papyrus Chester Beatty I (Fox 1985: 52; Lichtheim 1976: 182) identifies separate stanzas by rubricated headings. The first stanza is given here in fairly free translation. As also in the following examples, an attempt is made to represent the spirit and rhythmic structure of the originals, retaining the integrity and order of the units of sense central to the 'metrical' organisation rather than the syntax and the literal meaning of the individual words. A somewhat stilted English style is the unavoidable result.

Beginning of the Sayings of the Great Entertainress
One is <my> sister; without like,
Lovelier than any woman,
See her, like Sirius risen,
As herald of a good year,
Clearly radiant; glowing skin,
Lovely gazing eyes,
Sweetly speak her lips,
Without a word too much,
Tall neck; glowing breast,
True lapis her hair,
Her arms that outshine gold,
Her fingers like lotus (petals?),
Out-curving buttocks; in-curving waist,
Her thighs parade her beauties,
Model walk as she crosses the ground,
She ravishes my heart in her embrace.
She makes the neck of every man
turned to see her.
Joyous any she embraces,
He is like the prince of lovers,
She being seen, as she comes out,
Like that very only One.
[The comparison in the last line is to the goddess of love Hathor, who is also the eye of the sun.]

The manuscript is not written in 'poetic' format with 'line' divisions, but these are marked by red pointing above the hieratic text. In other love song manuscripts the stanza ends may be marked by the same 'period' sign as the section end in a schoolboy's exercise. Yet the written texts of the love songs are hardly school exercises. On one side of this papyrus are the love poems, hymns and business notes. On the other is the story of Horus and Seth, a long, mythologically based narrative. It is from the private library of one of the scribes from Deir el-Medina. The notation acts as a sort of punctuation, marking metrical breaks as an aid to reading, that is, oral reading or singing. The lines consist of an average of 4 or 5 words, and each line forms an independent unit of sense and syntax. 'Enjambement' is so rare as always to raise suspicion of error, although there is one possible case in the passage quoted here: 'She makes the neck of every man / turned to see her'. The overall metrical structure is more complex. The lines divide and relate to one another in groups, here of two and four, elsewhere also in triplets. Individual lines divide into two or three stress units. Without knowledge of the vowels our understanding of the metrical structure of the individual line may be limited, but it was probably based on a stress, not vowel length or quality.

This is evidently a song, that could be performed with musical accompaniment, yet its structure and style are the same as that of many other genres of text. There are manuscripts of the New Kingdom 'Wisdom of Amenemope' written in 'poetic' format. Each 'line' stands separate on the page, and the division into stanzas marked by rubricated headings. These stanzas or chapters, which vary in length from 6 to 36 lines, fall naturally into groups of 2, 3 or 4 lines. Individual lines divide into the normal 2 or 3 units. It is uncertain whether line divisions into 4 units were used. Possible examples of such a division may not be correctly understood. The length of line varies much more than in the love songs, but the number of units of stress is comparable (Grumach 1972: 161-5; Lichtheim 1976: 160-1).

The 26th Stanza

Do not sit in a beer house,
And join one greater than you,
Be he a youth great from his offices,
Or whether an elder by birth.
Befriend yourself a man your equal:

It is from a distance that God helps.
If you see your superior outdoors,
Follow behind him respectfully.
Give a hand to an elder sated with beer.
Respect him as his children (do).
The arm hurts not from baring it.
The back breaks not from bending it.
A man is not impoverished who speaks sweetly,
Or enriched when his words bristle.
The pilot, he sees from afar;
He doesn't act towards his boat's capsize.

The same principles turn out to be applicable to any continuous text. An autobiographical text from the tomb of the Sixth Dynasty official Neferseshemre Sheshi is a paradigmatic example of purely formulaic composition, involving the absolute minimum of individuality. The same lines are found time and time again in texts of the genre. 'Line' divisions are not marked in any way in the original inscription. (Sethe 1933: 198-200; Lichtheim 1973: 17).

I have come out from my town,
I have come down from my estate.
I have done Right for her Lord;
I have satisfied him with what he loves;
I have spoken justly; I have done justice.
I have spoken fair; I have reported fair.
I have taken (my) fair opportunities,
(For) I desired that I should be well in with the world.
I judged litigants to their satisfaction:
I saved the weak from the stronger;
I used my power in this.
I gave bread to the hungry,
Clothing <to the naked>,
Bringing ashore to the boatless.
I buried the one without a son.
I made a ferry for the one without a ferry.
I honoured my father,
I pleased my mother,
I reared their children.
          (So) he says;
He who is called Sheshi.

Autobiographical texts, whether formulaic in this way or containing more individual narrative, occur in private tomb and stela inscriptions. Their superficial purpose was to mark ownership and encourage the living to make offering to the deserving dead. They also had an important function in display and prestige. The genre goes back to a very early stage of Egyptian writing. Their formulae are found in almost the earliest continuous texts, and continue to be important until early Roman times. As a genre they appear in the Old Kingdom, and provide the earliest 'literary texts' we know. They are closely related in style and literary development to classes of royal text that first appear in inscriptions of the Middle Kingdom, and were of central importance to the development of written literature in Egypt (Helck 1972; Assmann 1983; Schenkel 1983). Idealising 'praise' or 'self-praise' of the king - whether in the direct form of an address with recitation of virtues (and later specific deeds), or more subtly in the framework of plot - is the central theme of much of this literature (Hermann 1938; Posener 1956; 1976). Any attempt to assess the relationship of such written genres to oral forms of display must be speculative, as is the assessment of the relationship between Egyptian oral and written literature in general (cf. Seibert 1967). However, such a central genre would logically have its roots in oral declamatory 'literature', for which African 'praise poetry' (Finnegan 1970) offers one analogy.

Even tomb texts could be performed orally. A standard appeal to the living for recital of the offering formula stresses that only 'breath of the mouth', is required; no expenditure and no tiring physical effort. The Middle Kingdom stela of Montuwoser (Sethe 1928: 79-80) ends: 'Now as for everybody who will hear this stela, who is among the living, he will say, "It is the truth." Their children will say to <their> children, "It is the truth. There is no lie there." And any scribe who will read out this stela, all people will come up to him.' The vision of curious visitors to the necropolis approaching for the entertainment of hearing an elegant biography read out is not completely unreal.

It can hardly be doubted that these formal inscriptions have an implied context of oral performance, which deeply influenced their structure. The format of such texts - formulaic autobiography and the most closely related classes of royal inscription, which especially include those condemned by historians as 'rhetorical' and comparatively useless - is the speech of the high official, the king, or sometimes a god. The inscriptions we have are mostly short - occupying no more than a couple of pages in print - and are not themselves direct records of performances, although they may be models or distillations of the practice. After all, part of the point of oral performance is that it is seldom fixed, but expands and contracts with circumstances. Among the elite there may have been much interaction between spoken and written forms of praise, although there is little indication of the circumstances under which rhetorical accounts of exploits - 'biography' or 'autobiography' - might have been performed in public praise or self-praise

The heading to the Armant Stela of Tuthmosis III states that it is a summary of what would be longer in speech: 'Collection of the deeds of bravery and might which this perfect god (=the king) did ...; that which the Lord of Gods, Lord of Armant (=Montu) did for him, that his victories might be magnified, and to cause his activities be related for millions of years to come. ... If one relates the deeds as a list, they are too many to put in writing' (Helck 1955: 1244,15-1245,2). There are also Middle and New Kingdom royal inscriptions that use the topos of 'dialogue' between king and officials to present the officials reciting praise to the king, and the king addressing the officials in self-praise (Hermann 1938). Little is known about the social context in which hymns of praise to Egyptian kings were used, although several are preserved, and the question cannot be pursued here. Yet in evaluating content, as well as linguistic and stylistic structures, it is helpful to evoke this analogy of 'praise' poetry designed for formal, rhythmic performance.

Such texts might be dismissed as unfair examples, genuine 'poetry', not 'prose', although these and related genres form a substantial proportion of Egyptian literature. However, the same stylistic features also occur in simple narratives. The following is the opening of the New Kingdom 'Tale of the Doomed Prince' (Lichtheim 1976: 200-3); line divisions are marked by red pointing on the original.

It is told there was a king;
A male child had not been born to him.
So the king prayed for a son from the gods of his domain.
They decreed that one be born to him.
He slept with his wife in the night.
She [conceived] and became pregnant.

She completed the months of bearing.
Then she bore a male child.
Came then the Hathors,
To fix for him (his) Fates.
        They said;
He will die by crocodile,
Or else by snake,
Or equally by dog.
Then they heard, who were by the child.
So they repeated it to the king.

This is not the metre of Classical or Western European tradition, but it is the criteria of oral literature. The extreme position among egyptologists (especially Gerhard Fecht, e.g. 1965; 1982) is that all continuous texts are 'metrical'. As one moves from obvious short songs to long narrative tales the tightness of composition varies (in line length, assonance, balancing of lines and half lines). Syllable count or specific metrical feet seem irrelevant to the system, but the stress count seems to remain regular. The essential structural patterns do not seem to alter. The assertion that all texts are 'metrical' has been too strong for many egyptologists to accept, although the nature of the style itself is evident in outline to all (Lichtheim 1971/2; Burkard 1983).

Most written texts can be sited on a scale between literary composition in metre by rules - a highly literate occupation, that will be exceptional in Egyptian texts - and the composition of texts for fluent, rhythmic performance (cf. Saenger 1982: 370; 380-1; 407-8; 411; Junge 1984: 251-2); texts built additively from small, relatively independent units that do not over-extend the listener's attention span, or cause him to lose the thread if he fails to hear every detail. Egyptian written 'stories' generally have all the devices typical of literature for oral performance, that help to hold or re-catch the attention of an audience, and allow the length and detail of a performance to vary according to audience reaction; formulaic phrases, particularly in the introductions to new sections; episodic structure - the plot breaking up into short sections that can be included, omitted, and sometimes transposed without destroying the whole; repetition of important sections in reported speech.

Such 'metricality', the use of formulae, and oral performance as the proper context of a work do not add up to 'oral formulaic' poetry, even under a mild definition; Egyptian literary works do not fit the Parry-Lord hypothesis. It would not seem helpful to class Egyptian literature as 'intermediate', on a scale between 'oral' and 'literate', although it was both recited and written, nor to try to isolate 'oral residues' in its content and form. The features of literary structure we are discussing must be related to the reading process as well as to oral performance. Learning to read by additive chanting of texts relates to an additive rather than subordinating syntactic ordering of clauses and the use of relatively short and discrete units of sense, whether this is an issue of language or of literary and metrical style (note Kalmar 1985). Simple sense units often add to or contrast with one another in simple patterns. These units may seem oral, but they are also convenient for practical reading.

Formulae are not only helpful in oral performance, whether as compositional or as mnemonic devices. They are also fundamental to much reading, and much written composition. The repetition of vocabulary and grammatical constructions, the 'formulaic' nature of logographic orthography, and the use of complete formulaic units of composition, are all aids to greater fluency in composing and reading script. Here Egyptian teaching methods and orthographic conventions, with their focus on whole words or phrases, put an extra premium on formulaic habits. 'Formulae' make script readable, however tedious they may seem when the text is printed for the silent reader, who reads more quickly, and is concerned more with meaning and less with form and performance. The ideal of varied, non-repetitive discourse, is essentially an ideal of written prose.

In Egyptian literature, more complex and varied syntactic patterns and more difficult styles are usually found in texts with shorter individual units and more obviously 'poetic' character. Narratives have longer units, which appear more 'prosaic', and they have less variety in syntax and vocabulary, so that some are very repetitive in language and structure. In the Middle Kingdom story of the Shipwrecked Sailor (Lichtheim 1973:211-5), almost every other sentence begins with the same verb form, which means, roughly, "It then happened that....". This is as helpful to the eye of the reader or reciter as to the ear of the hearer. However, such syntactically repetitive narrative represents only a single style. It is characteristic of the best written literature from Egypt that a variety of styles are welded together into a single work.

The story of the Eloquent Peasant (Lichtheim 1975: 169-84) places a series of complex rhetorical or poetic addresses of praise and criticism ('praise poems' where the peasant as performer tests the limits of poetic licence) within a simply expressed narrative framework, as the peasant is wronged and looks for aid and redress from an apparently reluctant lord. It is common for longer royal inscriptions of the New Kingdom to vary style or text genre in different sections. The greatest tour-de-force of Middle Kingdom literature, the story of Sinuhe (Lichtheim 1975:222-35), goes furthest in this direction beyond the conventions of simple narrative. It uses a very wide range of literary genres, both narrative and poetic, within the conventional framework of an autobiography, as well as striving for original and striking use of language (cf. Baines 1982). Conversely the Late Egyptian story of Wenamun (Lichtheim 1976: 224-30) presents something like a non-formulaic 'prose' narrative. It may be presumed that these last two texts - virtuoso works whose status as 'fictional literature' rather than 'genuine' tomb autobiography and official report has been questioned by some writers - were consciously composed in writing, in contrast with normal patterns of narrative; but this does not mean they were not expected to be recited in oral performance.

The practicalities and habits of reading place constraints on written style, and so standards of good style should be related to reading habits. They influence what accident has preserved, because they govern what was valued, and copied. They are as important as the specifically auditory aspect of performance, since most major literary manuscripts are likely to be the private copies of individuals and not texts used for repeated declamation. Oral performance is not in conflict with written composition. The classics of Egyptian literature are written compositions, not oral compositions that happen to be recorded in writing. Yet even the most carefully composed and 'literary' religious texts are also for recital in oral performance, which would often be from memory, without the use of a manuscript as a prompt.

Analysis of reading habits, and of learning to read, is critical to identifying what is oral and what is literate in any written tradition, and to comprehending that tradition's role in society. Literacy was not a single invention that immediately changed the life of all who attained it, any more than modern literacy is a social and intellectual panacea. There are many historical gradations of literacy and changes in its potential, from being an extension or form of memory for recording and a vehicle for the display of prestige, to its eventual status as a quasi-independent means of communication (which it never achieved in Egypt). This slow development is associated with other social and cognitive change. This self-evident interrelationship, whose exploration was pioneered by Jack Goody (1968; 1977), resists close definition. Egyptian evidence does not directly answer the questions of whether literacy is a cause, an enabling factor, or merely a concomitant circumstance of such change, or which changes may be termed consequences of literacy. Our material provides no neat answers to these fundamental questions, but it does suggest something of the reality of oral-literate interchange in the constant passage of language, texts, and written material in general, through both oral and written forms. We hope we have conveyed some of the potential of using primarily textual sources to formulate hypotheses, as well as giving some of the flavour of actual usage. We have looked at this principally through schooling and reading methods (for which comparative evidence supplies vital support), and we have related this approach to the structure of literary texts. An awareness of how writing was used, in the simple sense of writing it down and reading it back, is important for understanding its general position in society. This is a low-level approach to general questions, but may add to the discussion of the increasingly rich material available on different literacies, and help to reinforce awareness that literacy is a process, and not a fixed entity.

Bibliography

(**Note:** There is insufficient space here for detailed reference to Egyptian textual evidence. The basic study of Brunner (1957) cites many sources for Egyptian education in extenso. For literary and didactic texts in translation see Lichtheim 1973; 1976; 1980.)

Assmann, J. (1983) Schrift, Tod und Identität. Das Grab als Vorschule der Literatur im alten Ägypten. In J. and A. Assmann and C. Hardmeier (eds), *Schrift und Gedächtnis. Archäologie der literarischen Kommunikation*, 64-93. Munich: Fink.

Baines, J. (1982) Interpreting Sinuhe. *Journal of Egyptian Archaeology* 68, 31-44.

Baines, J. (1983) Literacy and ancient Egyptian society. *Man* NS 18, 572- 99.

Baines, J. (1985) Color terminology and color classification: ancient Egyptian color terminology and polychromy. *American Anthropologist* 87, 282-97.

Baines, J. and C.J. Eyre (1983) Four notes on literacy. *Göttinger Miszellen* 61, 65-96.

Bottéro, J. (1982) De l'aide-mémoire à l'écriture. In *Écritures: systèmes idéographiques et pratiques expressives*, 13-37 (Actes du colloque .... Univ. Paris VII 22-24 avril 1980). Paris: Le Sycamore.

Bresciani, E., S. Pernigotti and M.C. Betrò (1983) *Ostraka demotici da Narmuti* I (Quaderni di Medinet Madi, I). Pisa: Giardini.

Brunner, H. (1957) *Altägyptische Erziehung*. Wiesbaden: Harrassowitz.

Burkard, G. (1983) Der formale Aufbau altägyptischer Literaturwerke. *Studien zur altägyptischen Kultur* 10, 79- 118.

Callender, J.B. (1983) Sentence initial position in Egyptian. *Chronique d'Égypte* 58, 83-96.

Caminos, R.A. (1968) A fragmentary hieratic school-book in the British Museum (Pap. B.M. 10298). *Journal of Egyptian Archaeology* 54. 114-20.

Caminos, R.A. (1977) *A Tale of Woe: from a hieratic papyrus in the A.S.Pushkin Museum of Fine Arts in Moscow*. Oxford: Griffith Institute.

Chafe, W.L. (1985) Linguistic differences produced by differences between speaking and writing. In D.R. Olson, N. Torrance and A. Hildyard (eds), *Literacy, Language and Learning: the nature and consequences of reading and writing*, 105-23. Cambridge: Univ. Press.

Clanchy, M.T. (1979) *From Memory to Written Record: England 1066- 1307*. London: Edward Arnold.

Comrie, B. (1981a) The formation of relative clauses. In B. Lloyd and J. Gay (eds.), *Universals of Human Thought: some African evidence*, 215-33. Cambridge: Univ Press.

Comrie (1981b) *Language Universals and Linguistic Typology*. Oxford: Blackwell.

Cooper, J.S. (forthcoming) Before Babel: writing, language and speech.

Devauchele, D. (1984) Remarques sur les méthodes d'enseignement du démotique. In H.J. Thissen and K.Th. Zauzich (eds.), *Grammata Demotika: Festschrift für Erich Lüddeckens zum 15. Juni 1983*, 47-59. Würzburg: Gisela Zauzich.

Edgerton, W.F. (1941) Ideograms in English writing. *Language* 17, 148-50.

Fecht, G. (1965) *Literarische Zeugnisse zur "Persönlichen Frömmigkeit" in Ägypten*. Heidelberg: Carl Winter & Universitätsverlag (Abh. Heidelberg. Akad. Wiss., phil.- hist. Kl. 1965, 1).

Fecht, G. (1982) Prosodie. In W. Helck and W. Westendorf (eds), *Lexikon der Ägyptologie* 4, 1127-54. Wiesbaden: Harrassowitz.

Finnegan, R. (1970) *Oral Literature in Africa*. Oxford: Univ. Press.

Fox, M.V. (1985) *The Song of Songs and the Ancient Egyptian Love Songs*. Madison and London: Univ. of Wisconsin Press.

Gardiner, A.H. (1942) Writing and literature. In S.R.K. Glanville (ed.), *The Legacy of Egypt*, 53-79. Oxford: Univ. Press.

Gardiner, A.H. (1947) *Ancient Egyptian Onomastica*. Oxford: Univ. Press.

Gardiner, A.H. (1957) *Egyptian Grammar* (third edn). Oxford: Univ. Press for Griffith Institute.

Goody, J. (ed.) (1968) *Literacy in Traditional Societies*. Cambridge: Univ. Press.

Goody, J. (1977) *The Domestication of the Savage Mind*. Cambridge: Univ. Press.

Grumach, I. (1972) *Untersuchungen zur Lebenslehre des Amenope*. (Münchner ägyptologische Studien 23). Munich and Berlin: Deutscher Kunstverlag.

Helck, W. (1955) *Urkunden der 18. Dynastie* 17 (= Urkunden des Ägyptischen Altertums IV, 17). Berlin: Akademie-Verlag.

Helck, W. (1972) Zur Frage der Entstehung der ägyptischen Literatur. *Wiener Zeitschrift für die Kunde des Morgenlandes*, 63/4, 6- 26.

Hermann, A. (1938) *Die ägyptische Königsnovelle*. (Leipziger ägyptologische Studien 10). Glückstadt, Hamburg, New York: Augustin.

Householder, F.W. (1971) The primacy of writing. In *Lingusitic Speculations*, 244-64. Cambridge: Univ. Press.

Junge, F. (1984) Rhetorik. In W. Helck and W. Westendork (eds), *Lexikon der Ägyptologie* V, 250-3. Wiesbaden: Harrassowitz.

Kalmar, I. (1985) Are there really no primitive languages? In D.R. Olson, N. Torrance and A. Hildyard (eds), *Literacy, Language and Learning: the nature and consequences of reading and writing*, 148-66. Cambridge: Univ. Press.

Kaplony-Heckel, U. (1974) Schüler und Schulwesen in der Ägyptischen Spätzeit. *Studien zur altägyptischen Kultur* 1, 227-246.

Knox, B.M.W. (1968) Silent reading in Antiquity. *Greek, Roman and Byzantine Studies* 9, 421-35.

Lichtheim, M. (1971/2) Have the principles of ancient Egyptian metrics been discovered? *Journal of the American Research Centre in Egypt* 9, 103-10.

Lichtheim, M. (1973) *Ancient Egyptian Literature: a book of readings. I: The Old and Middle Kingdoms*, Berkeley: Univ. of California Press.

Lichtheim, M. (1976) *Ancient Egyptian Literature: a book of readings. II: The New Kingdom*, Berkeley: Univ. of California Press.

Lichtheim, M. (1980) *Ancient Egyptian Literature: a book of readings. III: The Late Period*, Berkeley: Univ. of California Press.

Megally, M. (1971) *Considérations sur les variations et la transformation des formes hiératiques du papyrus E.3226 du Louvre*. Cairo: Institut Français d'Archéologie Orientale.

Millard, A.R. (1970) "Scripto continua" in early Hebrew: ancient practice or modern surmise? *Journal of Semitic Studies* 15, 2-15.

Millard, A.R. (1986) The infancy of the alphabet. *World Archaeology* 18, 390-8.

Ong, W.J. (1982) *Orality and Literacy. The technologizing of the word*. New York and London: Methuen.

Pleyte, W. and F. Rossi (1869-76) *Papyrus de Turin*. Leiden: Brill.

Posener, G. (1956) *Littérature et Politique dans l'Égypte de la XIIe dynastie*. Paris: Champion.

Posener, G. (1976) *L'Enseignement Loyaliste*. Geneva: Droz.

Redford, D.B. (1984) The meaning and use of the term GNWT "Annals". *Studien zu Sprache und Religion Aegyptens zu Ehren von Wolfhart Westendorf, 1: Sprache*, 327-41. Göttingen: (no publ.).

Saenger, P. (1982) Silent reading: its impact on late medieval script and society. *Viator* 13, 367-414.

Schenkel, W. (1976) The structure of hieroglyphic script. *Royal Anthropological Institute News* 15, 4-7.

Schenkel, W. (1983) Wozu die Ägypter eine Schrift brauchten. In A. and J. Assmann and C. Hardmeier (eds), *Schrift und Gedächtnis. Beiträge zur Archäologie der literarischen Kommunikation*, 45-63. Munich: Fink.

Schenkel, W. (1984) Schrift. In W. Helck and W. Westendorf (eds), *Lexikon der Ägyptologie* V, 713-35. Wiesbaden: Harrassowitz.

Scott, N. (n.d.) *The Daily Life of the Ancient Egyptians*, n.p. (The Metropolitan Museum, New York).

Scribner, S. and M. Cole (1981) *The Psychology of Literacy*. Cambridge, Mass. and London: Harvard Univ. Press.

Seibert, P. (1967) *Die Charakteristik. Untersuchungen zu einer altägyptischen Sprechsitte und ihren Ausprägungen in Folklore und Literatur*, I. (Ägyptologische Abhandlungen 17). Wiesbaden: Harrassowitz.

Sethe, K. (1928) *Ägyptische Lesestücke zum Gebrauch im akademischen Unterricht* (2nd edn). Leipzig: Hinrichs.

Sethe, K. (1933) *Urkunden des alten Reiches* I (= Urkunden des Ägyptischen Altertums I) (2nd edition). Leipzig: Hinrichs.

Smith, H.S. and W.J. Tait (1983) *Saqqâra Demotic Papyri* I. London: Egypt Exploration Society.

Ullendorff, E. (1958) What is a Semitic language? *Orientalia* 27, 66-75.

Vachek, J. (1973) *Written Language*. The Hague and Paris: Mouton.

Volten, A. (1937) *Studien zum Weisheitsbuch des Anii*. (Det Kgl. Danske Videnskabernes Selskab. Historisk-filologiske Meddelelser. XXIII,3). Copenhagen: Levin and Munksgaard.

Ward, W.H. (1981) Lexicographical Miscellanies II. *Studien zur altägyptischen Kultur* 9, 359-373.

Williams, R.J. (1972) Scribal training in ancient Egypt. *Journal of the American Oriental Society* 92, 214-21.

Winter, E. (1967) *Der Entwurf für eine Türinschrift auf einem ägyptischen Papyrus.* (Nachr. Ak. Wiss. Göttingen, phil.- hist. Kl., 1967, 3). Göttingen: Vandenhoeck and Ruprecht.

What They Wrote On Clay

Mogens Trolle Larsen

> Writing is not a monolithic entity,
> an undifferentiated skill;
> its potentialities depend upon the kind of system
> that obtains in any particular society
> Jack Goody

Some 80 years ago the Swedish playwright August Strindberg published a volume of essays, "A Blue Book", in which we find his views on Assyriology and the decipherment of cuneiform :

> Young people! Do not read Assyrian, for that is not a language, that is rubbish! Just take a look at this little sign! ▷— It looks like the finger that is pointing towards unsafe ice, or the public convenience, or the place voi ch'entrate. That little sign first sounds as follows: as, dil, til, dili, ina, ru, rum, salugub, simed, tal.
> Do you believe in that?
> But it also has other values and meanings. Look! Aplu = son; Assur = assur; êdu = one; nadänu = to give.
> Do you believe in that?
> Or this: ▼ which sounds: dab, di, ti, du, dub, dug, dugn, ha, hi, sar, sur.
> And means 4 or you or which, or stand close, or Assur (everything means Assur) or sar tabu = be good, or tubbu = good, or kusbu = great luxury.
> Is this possible?
> Young men swallow such things raw! No doubt is possible, no contradiction, no absurdity, for the Professor has spoken!
> But if the preacher says that God created this Earth in beauty and perfection, and that Man has made it ugly and stupid through his wretchedness, then the disciple doubts. It is too simple and beautiful to penetrate into a perverted mind!

121

"Woe unto you, scribes and pharisees!" (Strindberg, 1921, 515-516).

Obviously, Strindberg was not convinced that such a system of writing could be correctly interpreted. It was complicated and ambiguous rather than simple and beautiful and could only appeal to perverted minds. The skepticism towards the decipherment of the cuneiform system of writing which he expressed was a rather late example of the general sense of unease, confusion and doubt with which the decipherers were met around 1850 when they presented to the learned world their interpretation of the writing on the Assyrian clay tablets. And it was indeed a very complex system which emerged from the efforts of scholars in England, France, Ireland and Germany who began to pore over the tablets and stones with the strange, wedge-shaped signs.

First, since the script consisted of a great number of signs, it was clear that it could not be an alphabetic system; in fact, it was claimed to be a complex mix of syllabic and logographic principles. Secondly, each of the hundreds of signs could, it was said, be read in several different ways; one sign could have a number of syllabic values (Strindberg's "as, dil, til" etc.), which introduced the principle of polyphony for the signs; but on top of that each sign could also function as a logogram, standing for a whole word or concept as in Chinese for instance (Strindberg's "Aplu = son" etc.). Finally, many different signs appeared to stand for the same syllable, which introduced the principle of homophony.

It was said by many that any system as complex as this would be impossibly ambiguous. Even a quite simple text would be of uncertain interpretation, since each sign could be read in so many different ways that there would be a series of possible readings.

What is one to say about a language which consists entirely of defects and vacancies, and where every word may be pronounced in all possible ways and mean anything at all? A language which cannot be translated unless you know the accepted meaning beforehand (Ibid., 503).

In 1857 one of the men who claimed to be able to read cuneiform, the mathematician Fox Talbot, asked the Royal Asiatic Society in London to arrange a test of the reliability of the claims; he suggested that the Society should ask a few decipherers to make independent editions of a newly discovered royal inscription in

Assyrian of which he gave his own interpretation. The Royal Asiatic Society handed over the text to Rawlinson, the grand old man at The British Museum, and to the Irish scholar Hincks and the French scholar Jules Oppert, both of whom happened to be in London at the time. When the four letters were opened and examined, it was decided that the results were close enough to warrant the conclusion that the script could in fact be read, so the built-in ambiguities did not, after all, form an insuperable hindrance to an understanding of the written message. The discipline of Assyriology was - if not born, then surely baptized and legitimized[1].

Since then scholars have busily prepared editions of tens of thousands of documents written in cuneiform and we have come to understand the language, script and culture of three millennia of recorded history from Mesopotamian texts. So, when the question of the ambiguity of the cuneiform system of writing has again become an issue in the learned literature, there is, of course, no question of siding with Strindberg and casting doubt upon the correctness of the decipherment. Rather, doubts have been raised about the capability of such a system of writing for rendering a variety of human ideas and experiences with freedom and precision, and such doubts have become part of an argument which underpins a special technological mode of explanation for some fundamental differences between alphabetic and non-alphabetic literatures.

Two basic claims are made:
1) that the clumsiness and ambiguity of cuneiform writing placed severe restrictions on any written message, so that in fact not every human statement could be faithfully recorded;
2) that the complexity of the system meant that widespread literacy was impossible to achieve; instead we have a system of what is called "craft literacy" in which total control over the script and a monopoly over the correct interpretation of any written message belonged to a group of specialists: the scribes.

These claims enter into the analyses offered by a number of scholars, among them the classicist Eric Havelock[2]. He is particularly interested in the contrast between the ancient Near East and

---

[1] See e.g. Friedrich 1957, 66-67.

[2] See for instance Havelock 1963, 117, or Olson 1977, 265-266; see for comments Larsen 1987, 217-225.

Greece, worlds which were dominated by different scripts as well as by civilizations which have often been seen as utterly different from each other in nearly every respect.

Havelock has tackled these differences in a very direct manner, by comparing two of the major literary works from these traditions: Homer's epics and the Babylonian Gilgamesh Epic. He concludes that essential differences between these texts can be explained on the basis of "the deficiencies of cuneiform as an instrument of acoustic-visual recognition." In fact, in his view cuneiform was such a cumbersome and ambiguous system that it was incapable of recording the spoken word clearly and with precision, which accordingly made it applicable only for certain, limited purposes. The literary texts which have been written down in Mesopotamia, with the Gilgamesh Epic as the most outstanding example, do not truly represent the poetic genius of this civilization but must be understood as "epitomes transcribed for recital on formal occasions". The real Babylonian literature can only have existed in oral form behind these formal documents as "a far richer epic, linguistically speaking", now hidden and lost forever, namely "the poetry of the people, on their lips, in their memories..." (Havelock, 1978, 9).

Havelock further concludes that the ambiguity of the writing system meant that the topics of written compositions would tend to "codify and standardize the variety of human experience so that the reader of such scripts is more likely to recognize what the writer is talking about" (Havelock, 1976, 35). Havelock appears to imply that the script had so little information-carrying capacity that new, surprising and unknown messages could not be recorded in a way that would ensure understanding on the part of the reader:

> the alphabet .. made possible the production of novel or unexpected statements, previously unfamiliar, or even "unthought". ... Previous transcription, because of the ambiguities of the script, discouraged attempts to record novel statements (Ibid., 50).

Obviously, this means that writing could be used primarily to perpetuate and preserve; cuneiform writing was in other words a strongly conservative factor in society - in contrast to the alphabet of course, which gave to every literate person total freedom of expression through a completely transparent medium of communication. Such ideas therefore easily lead to a technological model of explanation for what were clearly fundamental cultural differences between the worlds of the ancient Near East and Greece, where the introduction of an alphabetic system of writing comes to stand as an element of paramount importance. In the words of Eric Havelock:

> It is therefore no accident that the cultures of the Near East which preceded the Greek and are recorded in hieroglyph, cuneiform, or Semitic shorthand, seem on the basis of the record to be peculiarly occupied with such matters [religion and myth]. We normally take it for granted that such preoccupation was an inherent characteristic of these cultures, and it is often put down to the fact that they were at a more "primitive" stage of development. The reason I am suggesting is rather to be sought in a fact of technology (Ibid., 35).

He points specifically to the parts of the Old Testament which were written in what he calls "the Phoenician shorthand syllabary" as a proper test case:

> it remains true that these originals and their surrounding sentiments are syntactically repetitive, that typical situations recur, that the relationships between the characters are relatively simple and their acts take on an almost ritual quality. We feel the simple rhythm of the record as it unfolds. It is precisely these limitations imposed upon the possible coverage of human experience that give to the Old Testament its power of appeal, as we say, to "simple people" (Ibid., 34-35).

In order to discuss and evaluate such ideas it is clearly necessary to have a reasonably adequate understanding of the characteristics of the cuneiform system of writing, and I shall attempt to provide an extremely brief and non-technical description of its development. Secondly, I shall present a crude overview of the extant textual documentation from the three millennia of cuneiform writing in order to provide a basis for a reasonable discussion of the uses to which writing was put in this long span of time. And finally, I hope that some relationship can then be established between these two analytic paths on the basis of the hypothesis that there was a correspondence between the development of the writing system and the uses to which it was put.

Mogens Trolle Larsen

The Writing System

I do not wish in this context to enter the discussion concerning the relationship between "proto-" or "pre-"writing and "true" writing; I simply refer to the generally accepted view that the oldest documents which are so far known from the history of this planet, which carry signs constituting elements in a system of writing, stem from early levels of the ancient town of Uruk in southern Mesopotamia[3]. During the last centuries of the fourth millennium B.C. a vast metropolis developed here, with a population of probably in excess of 10.000 inhabitants and complete with gigantic ceremonial complexes (Adams, and Nissen 1972). I am personally happy to accept the suggestion that a Sumerian genius invented writing one morning in Uruk around 3100 B.C. (Powell 1981), and recent work has even provided some plausible ideas about the basis for this invention. Various scholars have pointed out that clay tokens of various shapes which are found in many places all over the Near East could have functioned as counters in simple administrative procedures. According to recent theories (Schmandt-Besserat 1981 and 1988), such counters were at a later stage placed in balls of clay, the point being that the numerical information provided by the counters could then be transported in time and space without any interference or tampering. The next step was to place a sealing on this clay ball to indicate authorization or responsibility for the operation involved, and some bright person then had the idea to also impress the counters in the surface of the clay ball: in this way one would not even have to break it open in order to consult the counters.

All of these steps clearly point to an administrative practice, where quantities of various commodities were handed over from person to person or from agency to agency.[4] The clay balls containing counters whose shapes had also been impressed on

---

[3] See Damerow, Englund and Nissen 1988 for a presentation of the German research efforts directed towards an analysis of the texts; for further discussion I refer to Larsen in press. General discussions of the history and development of cuneiform may be found in Gelb 1963, and Hawkins 1979; see also for a different perspective Sampson 1985, chapter 3 "The earliest writing".

[4] As pointed out in Larsen in press, 185, a comparison with e.g. the Peruvian *quipu*-system shows that we are dealing with a functioning structure of recording and notation rather than of "real" writing.

the surface together with a sealing, constituted a kind of anepigraphic document.

Writing was introduced into this system by way of a combination of drawings representing commodities and the impressed marks of counters: the head of an ox followed by two imprints of the counter denoting the unit "1" gives us a text. In the words of Roy Harris, such a combination of a type-symbol with a countable token

> will mean incorporating certain structurally superimposed features upon the system of signs employed. And this, in turn, is the thin end of the semiological wedge which will ultimately prise scriptorial and pictorial signs apart. For the combination of two primordially different signs in the same graphic system opens up communicational possibilities which were not inherent in either type of sign individually (Harris 1986, 139-140).

Some of the early pictographic signs were naturalistic, the head of a bull as the sign for "ox", a human foot for the concept "go", or a star for "heaven"; others are less easy to understand, and at least some may go back to the system of counters: a circle inscribed with a cross thus seems to have its origin in a special counter for sheep which left such an imprint.

A pictographic system does not, of course, reveal the language spoken by those who use it, but there is every reason to believe that the first texts in Uruk were written by Sumerians, and as the script developed it certainly became linked inextricably with the Sumerian language. This was of the polysynthetic type, combining unchangeable one-syllable roots with a host of pre-, in-, and suffixes, and these roots became the "readings" of the various signs when they began to be used also as syllables. By way of the rebus principle drawings of objects could also be used to stand for words which denoted concepts which could not be easily represented pictorially, but which resembled phonetically. Thus, the sign for the Sumerian word for "arrow", pronounced somewhat like /ti/, could also represent another word /ti/ which meant "life", and which might be hard to draw.

The script was elaborated upon in another direction as well, however. One sign could be used for several words or concepts which were related by way of meaning rather than pronunciation. The human foot, to take an example, could represent the verb "walk", which in Sumerian was something like /gin/; or it could be used for the verb "bring", which had a pronunciation like /tum/; or it could be used for another verb "stand" which in Sumerian would be /gub/. So the same sign could stand for a number of words, and eventually for their pronunciations in a system of syllabic writing. This practice, where the signs could represent a number of different words, certainly introduced a potential for confusion and ambiguity, but in the actual writing exercise it mattered little. The script was not designed to indicate how the words were pronounced, and in cases of doubt, where the context was not clear enough to show whether commodities were "brought" or whether they "stood ready", it was possible in the developed system of Sumerian writing to provide a suffix which could show whether the root ended in -m or in -b. However, because of the nature of the texts such precision was rarely needed.

Over time, as writing was used for many more purposes, this practice certainly did lead to a great deal of complexity and ambiguity in the system, and the polyvalence of each sign was apparently what Strindberg found most ludicrous. In fact, a modern signlist provides even more readings of the signs Strindberg mentioned, and the whole system does look forbidding. The reasons for this are contained in the fact that it existed during a period of three millennia and accumulated a great deal of complexity in the course of the centuries, and - very importantly - it underwent some very drastic changes both in structure and in use.

Like so many fundamental features in Mesopotamian culture, the writing system was both marked by conservatism in the sense that it retained its basic nature through the entire period, and also by change and ruptures which altered the way it was used. To take an example: a Sumerian scribe around 3000 B.C. could write the name of the sungod by way of two signs: a star representing divinity and a drawing of the sun rising out of the mountains; and a scribe in Babylon 2,000 years later would use the same signs. Their appearance would be dramatically changed of course, but that is not really interesting, for we can construct a long sequence which shows how the old drawing in time developed gradually from a recognizable representation to a pictorially meaningless sign; the significant thing is that whereas the old scribe wrote in a logographic system which had no, or very little relation to spoken language, the late scribe wrote in a basically syllabic system which in principle gave a phonetic rendering of his spoken tongue.

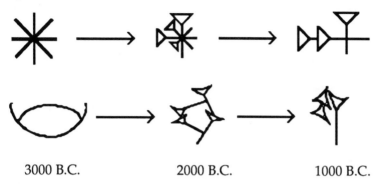

| 3000 B.C. | 2000 B.C. | 1000 B.C. |

The essential element in this transformation was the transfer of the script from one language, Sumerian, to another, Akkadian, which was completely unrelated, for this fostered tendencies towards a syllabic use of the cuneiform system of writing.

In the city-states of the third millennium B.C. the writing system was, as already mentioned, developed in conjunction with the Sumerian language. Not that the script represented spoken language, for it was used primarily as a logographic system with a very limited use of syllabic features for the writing of the most essential grammatical modifications of the unchangeable root. The many morphological elements which made up the complex Sumerian verbal structure, for instance, were as a general rule not reproduced in writing. Only the elements which were absolutely necessary - negations to take an example - were indicated. Reading aloud an early text accordingly must have meant introducing all of these grammatical elements, and it seems fair to conclude that any document could give meaning only to someone who knew the language and what the text was likely to say[5].

Sumerian writing developed as a mnemonic system of notation. It did not arise from the need to record verbal statements with phonetic precision, but was a bureaucratic invention designed to fulfill the needs of a growing administrative system. It was adequate for creating lists of commodities, objects, signs, titles etc., but the formulaic statements in a list had no direct basis in a speech act, whereas graphic indicators such as tablet shape, for-

---

[5] See for instance, Thomsen 1987, for some comments on the significance on the writing system for the understanding of the Sumerian language. See also Civil and Biggs 1966.

mat, writing conventions etc. offered information which had no equivalent in spoken language (Green 1981).

The distance between speech and writing is illuminated by the fact that in the early Sumerian texts the sequence of the signs in a phrase was arbitrary, or at least, it did not represent the sequence of spoken language. However, speech and writing gradually moved closer to each other during the course of the third millennium, and after around 2500 signs are generally written in the "proper" sequence, following the rules of spoken language. But it was only after Sumerian had died out as a spoken tongue that texts in this language were being written down in such a way that all grammatical elements are indicated, and the reason why Sumerian can be read with some confidence today by modern scholars is that they are standing on the shoulders of their Akkadian-speaking predecessors of the early second millennium, who studied and edited the Sumerian literary corpus which they had inherited.

For the traditional Sumerian system of writing it seems that Havelock's characterisations are quite appropriate. The early body of texts must be seen as a tiny literate island floating in an ocean of oral practices and traditions. Literary texts were not recorded in writing until about 2600 B.C., and being written in the "administrative" script designed for lists and functioning as a mnemonic system, these works should be regarded as sequences of cues, and not as "complete" renderings of the orally delivered compositions. In fact, in order to understand the text one would have to be acquainted with it in detail, which leads to the conclusion that the document was an aid for someone who was to give an oral performance. A few of these early compositions also exist in later, more fully written versions, and only when working on those is it possible for the modern Sumerologist to suggest a translation and interpretation. A simple example:

NN	dumu	na	na-mu-ri
NN	son	instructions	give
NN-e	dumu-ni-ra	na	na-mu-un-ri-ri
NN	to his son	instructions	he did give to him

The first line gives the early text's rendering of the phrase, whereas the second line gives a much later version, in fact some 700 years later, when grammatical elements are fully shown, and the translation of this line from a collection of wise sayings is "NN gave instructions to his son"[6].

Around 2000 B.C. Akkadian became the spoken language of the area and Sumerian lived on in the schools and in the writing system, but since most texts were now written in Akkadian the script itself changed. The Akkadian language is a Semitic tongue, utterly different in structure from Sumerian and of course totally unrelated. The need to record this language could be satisfied by a drastic extension of the phonetic principle which had hitherto played a limited role in the writing of cuneiform, and the result was a writing system which was predominantly syllabic while at the same time retaining a certain degree of logography. Most words in most texts were spelled out by way of syllabic signs whose values were based on the old Sumerian roots: *a-wi-lu-um*, the Akkadian word for "man", was written with four different signs, the first one A, being the Sumerian logogram for "water", to take a simple example. In a given text the scribe might, on the other hand, choose to use a logogram for the concept "man", and he would then write the sign that stands for lú, the Sumerian word for "man", which could represent any form of the Akkadian word. This is the same kind of shorthand which sometimes makes me write "4" rather than "four" (English), "fire" (Danish), or "arba'u" (Akkadian).

To give an idea of how this complex system functions in practice I shall present a brief passage from the Akkadian Gilgamesh Epic which illustrates the principles at work. I dispense with the copy of the cuneiform signs, which is the normal technical editing format, and simply give the transliteration:

> *i-lu-ma it-ti* STAR+SUN *da-ri-ish ib-ba-shu-u*
> *a-wi-lu-tum-ma ma-nu-u* SUN-*mu-sha*
> *mi-im-ma sha it-te-ne-pu-shu sha-ru-ma*

In accordance with normal transliteration practice, each sign is given, and hyphens indicate the signs that combine to spell individual Akkadian words; logograms are here indicated with their meaning. In consecutive transcription this piece of text would be:

---

[6] The example is taken from the text known as "The Instructions of Shuruppak", see Alster 1974

> *iluma itti Shamash darish ibbasshû*
> *awilutumma manû umusha*
> *mimma sha itteneppushu sharuma*

And in translation this is:

> The gods alone live forever under the divine sun;
> but as for mankind, their days are numbered,
> all their activities will be nothing but wind.

Such a predominantly syllabic system did not, of course, need nearly as many signs as a logographic one. The early texts made use of some 1200 different signs, which is a quite small number for a script of this nature; one may compare with the 50.000 signs used by the complete Chinese system, but the comparison is not very meaningful. The early Mesopotamian texts had a very limited repertoire and tried to deal only with a small part of the world, and the later Sumerian texts which became more demanding could rely on a certain degree of phonetization and on the polyvalence of the signs[7]. However, the developed Akkadian system of the early second millennium B.C. made use of some 150-200 signs, which sufficed for the production of unambiguous and relatively elegantly written texts. Cleverness or erudition could manifest itself through a higher proportion of logographic writings and by the use of "learned" syllabic values. A modern scribe who wishes to impress through his great learning often makes use of a complex syntax and a heavy use of loanwords and technical jargon, but for the ancient scribe such effects were available already on the level of the writing system itself.

In everyday documents such as private letters we find a trend in the other direction, towards a simplification of the syllabary and the use of only a few logographic writings. In such texts we typically find some 125-150 different signs, and in one particular group with which I am especially familiar there was a further simplification process. The so-called Old Assyrian texts all stem from private merchants' archives from the period around 1800 B.C., and they reflect the activities of a community which was heavily engaged in long-distance trade. Of some 15.000 texts covering a period of 40-50 years in one rather small settlement

---

[7] See for some statistics Edzard 1976-80, 561-562.

nearly one-half were letters, which indicates the very high level of written interaction. It seems that on average at least one letter arrived at this trading centre every day, many of them dispatched from colleagues some 1000 kms away.

The writing system used by these traders was clearly the result of a deliberate simplification process: signs which were easy to write, i.e. which were composed of as few individual wedges as possible, were selected for, distinctions between voiced and un-voiced, emphatic and non-emphatic and simple and doubled consonants were generally ignored, and there was a tendency to-wards the use of one syllabic sign of the type CVC to represent several vowels (for example: one sign for /lam/, /lim/, and /lum/).

About 100 signs are used frequently in these texts, logograms appear nearly exclusively in traditional shorthand writings for metals, textiles etc., the main elements in the trade, and in the writing of divine names. The tablets themselves, now scattered in museums all over the world, show the existence of a scale of scribal competence ranging from full mastery to a quite limited literacy. Some letters are calligraphic masterpieces, others are so crudely and clumsily written that it can be difficult to distinguish the individual signs - and it is possible to isolate individual hands in a number of cases.

It can hardly be doubted that in this particular community some degree of knowledge of reading and writing was fairly widespread, which is not in itself difficult to understand in view of the elaborate commercial system in which they functioned, and which could hardly have operated successfully without a high degree of literacy among the active merchants[8]. In this par-ticular context it is essential to point out that the cuneiform sys-tem was capable of such a drastic simplification that it became feasible for persons with enough motivation to learn to use it. The simplification certainly introduced a degree of ambiguity, but in practice this played a very small role - and as one who has read thousands of these texts I can say that it is not the ambiguity of the script which creates the problems for our understanding of them. It must be said, of course, that most of the letters are con-cerned entirely with the pursuit of profit, and that their contents are quite predictable in many instances, but difficulties of inter-

---

[8] See Goody 1986, chapter 2, entitled "The word of mammon" for a discussion of the importance of writing in such commercial contexts.

pretation in letters which have an "abnormal" subject matter are due primarily to our ignorance of the Old Assyrian dictionary and semantics - and there is no good reason to believe that such difficulties were felt by the ancient correspondents. I know of no statement in any text which complains that a message was hard to understand.

It is not possible to produce any meaningful estimate of the literacy rate in this, or for that matter any other period in Mesopotamian history. It has been suggested that the literacy rate in Egypt was around 1% (Baines and Eyre 1983, 65-74), and a similar figure seems reasonable also for Mesopotamia, although I believe we have to reckon with a certain amount of variation from one period to another. Among certain private, non-scribal professions a basic skill in reading and writing seems to have been common at certain times, but a great deal of study is needed before anything definite can be said in this field. Take the example of the famous Law Stela set up by king Hammurapi in Babylon around 1770 B.C., in which we find the passage:

> The man who has been wronged, who has a grievance, let him come before my statue named "King of Justice" and read aloud my inscribed stela and hear my precious words, and let my stela explain his grievance to him. Let him read his judgement, and may his heart breathe freely.

Without claiming that this passage indicates that a very large proportion of the inhabitants of Babylon could "read aloud and hear" such a text personally, it seems on the other hand reasonable to conclude that the words are quite meaningless unless at least some private individuals could be assumed to be able to read[9]. In this connexion it is also interesting to note that the word *tupsharrum* which meant a scribe, in the societies of this period appears to have been used to designate either an official in some administrative agency or a scholar. The title may perhaps be seen

---

[9] This passage has been used by Marvin Powell 1981, 436, as an argument against the assumption that such Greek or Roman practices as ostracism or the public use of writing for the dissemination of decrees or laws or for political propaganda necessarily are indicative of widespread literacy - "who would wish to deduce from this that most Babylonians were literate?", writes Powell. Obviously, that is not what I wish to do either, but I understand this text, somewhat like written Greek decrees of the *boule*, as an indication of at least some literacy in the non-scribal part of the public.

as corresponding in some sense to our academic titles, and the scholars ("Ph.D.s") were the specialists who studied the Sumerian heritage, who were bilingual, and who consequently controlled the entire array of expressive complexities built into the script.

The situation described here applies to the first half of the second millennium B.C., a period which was followed by a much more scantily documented phase in Mesopotamian history, lasting into the beginning of the first millennium. At this point the textual material again becomes extremely rich and diversified with the advent of the Assyrian and Babylonian empires. The writing system in the intervening "middle" phase began a process of what Gelb called "degeneration" (Gelb 1963, 202), by which he meant that it moved away from the phonetization which was characteristic of the preceding period and again became to a large extent logographic in nature.

These are such sweeping characterizations that they may be ultimately misleading, and they can only be meaningfully used if their true nature is understood. A less extensive documentation is still very rich in certain special areas, and the reason for the paucity of documents may in fact to some extent be due to the hazards of discovery rather than a reflection of a declining use of writing in the second millennium B.C. The growing number of logographic writings and the more complex use of the script is observable primarily in texts of a scholarly nature, and we may not be too well informed about the use of writing in other fields. Nevertheless, the tendency is reasonably clear.

In texts of certain learned genres the trend became especially pronounced, so that they were in fact written in a kind of fake Sumerian, with syllabic writings being restricted to a very small percentage of the entire text. The system could perhaps be referred to as a kind of shorthand, but it seems more likely that this use of the script served to hide and protect the content of the text by way of a screen of semi-cryptographic practices. A number of the logograms used were inventions which had no basis in any living tradition from Sumerian, by then not spoken for more than half a millennium, and we find different sets of specialized logographic writings in texts of different genres.

The documents themselves are quite explicit about the reason for this use of the script. In the colophons scribes often issue sharp warnings against letting uninitiated persons gain access to the information contained in the text. The intention was clearly to create a corpus of closed knowledge which was reserved for a caste of highly trained specialists.

The degeneration of the script, or what Oppenheim referred to as "a strange reversal" of the trends observable in the beginning of the second millennium B.C. (Oppenheim 1977, 238-239), is obviously linked to such scribal exclusiveness. However, this development can hardly be explained as a weakness or a kind of disease which appears as a logical consequence of the nature of the writing system. An explanation of such developments or such "devolution" must be sought elsewhere and should not be deduced from the nature of the script. But even a superficial attempt at such an explanation demands that we first provide a rudimentary sketch of the fluctuations which can be observed in the way in which the system was used, i.e. an investigation of the extant textual corpus.

The Development of the Textual Corpus

It should be clear that I cannot hope to provide a comprehensive overview of Mesopotamian documentary evidence in this context, so in order to proceed in an admittedly very ambitious, but hopefully not too absurd fashion I have chosen to isolate three main themes which will guide me through the hundreds of thousands of texts:

power and bureaucracy, private versus public and *science.*

Mesopotamia in the third millennium B.C. stands as the prototype of a successful "primary" civilization based on elite structures, *bureaucracy and social stratification.* Writing may be seen as an essential element in the exploitation of man, rather than in his illumination, as has been said with such force by Claude Lévi-Strauss in his chapter "Leçon d'écriture" from the book Tristes tropiques (Lévi-Strauss 1955, chapter xxviii). Writing's function as an instrument of power and control is illustrated for him by Egypt and China, whereas the kingdoms of Africa are the exceptions which confirm the rule; it was essentially their lack of a writing system that defined them as weak and transient phenomena. Without writing to "faciliter l'asservissement" they were unable to reproduce their system of centralized government for very long. It is logical, therefore, that when writing appears in China it is in the context of ritual and divination, defining the role of the king in relation to his subjects and to the cosmic powers; in Egypt the hieroglyphs were used for monumental texts and for administrative purposes, and here again it was on the figure of the king that the entire state was focused. The king is not evident in the earliest Mesopotamian texts however, but they did form part of the administrative apparatus of the central governing agencies, primarily the temples, so even if the political structures may have been different, it seems clear that the function of writing was basically identical[10].

It is not by any means a very weighty or surprising observation that writing served the needs of a controlling political machine in its earliest phase, but it does seem worth pointing to the single-mindedness of the exploiters of writing in Mesopotamia, for we can observe that no other purpose was served by writing for a period of some 600 years after its invention. In that span of time we find enormous numbers of lists of goods received, delivered, paid out as rations, still outstanding, of persons moving around in the administrative system as workers, officials, ration-receivers, prisoners-of-war or slaves - all elements in an administrative system of great complexity.

In the very earliest texts dating to around 3100 B.C. we can follow a steady elaboration and refinement of the administrative practices which were recorded (Green 1981). Special formats were developed for special types of information, more and more complex operations are committed to writing, and the persons involved become clearly designated by way of titles and personal names. The aim was clearly the establishment of clear routines and standardized behaviour - in the best tradition of Max Weber - more levels in the hierarchical structures, presumably larger units and closer control within the bureaucratic apparatus itself. Greater amounts of information can be stored, with more detail, and with precise definitions of areas of responsibilities.

These developments, observable from the very first documents available, continued all through the third millennium, and they reached their climax in the twenty-first century, the time of the so-called Ur III empire. From a short period of no more than 75 years we have tens of thousands of texts, practically all of them of an administrative nature. They reflect a society where a strictly planned economy, encompassing production as

---

[10] See for further comments Larsen in press, and the other articles by John Baines, Stephen Driscoll, Margaret Nieke and Michael Harbsmeier collected in that section of the volume.

well as distribution, resulted in the construction of what the leading Soviet Assyriologist has called "one of the worst totalitarian regimes known to history" (Diakonoff 1971, 20). Bureaucratic technique was perfected to a point where standardization and formularization allowed single documents to regulate transactions involving tens of thousands of persons, animals or objects, where each step of the most complex procedures was recorded by way of special formats and formulae, and where the disappearance of a single pound of wool out of several tons delivered would be found and noted with a frightening inevitability.

There *are* texts of other types: from the very start we have signlists or "lexical lists", and literary compositions and royal inscriptions begin to appear around 2600 B.C.; we even have a few texts which must be said to belong in the private sphere, though practically no letters. These private texts are nothing but a drop in the ocean, however, and it is an inescapable conclusion that writing in the third millennium was an elite phenomenon whose main use was to serve as an administrative tool[11].

Moving down a couple of centuries into the following Old Babylonian and Old Assyrian period we encounter a completely different picture, reflecting an appallingly sudden development of entire new genres and a vast extension of reading and writing practices throughout society. This is where the theme of private use of literacy has to be addressed.

Bureaucracy did not die out, of course. It never will. What happened was that a number of practices developed in the sector of public administration were diffused throughout the *private sector* as well, and adapted to suit new purposes. From archives discovered in private houses we now have thousands of such texts as testaments, records of adoption, deeds of loan and purchase, rentals, records of legal proceedings, partnership agreements, contracts of hire - just about every conceivable private transaction is recorded. The formulary of the public sector is expanded and transformed to become a unique system of precise recording.

A genre of particular interest is the private letter. From the entire third millennium we have no more than a handful of them,

---

[11] For an excellent discussion of elements in the pattern of literacy in specifically the third millennium see Postgate 1984; on page 8 he offers a schematic chart of the currently attested application of writing in Mesopotamia between 3200 and 1700 B.C.

but from the first centuries of the second millennium we have thousands. Any subject matter seems to have been deemed suitable for a letter, and at least in certain groups of the population it appears to have been quite normal to correspond with family, friends and business partners on a fairly regular basis, as already mentioned for the Old Assyrian texts. This growth of the letter as a genre is also characteristic of the administrative sector, where for instance diplomatic correspondence collected in palace archives now provide a fascinatingly intimate view of the concerns of the period. Both in these official archives and in the strong-rooms in private houses we also discover fairly large numbers of letters written or received by women.

Private archives were in evidence in all later phases of Mesopotamian history, down to the Neo-Babylonian and Persian periods. A recent study of archives and libraries discovered in the ruins of the ancient Assyrian capital Assur gives an impression of a relatively wide scatter of archives all over the town, and some of these were quite substantial (Pedersén 1985). However, where a "normal" private archive may have contained a handful of texts which proved ownership to land for instance (in the Neo Assyrian period such archives belonged for example to goldsmiths, doorkeepers, tanners, oil pressers and members of the local Egyptian community), the very large archives are found in houses belonging either to highly placed officials or persons who may be classified as "scholars": hymn-singers, incantation specialists etc. The truly large private archives appear to have been characteristic of the classic Old Babylonian and Old Assyrian phase during the first centuries of the second millennium, so the "degeneration" of the script does seem to have accompanied a decline in the use of writing in the private sector.

The Old Babylonian period was also characterized by a flowering of the *scribal schools*. A central concern for these establishments was the care for the Sumerian heritage, which meant writing down the many compositions which had so far been transmitted mainly, or even exclusively in oral form. The schools did much more than simply record, however, they became the focus for a whole scientific discourse on Sumerian. This involved the construction of dictionaries of Sumerian and Akkadian, the composition of paradigms of Sumerian grammar and phraseology, the translation of Sumerian texts, often in the form of interlineary Akkadian versions - and even the composition of new texts in the Sumerian language.

The motivations for this concerted philological effort are only in part understood. The writing system itself was one major reason, since the logographic basis for the script rested firmly on Sumerian lexicography. The script carried a load of meaning and information which could only be fully understood on the basis of a relatively extensive knowledge of the Sumerian language. It should also be kept in mind that the literate culture of Mesopotamia for centuries had been bilingual, and in this respect the writing system was clearly an essential element in the general cultural assemblage, sharing the same kind of relationship to the Sumerian past as for instance ritual, artistic conventions etc. Philology was an indispensable part of the translation of Sumerian traditions into the Akkadian world.

These schools also produced texts which had a much less clear relationship to this past, however, and a good example is the corpus of divination compendia which were being produced. These constitute the beginning of the peculiarly Mesopotamian preoccupation, which in the Hellenistic world resulted in the use of the term "Chaldean" as a general designation for a diviner. In the Assyrian texts of the first millennium B.C. the term "scribe" had the same meaning, which indicates the essentially literate character of the Mesopotamian divination practices.

Divination was known also in the Sumerian third millennium, but it was only in the centuries after 2000 B.C. that this subject became the concern of texts. At the same time we find the development of a systematic scholarly attitude towards divination, the creation of a flexible and highly precise technical terminology, and the establishment of a textual corpus based on clear principles of ordering and systematization. The same process can be observed in other scholarly areas, and one may mention mathematics which also flowered in this period, and which in the same way was characterized by an ordered collection and systematic structuring of observations[12].

Mesopotamian science is - as we now know it - marked by two peaks or formative and creative eruptions of energy: the classic period during the first half of the second millennium being the first one, the Golden Age in Mesopotamia when the classic formulation of its literature and science was created, based on a fusion of Sumerian and Akkadian traditions; and the last phase of the great Neo Assyrian and Neo Babylonian empires during the

---

[12] See Bottéro 1974 and Larsen 1987 for discussions and literature.

first half of the first millennium as the second. The accomplishments of the later phase are represented by the great scientific library discovered in the palace of Ashurbanipal at Nineveh, and it seems fair to say that they rarely reached beyond the frameworks created during the Old Babylonian period to construct new and different views of the world. On the other hand, the late scientific literature developed within a vastly changed social and political universe, again dominated by a strong centralized power. The imperial bureaucracies now dominate to such an extent that they easily come to figure in our reconstructions as pure examples of Oriental despotism, and although this may be a somewhat skewed view, writing did seem to become predominantly the tool of the political power, and it was not used as creatively in the private sector as had once been the case. However, there are a great many uncertain factors involved in such an analysis, one of them being the role that may have been played by the Aramaic alphabetic script which was certainly made use of in the private sector - even though it is impossible to determine how widespread it was.

Writing and Society

The two trajectories followed in this rough sketch merge into one reasonably clearly defined path which shows a clear correlation between the degree of centralization, the nature of the script, its field of usage, and the degree of social literacy.

The first stretch on this path is constituted by the phase of complex bureaucracy during the third millennium, reflecting and serving a centralized government and a highly stratified society; the script is logographic in character with a great number of signs, and it is used basically as a mnemonic device.

The second stretch is the first half of the second millennium, a time of decentralization, relatively small territorial states, and a strongly developing private sector which for instance controls foreign trade; the script is basically a syllabic system with a limited use of logograms, and the number of signs is reduced accordingly; in certain sectors a conscious simplification of the writing system means that a larger proportion of the population gains access to it and acquires at least a rudimentary literacy.

The final and third stretch is a fairly undefined one which should undoubtedly be treated with much greater care than has been possible here, but we may note a strong trend towards political re-centralization and bureaucratization; the script "degenerates" and becomes a complex tool which is manipulated by trained specialists.

On the basis of the development that can be described for the cuneiform system Havelock's insistence on the ambiguity and clumsiness of the script itself appears to me to have a limited relevance. In my view, Havelock suffers from what Roy Harris aptly calls "the tyranny of the alphabet".[13] For instance, he does not recognize the alphabetic character of the Semitic writing systems because they do not have signs for vowels, and in a memorable passage he claims that when Byzantium fell to the Turks

> her alphabet fell with her. The Arabic script of the invaders which supplanted it brought about a reversion to the inefficient syllabic shorthand, thus ushering in a new age of craft literacy, a severance between rulers and ruled, a revival of bureaucratic despotism and of religious monopoly of authority, while among the vulgar, habits of purely oral communication and preservation were re-established (Havelock 1976, 75).

This analysis has a double bearing on my argument: first, the absolute belief in the superiority of the Greek alphabet with vowels which in the words of Roy Harris

> fails altogether to take into account the fact that the practical utility of having separate signs for vowels will vary according to the phonological structure of the language concerned, just as will, for instance, the practical utility of having separate signs for voiced and voiceless consonants. What is viable as a writing system for one language is not necessarily viable for another, and the history of the alphabet amply illustrates this point (Harris1986, 36-37).

It makes little sense to set up the alphabet as a yardstick against which all other systems are measured - and obviously found to be deviations or primitive precursors. To believe, for instance, that the alphabet differs in essence from syllabic or logographic systems by constituting by nature a phonetic notation in contrast to

---

[13] Sampson 1985 presents a very sharply formulated critique of statements by Goody, MacLuhan and Havelock concerning the inferiority of a logographic system such as the Chinese: "bizarre statements" and "nonsense [which] is rather offensive" (164 with note 4).

the others is, in Harris' words "simply a fourth-form howler of the most elementary order":

> The alphabet was not devised by people committed to setting up a science of phonetics avant la lettre. They were interested in 'writing as writing', not in 'what it sounded like' ... Alphabetization is essentially a problem of re-deploying existing symbols in such a way as to reduce their number, but at the same time lose few or none of the facilities of 'word identification' which the previous writing system afforded. In essence it does not differ from the reduction of logographic systems to syllabaries (Ibid., 118-119).

Some of Havelock's observation are relevant for the Sumerian version of cuneiform, but it is not meaningful to claim that the fully developed syllabic system was incapable of representing "the complexities of human descriptive speech at its most concrete level". Nor is it credible to base a theory concerning the contrasts between such literary compositions as Homer and Gilgamesh on the differences between an alphabetic and a mixed syllabic/logographic system of writing.

In fact, the second observation to be made with reference to Havelock's remarks must be that serious historical analysis cannot be reduced to a question of technology; Havelock's theory concerning the change from Greek Byzantium to Turkish Istanbul as being due to the difference between a full alphabet and the Arabic "syllabic shorthand", is entirely unconvincing - if, in fact, one should accept this contrast as based on fact rather than on Eurocentric ideology.

On a more basic level the contrast between oral and literate must be brought into this discussion, but these categories likewise have their confusing and difficult aspects when introduced into such broad, historically defined problems. Walter Ong, for instance, has set out to describe the characteristics of something he calls "the oral mind". The psychodynamics of orality are characterized by an additive analysis of the world rather than a subordinative one; aggregative rather than analytic; conservative and traditionalist; close to the human lifeworld, and situational rather than abstract (Ong, 1982, chapter 3).

There is at least one serious difficulty with such characterizations, for they do not only apply to "oral" situations, but would be meaningful descriptions of the central concerns of for instance

Mesopotamian or traditional Chinese science, and you could hardly call these societies "oral". On the other hand, science and scholarship here may be compared to what Goody calls the "guru-type" traditionalism found for instance in India, where bookish knowledge acquires an authority and indeed sacredness which imposes a total lack of flexibility. In "guru-type" systems we find "the antithesis of the spirit of inquiry which literacy has elsewhere fostered" (Goody 1968, 14), and this "elsewhere"-land can without a doubt be located in time and space: it is the same classical Greece that Havelock is talking about. Here the spirit of inquiry was fostered by not just literacy, but alphabetic literacy.

I have no intention of going into the questions raised by the traditional contrast between the *chiaroscuro* of the devious Oriental mind and the blazing light from the Acropolis. I subscribe to Havelock's refusal to find the reason in a theory of racial superiority (1976, 36), but the recourse to a technological explanation based on the alphabet is not a meaningful alternative.

With respect to the cuneiform system it may be shown, as I hope to have done, that it can be used in quite different ways in varying social and cultural situations, and the late complexity has to be understood and evaluated as an historically defined problem.

And as for Mesopotamian literature and science it seems to me futile to try to understand these phenomena in terms of technological backwardness. This is not a blanket denial of the relevance of technology, and especially in this context of course of communication technology, for our understanding of the historical process. The Mesopotamian record shows with great clarity how writing played a vital role in the intellectual development in for instance divination (Larsen 1987); when it was introduced into this field about 2000 B.C., where oral practices had until then been dominant, it led to a vast extension of it. It allowed the storing of large numbers of individual observations in a system of precise and detailed description, and a series of compendia were created, each containing huge numbers of omina which related to special domains of divination (the entrails of sacrificial lambs, the flight of birds, the shape of drops of oil on water, dreams, etc. etc.). These texts were organized on the basis of logical rules which determined where and in which way observations were to be described and located in relation to each other, and this gave rise to a precise structuring and an elaborate terminology. However, the contrast between these lists[14], the primary genre of Mesopotamian scientific endeavour in all fields, and Cicero's *De divinatione* with its reasoned discussion of the philosophical background for the whole exercise, is hardly to be explained in terms of technological differences between cuneiform and alphabet. It has been suggested that the bulkiness of the clay tablet as a vehicle for written information meant that texts had to be kept rather short:

> Cuneiform is a beautiful system of writing that appeals very much to the senses. It is a matter of profound pleasure just to watch the signs appear under one's stylus and to feel the plasticity of the clay in one's hand. However, even the most ardent devotee might well change his mind, were he required to carry a cuneiform copy of Herodotus from Babylon to Damascus on his back (Powell 1981, 435).

This rather odd idea obviously has *some* merit, but it is hard to regard it seriously as an adequate explanation of why there was no Babylonian Herodotus or Cicero. Powell himself concludes a little later that "the introduction of the alphabet, by itself, has had little effect upon the reduction of functional illiteracy, and thus, its importance in the history of human development has been overestimated" (Ibid., 436).

However, the important point to make is that the presence of the Greek alphabet in Babylon would hardly have created a Mesopotamian Homer, or for that matter a rational, scientific attitude among the diviners. Things are more complicated than that, and there is no escape from the painstaking analysis of the "cultural causes", the basic understanding of the intellectual universe in which our ancient documentation was shaped, even though technology may seem to offer miraculously easy shortcuts. In fact, looking at this problem from the point of view of Greek science we see that scholars find that it was *not* the presence of the alphabet in Greece which was responsible for "the Greek miracle". In the most recent comprehensive account of the growth of early Greek science Lloyd points to what he calls "the distinctively Greek factor" which he seeks:

> in the development of a particular social and political situation in ancient Greece, especially the experience of radical po-

---

[14] See discussion in Goody 1977, chapter 5.

litical debate and confrontation in small-scale, face-to-face societies (Lloyd 1979, 266).

- which surely must indicate that the emphasis is on the oral rather than on the literate nature of the situation.

Bibliography

Adams, R. McC. and Nissen, Hans J. 1972 *The Uruk Countryside: The Natural Setting of Urban Societies.*, Chicago.

Alster, Bendt 1974 *The Instructions of Suruppak*, Mesopotamia 2, Copenhagen.

Baines, John, and Eyre, C.J. 1983 Four notes on literacy, *Göttinger Miszellen* 61, 65-96.

Bottéro, Jean 1974 Symptômes, signes, écritures en Mésopotamie ancienne, in J.-P. Vernant et al., *Divination et rationalité*, Paris, 70-197.

Civil, Miguel and Biggs, Robert D. 1966 Notes sur des textes sumériens archaïques, *Revue d'Assyriologie* 60, 1-16.

Damerow, Peter, Englund, Robert K. and Nissen, Hans J. 1988 Die Entstehung der Schrift, *Spektrum der Wissenschaft* 2, February, 74-85.

Diakonoff, Igor 1971 On The Structure of Old Babylonian Society, in H. Klengel (ed.) *Beiträge zur sozialen Struktur des alten Vorderasiens*, Berlin.

Edzard, D.O. 1976-80 Keilschrift, in *Reallexikon der Assyriologie* 5, Berlin - New York, 544-568.

Friedrich, Johannes 1957 *Extinct Languages*, New York.

Gelb, I.J. 1963 *A Study of Writing*, Chicago.

Goody, Jack 1968 Introduction, in *Literacy in Traditional Societies*, Jack Goody (ed.), Cambridge.

Goody, Jack 1977 *The Domestication of the Savage Mind*, Cambridge.

Goody, Jack 1986 *The Logic of Writing and the Organization of Society*, Cambridge.

Green, M.W. 1981 The Construction and Implementation of the Cuneiform Writing System, *Visible Language* XV Number 4, 345-372.

Harris, Roy 1986 *The Origin of Writing*, London.

Havelock, Eric A. 1976 *Origins of Western Literacy*, Monograph Series/14. The Ontario Institute for Studies in Education. Toronto.

Havelock, Eric A. 1978 The Alphabetization of Homer, in Eric A. Havelock and Jackson P. Hershbell (eds.) *Communication Arts in the Ancient World*, New York.

Hawkins, J.D. 1979 The Origin and Dissemination of Writing in Western Asia, in P.R.S. Moorey (ed.) *The Origin of Civilization. Wolfson College Lectures 1978*, Oxford.

Larsen, Mogens Trolle 1987   The Mesopotamian Lukewarm Mind. Reflections on Science, Divination and Literacy, in F. Rochberg-Halton (ed.) *Language, Literature, and History: Philological and historical studies presented to Erica Reiner*, American Oriental Series 67, New Haven, Conn., 203-225.

Larsen, Mogens Trolle in press Introduction: Literacy and Social Complexity, in John Gledhill, Barbara Bender and M. Trolle Larsen (eds.) *State and Society*, London, 173-191.

Lévi-Strauss, C. 1955 *Tristes tropiques*, Paris.

Lloyd, G.E.R. 1979 *Magic, Reason and Experience*, Cambridge.

Olson, David R. 1977 From Utterance to Text: The Bias of Language in Speech and Writing, in *Harvard Educational Review* 47.

Ong, Walter J. 1982 *Orality and Literacy. The Technologizing of the Word*, London and New York.

Oppenheim, A. Leo 1977   *Ancient Mesopotamia. Portrait of a Dead Civilization*, revised edition completed by Erica Reiner, Chicago.

Pedersén, Olof 1985   *Archives and Libraries in the City of Assur. A Survey of the Material from the German Excavations*, Part 1, Acta Universitatis Upsaliensis, Studia Semitica Upsaliensia 6, Uppsala.

Postgate, J.N. 1984 Cuneiform Catalysis: The First Information Revolution, in *Archaeological Review from Cambridge* volume 3:2, a thematic issue entitled "Archaeology & Texts".

Powell, Marvin A. 1981   Three Problems in the History of Cuneiform Writing: Origins, Direction of Script, Literacy, *Visible Language* Volume XV Number 4, 419-440.

Sampson, Geoffrey 1985   *Writing Systems. A linguistic introduction*, London.

Schmandt-Besserat, Denise 1981 From Tokens to Tablets: A Reevaluation of the So-called "Numerical Tablets", in *Visible Language*, Volume XV Number 5.

Schmandt-Besserat, Denise 1988 Tokens at Uruk, in *Baghdader Mitteilungen* 19, 1-175.

Strindberg, August 1921 *En blå bok*, 1-3. Stockholm.

Thomsen, Marie Louise 1987   *A Handbook of the Sumerian Language*, Mesopotamia 10. Copenhagen.

Literacy and Society in Medieval Denmark

Karen Schousboe

Studies of literacy[1] seem to fall into one of two categories: either they advocate the extreme view that nearly every social or cultural change at a given time is the result of a technological or demographic change in literate activities; or they grant literacy no explanatory role at all as regards such changes. Two examples should suffice.

Since the sixties, Elizabeth Eisenstein has been working on a huge investigation of the consequences of the invention of the printing press. Not only has she made this phenomenon responsible for the dissemination of a vast amount of literature in the early Renaissance; she has also consistently attributed to this technological change phenomena such as the evolution of science, nationalism (by way of so-called 'national' languages), the emergence of uniquely and individually famous artists, unspecified cultural diffusion, etc. Her point of view is very well expressed in the title of her book - 'The Printing Press as an *Agent of Change'* (Eisenstein 1979, my italics).

So on the one hand we have studies like these, designating literacy as the 'prime mover'. On the other we have historians like, for instance, Vovelle, who studied the religious behaviour of the common people in Provence in the late seventeenth and the eighteenth centuries. Analysing the changes in the dispositions in wills and the descriptions of burial ceremonies found there, he described in minute detail the so-called secularization of death. By amassing an enormous amount of material, he also found that this secularization was unevenly distributed through-

---

[1] The concept of literacy is used here in the restricted sense - to designate a mere proficiency in reading and writing. In medieval society literacy was defined as the ability to read and write latin. (See Bäuml 1980; Clanchy 1979).

out the countryside. Vovelle tried to discover what caused this difference in ritual observations from one village to another. One of the possible explanatory factors he investigated was literacy. Insofar as it could be deduced from the signatures of wills, he produced important statistics concerning the incidence of literacy. But Vovelle found that there seemed to be no statistical correlation between the rate of literacy and the religious behaviour represented as a process of secularization (Vovelle 1973).

On one side, then, we have this systematic, albeit very depressing investigation of the correlation between literacy and a specific cultural change, and on the other a causal linking of technology, literacy and the restructuring of society in the 16th century. Thus Eisenstein and Vovelle represent two different ways of approaching the problem of the implications of literacy, as well as two different modes of scientific explanation. In this paper I have chosen a third alternative, and will try to propose a different approach.

It seems to me that what we would really like to know is whether or not literacy, broadly speaking, was a necessary prerequisite for specific types of social organization, ways of life, world views, etc. And, further, whether or not literacy was a necessary prerequisite for *changes* in these. From this point of view, the factor investigated is not assumed to be a cause; nor are we only considering statistical correlations: we are discussing the exact significance - that is, the necessity - of the actual phenomenon, in this case the tool of literacy, for the understanding of the socioeconomic organization in question.

I have mainly been concerned in my studies with two periods in the history of Denmark: I have worked with the late eighteenth-century countryside and the transition from a so-called peasant economy to cash-crop farming. Secondly, I have worked with the overall social transformation in late medieval Denmark from 1400-1600. Characteristic of both periods are overwhelming changes in cultural organization, and it seems that literacy was in some way implicated in these changes; at least, both periods were characterized by additional significant changes in the use of literacy.

An exhaustive registration of Danish peasant diaries notebooks, accounts, etc. from around 1800 has shown that most of these records were essential aids to the rationalization of economic enterprise which followed the so-called Agricultural Reforms of the 1780s. In the eighteenth century the peasant had paid his rent almost exclusively in kind, that is, primarily in the form of corvée and grain and dairy products. Because of the reforms the landowners were compelled to commute the rents to payments in ready money.

In addition to this, the peasants gradually became owners of their farms, and thus became deeply involved in a money economy. It seems that a necessary prerequisite for the success of these new economic enterprises was a detailed day-to-day registration of prices, wages, weather, agricultural output and the like. The substantial outcome of this was a renewed interest not only in the ability to read, but also in being able to write (accounts, letters, petitions, etc.) (Schousboe 1982). Another consequence was more directly due to the rise in the economic surplus: this was invested in the self-conscious formation of a (new) peasant culture built out of bits and pieces from the ways of life of the eighteenth-century (noble) landowner, the bourgeois citizen of the beginning of the 19th century, plus some residual features from the peasant life of preindustrial Denmark (Schousboe 1983; Christiansen 1978).

In this paper I shall illustrate the proposition by presenting some preliminary results of an ongoing study of late medieval Danish society. Was the use of literacy a necessary prerequisite for economic and social, as well as cultural (re)organization in Denmark from 1200-1600? However, I shall not attempt here to give a full account of the transformation of society as a whole: instead I concentrate on the economy of 'rural' Denmark; and especially on the way of life of the nobleman and his bailiffs and retainers.[2]

Denmark around 1400

At that time the bulk of the population in Denmark - as in the rest of Europe - made its living from one type or another of subsistence farming. We have no exact figures for the size of the population. It has been estimated at a figure between 500,000 and one million, although the sources are extremely sparse (Paludan 1977: 414-415). Today the Danish population runs to about five million, half of whom live in the countryside. This means that,

---

[2] This article is a presentation of part of a research programme over the changes in the economic and social organization and ways of life in late-medieval and renaissance Denmark. See (Schousboe 1984) for a preliminary report on the whole project.

to visualize some of the demographic realities of late medieval Denmark, we would have to imagine travelling through Jutland, avoiding the towns, and meeting only every fifth person. Estimating thus, we have been discounting the fact that we have no way of assessing the percentage of people living in the towns or cities as opposed to the countryside. We do know that the cities were so-called agricultural towns, dependent on their own agricultural production, and we know from a later period that the population in these towns amounted to about 1500-2000 people. Only a couple of cities had as many as 4-6000 inhabitants (Olsen 1943; Ladewig Petersen 1980). Very small towns, in other words - most of them not much bigger than an ordinary village, and all of them inhabited by a number of peasants alongside the artisans, tradesmen, nobility, clerics and merchants proper. The population appears to have been equally mixed in the countryside. Naturally, the majority were peasants, but they were mixed with artisans, tradesmen, gentry, etc. Looking further at the occupational profile of the peasants we would find - as far as it is possible to ascertain - that they obtained their subsistence not only from farming but also from part-time small-scale trading, handicrafts and in particular fishing, in the season - catching herring in the Sound and selling them to the Hanseatic merchants of the North German coastal cities (Stoklund 1958). Some of them - we don't know the actual percentage - seem to have been in a mixed social position, verging on the borderline between peasantry and gentry (Prange 1964; Dahlerup 1969, 1971). We may conclude that the population in the countryside was occupationally, if not culturally, mixed. It does not seem very profitable to me to discuss the differences between the ways of life of the dwellers in each geographic category. I have found it more useful to consider the diffuse similarity between their economic profiles as the main characteristic.

This decision is reinforced by another factor: the signs of extensive migration to and from towns, regions, the countryside, etc. (Hørby 1980; Christensen 1976). As far as I can see, people did not belong to a particular village or other geographical setting or region; they were much more like nomads, moving to and from estates, towns, regions, etc. Their connections were not with the locality, but with groups of people, guilds, the households of lords, clerical institutions and the like.

One indication, among many others, of this is the use of surnames or nicknames. People did not normally take their names from a particular locality or homestead, as they did, for instance, in the 19th century. Instead the names referred to some personal feature like colour of hair, mental disposition, a quaint way of life or something of the kind (Skautrup 1944: Vol. 2, 111-15; Hornby 1948).

So, around 1400 we have a Denmark characterized by a fluid and migratory population. Yet these people constituted the workforce in a feudal, that is tributary, economy. How were they controlled?

A feudal lord in the 13th century would possess one, two, three or more estates. At the centre of the estate there would be a large unit farmed by the combined efforts of the lord and his bailiff, or *villicus* (Riis 1970; Ulsig 1981). Around the manor were situated a number of very small units with perhaps no more than five or ten acres of land, affording rent in the form of a few coins and a large amount of work on the demesne (the size of which might be from a quarter to a half of the total village, or even larger). The dominant feature would be the huge size of the manor as compared to the cluster of small-scale peasant holdings around it. Thus we have a picture of the landholdings of the lord or seigneur as closely concentrated.

Around 1400 - the period of the demographic and social profile described above - the form of economic organization had changed. At this time the feudal lord lived on rent paid in goods by yeomen living on normal-sized farms (50-75 acres). The demesnes had been split up or the land had been parcelled out. Moreover, the smaller-sized units had been fused together. To this must be added the fact that the farms or land controlled by one single nobleman or kin-group were nearly always scattered all over the country.[3]

If we look, then, at the changes in economic organization between the situation in 1400-1450 and in 1600; we get a different picture again. By that time the estates had once more become

---

[3] The background for this change in economic organization is -though still debated - normally thought to be as follows: The primary fact is the demographic decrease in the size of the labour-force post 1300-1330. This reduced the size of rent to half or one third of the original level. In order to get desolated land tilled, peasants, who now were in a better bargaining position, got access to "unlimited" land resources. The economic crisis primarily drabbed the landowners - nobles, churches, cloisters as well as the Crown. This induced a proliferation in the process of pawning, selling or buying land, thus furthering the splitting up of estates, formerly well rounded up.

what we perceive as 'real manors' - very large farming units surrounded by a full concentration of peasant farms paying rent in cereals, dairy products and heavy corvée. The question is: how were these different forms of estate controlled? How was rent collected? What kind of literacy was required for essential administrative purposes in each period?

Literacy and Economic Organization in 13th-Century Denmark

Taking the first situation, from the 13th century, into consideration, we must acknowledge that we don't know very much. Most people must have been familiar with the art of reading, many with writing. First of all, we know that ordinary people had some familiarity with the use of the runic alphabet - were able to read and write it. For a short period (1065-84) coins were stamped with runic inscriptions. We may presume that people were able to recognize these inscriptions in order to evaluate and accept the coins (which were exchanged, at least in principle, every year). Apart from these and the more monumental inscriptions we know of, runes were used by artists on murals, baptismal fonts, censers, tombs, etc. We have a single 'tourist' inscription, owners' names carved on personal objects, etc. We know from the excavations in Bergen in Norway that letters were carved on small pieces of wood used for written communication (Liestøl 1968). Finally, runes were used for magical purposes. Danes must have been generally familiar with runes, and thus must have been able to read and probably write.

The convincing argument of the runes brings us to the next body of evidence: the legal texts. The first long texts in the vernacular we know of are written with the Latin alphabet. These are legal texts presenting the regional laws. It is generally assumed that they were compiled and written down simultaneously during a very short period, c.1170-1210 (*Skaanske Lov* and *Sjællandske Lov* (Skautrup 1944: 209). The third regional law, *Jyske Lov*, was compiled and edited in 1241.

We know of several written lawbooks from various sources, although only a few have been preserved from the 13th century. One of them (dated c. 1300), the so-called *Codex Runicus*, interestingly enough presents the laws of Scania, the ecclesiastical law, and some historical writings written in runes - i.e. in the 'vernacular' alphabet as well as in the vernacular. Finally, it must be mentioned that Royal commandments, although originally written in Latin, would be translated into the vernacular and recited at local courts to lay people - the peasants. To conclude: every grown-up must have had some familiarity with the idea of writing in Latin as well as in the vernacular; thus so must the landowner or feudal lord.

What would he know of administrative practice? We know that large ecclesiastical institutions possessed administrative compilations such as cadastres, accounts, etc. Episcopal cadastres are preserved from *Ribe* (1291), *Aarhus*, (1315) *Roskilde* (1370). The last of these refers to an older version dated c. 1270. We know of one outstanding example from the Royal administration - *Kong Valdemars Jordebog* - the bulk of which must be dated c. 1230. These cadastres were written in Latin; but compilations like these must have been fairly well known, used as they must have been not only for fiscal purposes, but also for legal ones (in the event of lawsuits).

Arguments *e silentio* should always be avoided in the discussion of medieval history. We cannot be sure that some large landowners did not use written accounts in their administration. However, absolutely no traces of such accounts are extant. On the other hand, we know that the lord would have had written documents in his possession, documents testifying to his rights to real property. He would use these occasionally in the event of lawsuits. But these documents were never in the vernacular. The earliest document written in Danish is dated 1371 (Skautrup 1944, I : 205). We know of at least 1000 documents from the 13th century, and not one is in the vernacular. It seems reasonable to presume that at least a few would have been preserved if there had been a more general practice of writing in Danish. Apart from these legal documents, and the odd will, it seems that writing was not used in the administration of the feudal estate. And this can be corroborated by a logical argument.

The lifestyle of the 13th-century lord was, as far as we can ascertain, much more locally orientated than was the case later on. He would live on the manor when not taking part in warfare. His landholdings would be concentrated around his manor, not dispersed as was the case around 1400 (Ulsig 1968). Another sign of his local orientation is the fact that a lot of the church-building which went on in this period was located near manors and funded by lords, for whom pulpits were built, and who were later buried there (Nørrelund 1928; Hørby 1980). Usually the bailiff -

the *villicus* - would have some sort of sharecropping contract with the lord, paying a very large percentage of the harvest. He would often be supplied with a written account of the harvest, detailing the value of the farm. We may presume that the lord, on the other hand, would be well aware of the extent of land as well as the proper yield. This would be facilitated by the system of land evaluation, the *bol* system. The lord would own a part of the village, not usually a precinct (although this could be the case in Jutland). Farming with the cooperation of the village, he would easily be able to supervise the yield.

In my opinion, the lord would not need to receive written accounts or be in possession of formal cadastres. Literate activities might easily have been limited to what could be handled by the odd scribe or notary.

Whether private letter-writing was essential to the way of life of the nobleman at that time is a more difficult question. With one exception, there are no private letters extant from Denmark prior to 1400. There must have been some letter-writing, though, judging from some material preserved from Bergen in Norway. We know of a copybook kept at the episcopal seat which numbers letters from 1304 until after the Reformation. Many of these are truly private in character. A very interesting group of them consists of letters from the Bishop in the early 1330s. He would receive letters from nobles (one or two a year) and would answer in the vernacular. This goes for the correspondence with the Royal administration too. In fact, the only letters written in Latin would be those meant for the Papal administration and its representatives (often foreigners). It appears from these that the Bishop was very preoccupied with letter-writing as a form, as he was constantly excusing the insignificance of his letters, their small number, and asking nobles in the Royal administration whether a letter to the King was too long, or should have been written at all, and so on. Judging from the evidence of the copybook, there appears to have been an ongoing correspondence, although it was by no means prolific. Most interesting, however, is the fact that only one original private letter from this period is preserved. If Arne Magnusson had not made his copy of almost the whole collection around 1600, we would never have been in a position to evaluate the private letter-writing of this period in Norway.

Although we are not in a position to find out whether private letters were exchanged in Denmark, this leads us to the conclusion that it might very well have been the case. However, the only evidence of prolific letter-writing in Denmark prior to the fifteenth century comes from two large administrative bodies - the Church and the Royal administration. There is evidence of this as early as the period just after 1170 - the letter collection of *Abbed Vilhelm* (an abbot of French origin, later canonized). From his hand we have a number of letters - partly stereotypes, partly real letters. Some of these pertain to the international sphere of diplomacy and concern the marriage between Ingeborg, sister of the Danish King, and the French King Philippe Auguste. The evidence of the art of letter-writing appears to reveal the fact that letters were used for extensive long-distance communication within the diplomatic or administrative sphere, not as a fore-runner of the daily telephone call. This ties up beautifully with the Norwegian example of letters used by the episcopal see for long-distance communication. We may presume that the fact that the nobles resided in specific localities and the non-existence of long-distance kin-connections did not encourage the estab-lishment of a wide communicative network based on letter-writ-ing. We may conclude that an extensive use of writing in admin-istration was closely connected with the size of the institutions - episcopal sees, the Royal Chancellery, monastic orders, etc. It seems, too, that there was a significant correlation between the apparently localized character of the lifestyle and economic organization of the ordinary lord and the apparently non-existent use of literacy in his administration and day-to-day practice.

Literacy and Society in 15th-Century Denmark

Can we detect a similar logical correlation in late medieval Den-mark? The period is certainly characterized by a number of significant changes in the use of literacy. The most important one has already been mentioned: the shift from Latin to Danish and/or Low German in the documents. The first document in Danish is dated 1371: this is rather late compared to what was the case in the neighbouring countries. England and Norway used the vernacular during the whole period for legal and admini-strative purposes alongside Latin (Clanchy 1971: 151ff; Skautrup 1944, I: 205). In Germany the earliest example is from 1240, from Sweden we know of examples from the 1340s and later. It is an intriguing fact that Denmark was rather slow in this respect. Fur-ther, we know that the use of the vernacular must have been in-stigated by the Royal administration (Skautrup 1944, II: 29-30).

The reasons for this initiative are obscure, although we may presume that it ties up somehow with the increased contacts between the Nordic countries formalized, for example, in the political and royal union, *Kalmarunionen*. At the same time we hear of the first local lay schools. For instance, *Malmø*, one of the most important cities in the Sound region, was permitted in 1404 to educate the children of burghers in the art of reading and writing.

Simultaneously with this secularization of the school system, handwriting changed from so-called 'book writing' to a cursive script (called *lettre parisienne*), and, supposedly to ease writing, the abbreviations became so numerous that the texts are rather difficult to read today (Brøndum-Nielsen 1943: 64-65).

Finally, paper was introduced. We know that the total amount of parchment used for a specific Icelandic saga came from about 100 sheep (*Kulturhistorisk Leksikon for nordisk Middelalder*, sub *Pergament*). Compared to this, paper was much cheaper. It would not be reasonable to explain the proliferation of written texts in the fifteenth century in terms of these technological changes, but we might consider them as necessary prerequisites for this proliferation. We know of about 3800 documents from the period 1351-1400; about 6650 have been preserved from 1401-50; and from 1451-1500 the number totals about 9200 (Skautrup 1944, II: 14). This growth cannot be explained merely as the result of a change in methods of preservation (indeed paper is more perishable), nor by the difference in time (a mere 150 years). Most of these documents concern landed property. We may presume either that the use of written deeds had become more extensive or that the buying and selling (or mortgaging) of land were more widespread in this period. Both explanations, in fact, seem reasonable.

Fourteenth-century Denmark was marked - as was most of Europe - by the demographic crisis following plague, hunger, the overexploitation of land, etc. It is generally assumed that the crisis, which set in as early as the turn of the century, was full-blown by mid-century. Around 1350 we have the first explicit statements on the problems ensuing on the diminution in the workforce. Apart from the immediate deaths from hunger and plague, it thus seems certain that the longer-term effects of the crisis first and foremost affected the great landowners, whether Church, Crown or nobility.

Rents were reduced to half or one third of their former level, the great estates were parcelled out, the small cottages were turned into ordinary farms tilled by wealthy tenants, etc. The diminishing income of the lord meant that his economy had to be reorganized. Formerly it must have been based on the actual income from the agricultural production of the demesne, with its heavy accent on grain products. Now he leased the landholdings out, sometimes receiving no rent at all, more often a small manorial due, fixed and unchangeable. Where possible, he sold or mortgaged out land for ready money, thus adding to the extensive splitting-up of landed property. As a third measure, he would try to restructure the large *Wüstungen,* using them for cattleraising and dairy production. Finally, he would go into international merchant ventures, entering into investment partnerships with merchants from the Hanseatic League. The question I want to raise is: was there a significant and logical correlation between these changes in economic organization, ensuing changes in ways of life and the changes in the use of literacy described above? In order to answer this question, I shall outline the lives of two nobles and their use of literacy.

Two Nobles and their Ways of Life, 1400-1500: Sten Basse and Mourids Nielsen (Gyldenstjerne)

Sten Basse was a very wealthy noble, decidedly in the upper stratum. Despite this, the structure of his economic situation was not unique, compared with that of his less fortunate peers.

We know of his life from approximately 150 sources, i.e. written documents in which he is mentioned.[4] The overwhelming majority of these are deeds concerning landed property. There is no doubt that he made extensive use of writing in his constant endeavours to enlarge his landholdings. We can follow some of these processes through time. Initially, he would acquire a mortgage on the land, which could be documented by a witnessed, signed and sealed paper. The next step would be to acquire the actual ownership, and later on Royal confirmations (so-called *låsebreve* or title deeds). He controlled a number of estates scattered all over Zealand and Funen, several of which belonged to his wife, and all of which probably belonged to a more limited extent

---

[4] For a detailed and documented presentation of Sten Basses way of life and mentality, see (Schousboe 1985).

to his strict sphere of dominance. The size of each of these demesnes would vary from the size of three farms to that of half a village. The whole village around this might belong to the estate, but often enough this would not be the case.

Yet his wealth did not stem primarily from the land he controlled. We measure his wealth by the number of estates and peasant farms he exercised control over, but we must not misinterpret the situation as if these estates were the background of his economy. Primarily, he belonged to the King's inner circle, and was thus enfeoffed with one of the most important castles, the castle of Nyborg. On what conditions we do not know, but generally it seems that such enfeoffments were not accompanied by a direct economic advantage. What we know is that Sten Basse used this privileged position to enter into joint ventures with merchants from the Hanseatic League. The evidence, although it is sporadic, tells us that in 1421 he and his wife joined the local merchant guild in Nyborg, that they were allowed by the magistrate to trade freely and without hindrances in and out of Nyborg, and that he took part in a joint venture with one Hans Hagemeister, a merchant from Lübeck, who acknowledged in a written statement that he was the *Knecht* of Sten Basse, and that he was trading in his goods and to his benefit. This explicit evidence is corroborated by a number of other cases. First and foremost, some of the sums he acquired mortgages for in farms or land located near Nyborg were not (as normally was the case) round figures - we may presume that these were payments for goods received, as we know was the case later on. In these dealings he used a citizen and official of Nyborg as his retainer. What he traded in remains obscure: only one case gives us a hint.

From the castle of Nyborg he was supposed to monitor the transit trade of the Hansa to and from Norway and England (in its attempt to avoid the Sound dues). We know that he was accused at least once by the Hansa of acting as a freebooter. During one of the frequent conflicts with the Hanseatic League he had captured a ship carrying salt and canvas, a cargo representing the two dominant kinds of merchandise imported to Denmark in that period. Salt was the main preservative, totally necessary for the large-scale herring catches and thus for the fishing enterprises in Denmark in this and the preceding century, as well as for the export of butter and other dairy products. Cloth - fine, imported fabrics, cut out and used for extravagantly multicoloured clothes

- was one of the main symbols of wealth and power, although in this case the textiles must have been meant for packing.

We know that some of the land he bought outside Nyborg consisted of pastures, and generally it appears that the new estates were located in traditional cattle-raising areas. It seems logical that he was involved to some extent in exporting cattle and dairy products (perhaps some grain) through commissionaires from the North German trading cities, importing salt and luxury goods, selling them to the less affluent local inhabitants and receiving payment in export goods and occasionally land. This organization of trade is documented in great detail in sources from the end of the 15th century, and there is nothing in the scarce source material concerning Sten Basse to gainsay the general picture presented here.

As far as we can see, his way of life was marked by this economic profile. In the first place, his life centred around the city and castle of Nyborg, where he had living quarters. Over and above this, he owned a number of merchant houses and warehouses in the city: at least one of them was rebuilt by Sten Basse on a large scale, thus confirming his wealth and power. The living quarters were situated at the sunny side of the church, opening up on the other side to a yard which ended at the wharf. Here a number of warehouses were placed. Just opposite the house by the church he built a chapel where eternal masses were to be said twice a day.

Part of this pattern, however, was his close connection with the Royal administration, and his continuous participation in the political dealings with the Hansa. He seems to have acted as a trusted negotiator on behalf of the King on several occasions. The period was characterized by alternations between diplomatic negotiations, small-scale conflicts and wars between Denmark, the Holsteins, the Hansa, the Teutonic Order (in control of the Baltic countries) and the Swedes. We see Sten Basse enmeshed in this political web along with those we may presume were his close brothers-in-arms, Peder Oxe, the Captain-in-Chief at Elsinore (the King's main castle), and perhaps Erik Krummedige, the Chief at Aalholm, which controlled the main gateway into the South of Denmark.

If we try to follow him, we find that he was present at the most important negotiations, sometimes far from his commercial stronghold, sometimes in the heart of the territory of his trading partners, the Northern cities of the Hansa, primarily Lübeck. We know that at one point he was stranded for the whole of the winter in *Stargarde* in Pomerania, unable to come 'home', that is to return to Denmark. In order to round off this account of the main characteristics of his way of life - his interlocality or constant moving about - we must note where he chose his burial ground. It was not in the local church as was normally the case in the 13th century, but in a large and very important monastery, to which he had donated much landed property. It is an intriguing fact that this monastery, *Antvorskov,* was situated far from his estates.

What role did writing play in his economy and way of life? Of the three economic spheres dominating his life - the demesnes, trade and politics - each in its own right demanded some measure of proficiency in reading and writing. But did they require that Sten Basse personally mastered these arts?

To take politics first: it is unfortunate, since it is pertinent to the question of the implications of literacy, that the history of the art of political negotiation is as yet unwritten. The period during which Sten Basse was 'on stage' (1408-1448) was marked by continuous negotiations between the Crown and its political counterparts elsewhere - especially the Holsteins, the Hansa, the Teutonic Order, the German Emperor, the Roman Catholic Church, England, and - above all - Norway and Sweden, the three Northern Kingdoms having been united under one crown, that of *Eric of Pomerania.* The political story of this period has been written from the point of view that the endless number of documents - treaties and contracts witnessing the negotiations - actually did constitute the legal basis underlying political administration. To this extent the political historian is in accordance with the general concept of written documents of the early fifteenth century. There is no doubt that written and sealed documents were considered to be of paramount importance. Much time, energy and money was spent obtaining written documents detailing and witnessing specific agreements.

The prelude to the drawing up of a document consisted of endless oral talks and negotiations. We know that Eric of Pomerania was considered to be a brilliant orator. But we also know that he was a stubborn negotiator, demanding legally specified terms, in writing and sealed. Sometimes, though, he used an old trick to renege on the actual fulfilment of the terms - not sealing the papers himself. Taking part in this sort of politics would require a capacity not only for oral performance, but also for quibbling. It would require the services of scribes and notaries as well as an ability to check the written results personally.

We may conclude that Sten Basse had to have access to skilled scribes and lawyers, and that he must have been able to read. He must have been able to familiarize himself with written instructions from the King, and to formulate in a form suitable for writing in order to dictate to scribes; and he must have been able to check the results, the political treaty in the form of a written text. But we do not have to assume that he had to master the art of writing himself.

Was the ability to write a necessary prerequisite for his trading activities? We know very little about the organization of trade from the archive of Sten Basse. This is coupled with the fact that very little systematic investigation has been done concerning the Danish end of the trade that went on (Ilsøe 1966). But it appears that the dealings between the principal (consignor) and the commissionaire were organized as follows. Their relationship would be of reasonable long standing. The commissionaire would receive goods (agricultural products) in the Hanseatic cities and market them there. Then he would send a written and very detailed account to the principal along with requested luxury articles, salt and hops. Reciprocal gifts would be included in the consignment to stabilize the long-term relations between nobleman and merchant. Two things seem to have been necessary for this kind of arrangement. First, the merchant had to be able to read and write - to do accounts. Secondly, the lord had to have the opportunity of getting news about prices (this would be necessary for him to be able to check the loyalty of his commissionaire). He would of course depend upon the political sphere (and his own travels) to acquire this necessary information. He would also need a scribe through whom he could correspond with the merchant. But as yet Sten Basse would not be required to write in person. Yet he would need to have a number of different people on his payroll whose main task would literally be to 'keep tabs' on one another.

Finally we may ask if literacy was a necessary prerequisite for running the estates. Extensive travelling must have made it impossible for Sten Basse to supervise agricultural production in person. Consequently, he had on his payroll a number of bailiffs and retainers, usually from the lower or lowest gentry. The bailiff dealt with the day-to-day farming of his manor. Moreover, he was the curator in the endless lawsuits typical of the 15th century due to the splitting up of the estates in the previous century. But first and foremost he was responsible for collecting the rents. The rent from a farm consisted primarily of victuals, typically four to ten bushels of barley or rye, a few coins, a fat swine, some butter and one or two chickens. The noble or his bailiff would go around the countryside accompanied by a small army of retainers, gathering the rents due from the farms. The formal framework of this extraction was of course the combined threat of violence and the offer of protection against the noble neighbours. Once in a while this would have to be acted out as a real drama (in order to make the threat effective) - the feud. The lords would fight it out, burning the farms and crops of the peasants. Normally, though, in more peaceful periods, the threat of violence would be enough. We may presume that the bailiff would be in charge of this process of extracting rent whenever the lord was away - which was generally the case. The bailiff would then have to present the lord with a detailed account of rents collected. We may presume that most estates had the surrounding farms registered in a so-called *jordebog* ('land book') - the manorial equivalent of a cadastre. For the bailiff this would function as a manual for the collection of rent, as a register with which the lord on inspection could compare the accounts of the bailiff, and as a background for obtaining probate. Evidently the bailiff himself would need to be able to read and write. We know of a number of Sten Basse's bailiffs, although the administration of his estates is badly documented. One bailiff was Claus Iversen, who had been bailiff at Lykkesholm for six years. In 1442 he and Sten Basse met at a conciliation conference in the church of St. Mary in Nyborg. Present were the (new) Captain of Nyborg, another nobleman, four priests and two burghers. Sten Basse asked Claus Iversen to present his accounts. The bailiff answered that he would not 'lay before him' other accounts than those he had formerly 'given' to him. We do not know what the outcome of this legal wrangle was, except that Sten Basse filed a formal lawsuit at the High Court in Odense later on. However, we can deduce from this episode that the written accounts were controlled and formulated by Claus Iversen. The serious character of the charge against him indicates this.

The case of Sten Basse makes it clear that his way of life required a network of administrators and retainers with the full ability to read and write, although his own lifestyle did not require such proficiency from him personally. This becomes clearer still when we consider the case of *Mourids Nielsen (Gyldenstjerne)*.[5]

Mourids Nielsen (Gyldenstjerne) (c. 1446-1503) was a nobleman with an even more scattered estate. He administrated manors in the northern part of Jutland, in the middle of Zealand and in Scania. Like Sten Basse he took part in trading, selling grain, herring, cattle and horses to the South. His market, however, had shifted to some extent to the Northwest of Germany. Finally, he was a trusted servant of the King, taking part in the Royal administration, negotiations and politics on the international scale. On occasion he would be asked to serve on diplomatic missions, at Royal weddings, important negotiations, in warfare, etc. For half of the year he would be travelling through the country to take part in these activities. For two or three months in the winter he seems to have been preoccupied with taking care of his estates. He seems to have taken a special interest in one of them - *Aagaard* - probably because of the rich pasture of the coastline and the fishing in the *Limfjord*. We know that he travelled around the countryside in person to a certain extent, accompanied by a small force of about ten people and a scribe, collecting rent: the day-to-day accounts of the scribe are preserved in the form of a diary. But primarily he appears to have depended on bailiffs, with whom he kept up an extensive correspondence.

Alas, only fragments of this correspondence have been preserved. But it appears that he would use his personal scribe (called *Esben Skriver* or Esben the Scribe) as a messenger and administrator, monitoring, for example, the bailiffs and their accounts. One letter sent by him from Markie is preserved, in which he writes to Mourids Nielsen telling him about the bailiff and his administration, quoting prices and passing on rumours from the court that he has picked up in Copenhagen and the like (Christensen 1914 II, No. 143). We also have what might be termed the 'counterpart' of this letter - a detailed account from the bailiff to the knight *Henrik Krummedige* in the form of a letter sent along with the scribe who came to check and collect the income administered by the bailiff (Christensen 1914, II, No. 146).

---

[5] The preliminary sketch here presents the results of an ongoing investigation into the life of Mourids Nielsen Gyldenstjerne based on his papers in his private archive in The Danish State Archive, Copenhagen.

When entering the service of a noble like Mourids Nielsen Gyldenstjerne the bailiff might sign a contract affirming his intention to be loyal. Secondly, they would draw up an inventory of cattle, goods, grain, ploughs, tools, cooking and brewing utensils, etc. Both parties would sign this and copies would be made for the security of both. We know of two such inventories, one which *Hans Bagge* had made when he took charge of *Bregentved* in August 1495, and another inventory of *Aagaard,* which was drawn up when Mourids Nielsen invested *Oluf Skriver* (Oluf Scribe) with the keys and the responsibilities of a bailiff. This position involved as a bounden duty the production of detailed accounts. This becomes obvious from a trial. Mourids Nielsen Gyldenstjerne had left Aagaard to go to Sweden in the service of the King. I quote:

At the time when My Lord left the country and went into the service of the King he entrusted the bailiff with his property in Jutland and gave orders regarding how the bailiff should manage. He also entrusted him with a key to his personal belongings [the jewellery, silver plate, and documents concerning the real property]. The documents were only to be taken out in the presence of other noblemen. He then left, instructing the bailiff to send money and supplies when requested. He did not do so, and Mourids furthermore received notice that the bailiff had gone into the service of another lord and stolen his goods. As a reaction to this Mourids obtained a letter from the Royal administration and had it sent out to the local courts to be read aloud there. The letter extended protection to his land and ordered that there should be no contesting of his rights until he returned. He came back just before Christmas and called for a court session in order to convict the bailiff.

It appears that the bailiff had a concise account written down, which he had given into the custody of the abbot of the local monastery. He was allowed to produce these account books, but unfortunately this did not succeed in convincing the judges of his innocence. We know that he was hanged as a thief (Rasmussen 1884: 265).

Sola Scriptura

There is thus not much evidence for the 15th century of the need for the people in power - that is, the nobles - to be able to read or write. We may presume, though, that they mastered the art of reading a written text - a letter, an account or written instruction. Primarily, there is ample evidence that their special proficiency was to master the art of eloquence. Giving speeches, presenting problems and points of view in the oral mode, however, also involved an ability to take part in the never-ending ritualized contexts of processions, pious churchgoing, large ceremonial gatherings, feasts, etc.

In this there was a sharp distinction between the so-called rulers and their administrators - of whom it was required, as we saw, that they were extensively able not only to read, but also to write. Indeed, as was the case in the last example, the life of such a bureaucrat might very well depend upon his proficiency in this respect. Personal proficiency in reading and writing became the most important tool of these functionaries, and their trademark of excellence.

With the formation of a distinct social category of scribes, burghers, merchants, artisans, etc., writing and epigraphics also emerged as a central mode of ornamentation. In the beginning writing was first and foremost used on tombstones by these groups, as opposed to the reliefs or effigies of the nobility. Later it became the fashion to place inscriptions - apothegms, biblical quotations or proverbs - all over the houses and utensils of burghers. This was in direct opposition to the nobility's excessive use of heraldic devices on the same objects.

It would of course be daring to consider the whole question of the iconoclasm of the Reformation as an overall product of this phenomenon. But it is an intriguing fact that, while the nobility persisted in displaying a whole range of spectacular behaviour - processions, feasting, jousting, etc. - the burghers turned their way of life into a private, secluded affair. Absorbed in silent reading or writing, the citizen was consciously opposed to the outward, near-dramatic playacting of the nobility. Literacy was thus not only a necessary prerequisite for the economic organization of late medieval Denmark. It became a powerful symbol of the lives of the citizens as opposed to the way of life of the nobility. It thus became the key symbol in the 'cultural' struggle over who should profit - the controllers of people or the controllers of words. And at the dawn of the German and Danish Reformation this struggle even took the form of a real civil war. As is well known, the early phases of the 16th-century peasant revolts coincided precisely with the iconoclastic campaigns and riots of this Reformation (Christensen 1979).

Conclusion

The widespread literacy of late medieval Denmark was a social phenomenon which helps us to understand the overall shift from a decentralized manorial economy towards a new, centralized - but large-scale - form of organization.

On the other hand, it was neither the cause of this decentralization and recentralization, nor of the specific cultural and social polarization of society after 1500. But we may safely assume that literacy came to play a major role insofar as it presented itself as the logical 'tool' for administrative practice, in fact the prerequisite for this whole process of reorganization. Consequently, as *the* tool of the 'artisan' - the scribe - it came to be the core symbol of that process and especially of the subject - the bureaucratic administrator.

Bibliography

Brøndum-Nielsen, Johannes and Jørgensen, Poul Johannes (1932-61) editors *Danmarks gamle Landskabslove med Kirkelovene*, I-VIII.

Brøndum-Nielsen, Johannes (1943) Palæografi, *Nordisk Kultur* XXVIII, København.

Bäuml, Franz H. (1980) Varieties and Consequence of Medieval Literacy, *Speculum*, vol. 55, 2 p. 237-265.

Christensen, Axel E. (1976) Senmiddelalderlige Fæsteformer som forudsætning for forordningen om livfæste af 1523, *Danmark, Norden og Østersøen. Udvalgte afhandlinger*, København.

Christensen, Carl C. (1979) *Art and the Reformation in Germany*, Ohio.

Christensen, Palle Ove (1978) Peasant Adaptions to Bourgeois Culture, *Etnologia Scandinavia*, Lund.

Christensen, William (1914) editor, *Missiver fra Kongerne Chr. I's og Hans's tid*, I-II, København.

Clanchy, Michael T. (1979) *From Memory to Written Record: England 1066-1307* , Edward Arnold and Harvard University Press, London and Cambridge, Mass.

Dahlerup, Troels (1969) Lavadelens Krise i dansk Senmiddelalder, *Historisk Tidsskrift* XII rk. 4 p. 1-41.

Dahlerup, Troels (1971) Danmark. *Den nordiske adel i senmiddelalderen. Struktur, funktioner og internordiske relationer. Rapporter til det nordiske historikermøde i København 1971 9-12 august*, s. 45-80.

Eisenstein, Elizabeth (1979) The printing Press as an Agent of Change. *Communications and Cultural Transformations in Early Modern Europe*, vol. 1-2, Cambridge.

Hornby, Richard (1947) Fornavne i Danmark i Middelalderen, *Nordisk Kultur* VIII, Oslo.

Hørby, Kai (1980) Middelalderen, *Dansk Socialhistorie*, vol. 2, p. 77-304.

Ilsøe, Grethe (1966) Dansk Herremandshandel med Hansekøbmændene i Senmiddelalderen. *Middelalderstudier tilegnede Axel E. Christensen.*

Kulturhistorisk leksikon for nordisk middelalder Vol. 1ff, 1956ff.

Ladewig Petersen, E. (1980) Fra Standssamfund til rangssamfund 1500-1700. *Dansk Socialhistorie*, vol. 3, København.

Liestøl, Aslak (1968) Correspondence in Runes, *Medieval Scandinavia*, vol. 1 p. 17-28, Odense.

Nørlund, Poul (1927) Jordrotter paa Valdemarstiden, *Festskrift til Kr. Erslev*, p. 141-70, København.

Olsen, Gunnar (1943) De danske Købstæder gennem Tiderne. *Vi og vor Fortid* No. 10, København.

Paludan, Helge (1977) Tiden 1241-1340. *Gyldendals Danmarkshistorie* Bd. 1, p. 401-511, København.

Prange, Knud (1964) Bonde af Thy. En standshistorisk Studie. Landbohistoriske Afhandlinger, *Bol og By* vol. 5, p. 47-70.

Rasmussen, M. R. Kall (1884) Dokumenter vedkommende Rigsraaden Mourits Nielsen (Gyldenstjerne) til Aagaard. *Danske Magazin*, 3. rk. 3. vol. no. 4.

Riis, Thomas (1970) Villici og Coloni indtil 1340. Et forsøg på en begrebsanalyse. *Landbohistoriske Studier tilegnede Fridlev Skrubbeltrang på halvfjerdsårsdagen d. 5. august 1970*, p. 1-20.

Schousboe, Karen (1982) Bäuerliche Anschreibebücher des 18. Jahrhunderts aus Dänemark. Ottenjahn, Helmut und Wiegelmann, Günter, editors, *Alte Tagebücher und Anschreibebücher*.

Schousboe, Karen (1983) *En fæstebondes liv. Søren Pedersen Havrebjerg. 1776-1839.* Odense.

Schousboe, Karen (1985) *Sten Basse - Erik af Pommerens Befuldmægtigede (-1400-1448). En Studie i senmiddelalderlige livsformer og livsopfattelser.* Manus.

Skautrup, Peter (1947) (1968) *Det danske Sprogs Historie, I-IV.* København.

Stoklund, Bjarne (1958) Bonde og Fisker. *Handels- og Søfartsmuseets Årbog.*

Ulsig, Erik (1968) Danske adelsgodser i Middelalderen. *Skrifter udgivet af det historiske Institut ved Københavns Universitet,* vol. 2, København.

Ulsig, Erik (1981) Landboer og bryder, skat og landgilde. De danske fæstebønder og deres afgifter i det 12. og 13. århundrede. *Middelalder, metode og medier. Festskrift til Niels Skyum Nielsen,* p. 137-166.

Vovelle, Michel (1973) *Piété broque et déchristianisation en Provence au XVIIIe siècle: Les attitudes devant la mort d'après les clauses des testaments,* Plon, Paris.

Reading the Signs at Durham Cathedral

M. T. Clanchy

Literacy by that name is only a century old (the word first appears in 1883 according to the Oxford English Dictionary), whereas writing in various forms has been in use for five thousand years (or much longer, when prehistoric man's ability to mark out his world is taken into consideration). The modern definition of literacy as the 'ability to read and write' assumes an objective. In the twentieth century reading and writing have been directed at the mass of the population through compulsory schooling in the industrialized nations and literacy campaigns in the Third World. Those men and women, who are able to read printed directions and write or sign when required to do so, are described as functionally literate. Past societies, on the other hand, reveal a diversity of priorities and objectives in their uses of writing. Historical study is therefore essential for understanding what the ability to read and write signifies beyond functional competence.

The growth of literacy in medieval Europe is often seen as a halting progress towards the invention of printing in 1450. Advance would have been much faster, it is assumed, if lay people had been allowed to read the bible for themselves and the church had willingly surrendered its monopoly on learning. By this line of thinking the modern objective of functional literacy is imposed on the past and the significance of writing in medieval culture is largely obscured. In *De Laude Scriptorum* ('In Praise of Scribes') the abbot of Sponheim in 1492 reacted to the first printed books by exhorting his scribes to copy them out on to parchment. The principal function of writing, in his view, was not to provide information for the masses but to ensure that posterity possessed the necessary signs of salvation in holy scripture. For this purpose, printing was too superficial and impressionistic a process. 'If writing (*scriptura*) is put on parchment, it can last for a thousand years, but how long will an impression (*impressura*) on something paper last?', he demanded (Clanchy 1983: 10).

This question is rich in paradoxes, as most early printed books were produced on such high quality paper (or even vellum) that they have lasted very well, and furthermore *De Laude Scriptorum* was itself disseminated as a printed book. Nevertheless the abbot's question is important for the point of view it reveals. He was looking back over a millennium of monastic scribal tradition to the earliest parchment books and the illumination of scripture in Carolingian and Ottonian manuscripts. He apprehended that printing marked the end of the scribal culture which we now call medieval. His *De Laude Scriptorum* was its panegyric.

Although medieval manuscript culture is beyond recovery as a means of production, its values can be confronted, if not recovered, by examining its artefacts where they still exist. From the fifteenth century onwards, thousands of medieval manuscripts were rescued from neglect or deliberate destruction and concentrated in libraries. Such huge collections as the Vatican Library and the Bibliotheque Nationale serve the researcher well for every purpose except seeing manuscripts in their original cultural context among other medieval artefacts. For that purpose, more modest and local accumulations of documents, which are still retained on their original sites, are more helpful. In Britain, Durham cathedral is a site of this sort. The researcher there is presented with the fifteenth-century list of its charters instead of a modern archivist's rationalization. As a consequence of being so conservative, Durham has preserved artefacts of writing of unusual types. In the space of this article it is only possible to describe a few items in order to show how writings were part of a larger system of signs.

Durham cathedral was a monastery and a shrine, as well as the see of the bishop. The cathedral building is itself a sign, as it marks the place where in 995 A. D. the bearers of Saint Cuthbert's miraculous body could move him no further. They therefore built a shelter of branches over his shrine, which had developed by 1200 into the magnificent church we see today (Coldstream and Draper 1980: 1-169). The word *signum* in medieval Latin was rich in meaning. In addition to describing a 'sign' or 'signature', it was the term used for a miracle. Thus the frequent occurrences of healing at Cuthbert's shrine were *signa* ('signs') of his power. The cruciform shape of the cathedral, aligned to the rising and the setting of the sun (as medieval churches were required to be), makes a massive sign of the cross on the landscape. It marks the supreme miracle of man's redemption by Christ, as well as the immediate miracle of Cuthbert's undying presence.

Adam son of Ilbert's Charter

The sign of the cross was equally an individual's autograph mark or 'signature'. Thus the twelfth-century charter illustrated here [ill. 1] surrendering two villages to Durham priory (Dean and Chapter Muniments: 4.7. Spec. 9a) declares: '*Ego Adam signum hoc sanctae crucis propria manu subscripsi*': I Adam have subscribed this sign of the holy cross with my own hand'. (This charter also bears the autograph crosses of Adam's sons, Elias and Bertram, so that they likewise guarantee his grant to Durham.) Adam formed his cross on the parchment in much the same spirit as the cathedral builders made their mark on the landscape through their handiwork, although the scale and materials of the two operations differ. Because Adam's cross is done in pen and ink, it is described as being 'written' (the Latin is *subscripsi*), although whether Adam could write in a modern sense is doubtful. He certainly did not use a consistent signature, as a duplicate exists of this charter in which the crosses of Adam and his sons differ markedly (Dean and Chapter Muniments: 4.7. Spec. 9b.; Greenwell 1872: 126-7). In each case the *signa* are described as being subscribed 'with their own hands'. (Charters were quite often produced in duplicate or triplicate but it is unusual to show such divergent *signa*.)

In the text of both charters Adam is described as 'Adam son of Ilbert the Cementer'. A *cementarius* was a mason and Ilbert had perhaps been one of the builders of Durham cathedral. Such a man had little use for literacy in the medieval sense of Latin letters, although masons sometimes used distinctive marks to indicate which stones they had worked or cut and important ones were described as 'Master' like professors in the schools. A master mason, like a scholastic master, needed intelligence or genius (*ingenium*). Thus at Durham the architect of Bishop Puiset (1153-95) described himself as *Ricardus Ingeniator*, 'Richard the Ingenious One' or 'Engineer' (Greenwell 1872: 140; Raine 1835: 111-2, 302). The fact that he was called *simplex et laicus* ('a lay simpleton') by Reginald of Durham is not a contradiction, as the clergy described anyone who was unlettered in Latin in that way.

Judging from the seal on Adam's charter (the duplicate has lost its seal), which presents him as an armed man on horseback, he had advanced from his father's profession of mason to the superior status of knighthood. A knight was typically no more a man of letters than a mason was. He dedicated himself to knighthood by offering his sword on an altar. 'Who would demand of an *illiteratus*,' asks John of Salisbury in *c* 1160, 'whose duty is to know arms rather than letters, that he should make a literate profession?' (Webb 1919: vol.2, 25) 'Knights', John adds, 'offer not a schedule (*cedulam*) but a sword'. Appropriately enough, the knight on Adam's seal holds his sword aloft as a symbol of power. The sign of the cross could be formed or invoked in many materials: in the mason's stone, the scribe's parchment and ink, or the knight's cross-shaped sword itself.

The sense in which Adam 'subscribed' the charters in his name cannot be confined within the modern functional definition of literacy. He may have made his sign of the cross in the manner of his father who was a mason, or as a knight dedicated to arms (as his seal suggests), or even as a 'man of letters' (*literatus*), as there were knights who had learned Latin when boys. Adam also signed in more ways than with his cross in ink, as his seal spelled out his name, through its circular inscription *SIGILLUM DE ADAM FILII ILBERTI*, and it too bore the sign of the cross. The image of the knight served as an additional sign of Adam's identity, although it is a little too early in date to display heraldic symbolism distinctive to him. When Adam made this grant to the Durham monks, he may also have formed signs beyond those still preserved in ink and sealing wax. He probably crossed himself with his right hand, as well as subscribing a cross on the parchment, and the charter mentions an oath 'for the love of truth and the reverence of the blessed father Cuthbert'. This oath was probably taken over some of Cuthbert's relics in the cathedral. These affirmations of voice and gesture, which were done 'in the presence and hearing of many worthy men' (the charter states), may have been a more significant part of the ceremony at the time than the making of the written record. Even in the functionally literate society of twentieth-century Europe or North America, bride and groom may still consider their exchange of vows and rings as more significant parts of the wedding ceremony than signing their names in the marriage register.

Written record in its alphabetic form is a medium with obvious limitations because script represents nothing more than cues for words (Ong 1982:75). It cannot reproduce the context of feeling and action in which the words are first formed into a text. In medieval contexts this difficulty was compounded when Latin was the language of record because it was nobody's mother tongue. In Adam son of Ilbert's charter, as in other twelfth-century documents at Durham, the participants attempted to overcome these limitations by producing an artefact which transcended letters through its sacred *signa* and impressive seal. Such an artefact looks primitive and odd to us modern literates because we have been schooled to accept writing at its face value, whereas medieval people were not satisfied with that.

The Durham Knife-handles

Adam's charter is unusual in combining a seal with an autograph cross, and in making the significance of the cross explicit, but it is not unique. More extraordinary are two knife-handles kept in the Durham archives (Dean and Chapter Muniments: 3.1. Spec. 72 and 4.3. Ebor. 4). The one illustrated here (Ill. 2) has an inscription carved shakily on its haft saying: *Signum de capella de lowic*, that is, 'the sign for the chapel of Lowick'. There is more writing in Latin on the other side of the haft, repeating *de capella de Lowic* and adding: '*et de decimis de Lowic totius curie et totius ville*' ('and for the tithes of Lowick of the whole court and the whole village'). To the handle is attached, through a hole pierced in its head, a parchment label with a Latin text explaining that 'this is the agreement' between the monks of Lindisfarne and Sir Stephen of Bulmer: he acknowledges that the monks ought to have the tithes of Lowick and some other property. (Lindisfarne is the 'Holy Island' off the Northumberland coast, where Cuthbert himself had lived. With the removal of Cuthbert's body to Durham, the Lindisfarne monks became subject to Durham cathedral priory.)

This 'sign' of the knife-handle with its label serves the same purpose as Adam son of Ilbert's charter with its seal and autograph crosses. It is a durable and personal record or proof of Stephen of Bulmer's grant to the monks. The knife-handle is to be read as a sign of his gift and, to ensure that its significance was understood, a monk at Lindisfarne or Durham inscribed it. The inscription had to be spelled out for posterity in Latin letters, with great difficulty on the hard horn of the knife-handle, because it was the knife itself that was the real sign. Had the evidence of the knife not been paramount, the monks would have thrown it away and kept only the parchment label.

Why use a knife for this symbolic purpose? I have already published an explanation in *From Memory to Written Record* (Clanchy 1979: 206-7), so I will do no more here than summarize and make some observations. An explanation is supplied on the back of the parchment label. It records that Stephen's wife, Cecily, and his steward, Aschetin, 'at the command and in the place of their lord', crossed over to the Holy Island (Lowick itself was on the mainland) and 'offered to God and Saint Cuthbert and the monks' the chapel and the other property. The knife was presumably the 'sign' of Stephen's agreement, which Cecily and Aschetin offered on the altar of Saint Cuthbert's church at Lindisfarne. This is suggested because there are other instances in the twelfth century from Durham and elsewhere, of knives being offered as symbols on altars, although the knives themselves are no longer extant. The Lindisfarne knife may have been Stephen's own; as James Raine suggested, it could be: 'the very knife itself by means of which he was aided in his meals, in the carving of his venison from his park at Baremoor, or of his salmon from the Tweed' (Raine 1852: 77). Alternatively, it may have been the knife with which Aschetin the steward ceremonially carved his lord's meat at table.

The full significance of the use of knives - and other objects such as swords, rings and cups - as symbols of gifts is too large a subject to explore here. A remarkable feature of the two Durham knives, which is not referred to in the texts accompanying them, is that in each case the blade has been broken close to the haft. If this was done deliberately at the time of the ceremonies they concern, the breaking may symbolize finality. In the context of medieval uses of writing, the most interesting aspect of the Durham knives is the relatively late date at which they were used as symbols. Stephen of Bulmer was a substantial landlord who died after 1172. Such a man would have been expected to have a seal. If he possessed one, why was it not taken to the Holy Island, instead of a knife, by Cecily and Aschetin to ratify his gift? The answer may be that the knife was considered by all parties, including the monks, to be the most appropriate symbol because it could be offered on an altar. Sealing a charter was an impressive ceremony when it was done in the seal-owner's presence, as the witnesses saw the lettering of his name and the image of his status being impressed on the wax. But, because Stephen was absent, his seal could not be used in this convincing way. Similarly his absence meant that he could not make an autograph sign of the cross on the charter in the presence of the monks, as Adam son of Ilbert, had done.

Why, then, did Stephen of Bulmer not send a message to the monks and sign it? The answer is that this is precisely what he did do. For literates today, 'sending a message' suggests writing a letter, and 'signing it' means appending a signature. Stephen, on the other hand, directed an oral message through his wife and his steward and he signed it with a knife. As with Adam son of Ilbert's charter, it is impossible to say whether Stephen's signing in this way implied literacy or illiteracy. Stephen's kinsman and contemporary, Bertram of Bulmer, is known to have employed a household knight who was a cleric and a *literatus* (Clanchy 1979: 194). The knife is not a sign of Stephen's illiteracy but of the special circumstances of his grant: his wife and steward had to present the monks of Lindisfarne with a sufficient proof in his absence. It is just as likely to have been the monks who suggested that a knife should be the *signum* as that Stephen did. To the monks the knife was presumably like a saint's relic: it was a tangible object which could be labelled and kept as a symbol of power.

Although Stephen's sign of a knife can be accounted for within this reconstructed thought-world of the monks of the Holy Island, the fact remains that it was an unusual form of proof in the second half of the twelfth century. By 1200 documents had to have regular seals in order to be acceptable as evidence in the king's court. This is shown by the other Durham knife which was exhibited by the prior of Durham as evidence in King John's court at Westminster in 1213. The knife was attached, as it still is, by a hole in its haft to a parchment document (like the Lindisfarne knife). The defendant in the case objected that the document had no seal but only 'a certain knife which can be put on or taken off' (Clanchy 1979: 24). Although the prior of Durham eventually won this lawsuit, he did not deny the invalidity of this title-deed. Nevertheless he kept it and took it back to Durham, where it still remains. Like the Lindisfarne knife, it was of relatively recent origin, as the document attached to it bears the date 1148 A.D.

Durham cathedral has retained from the twelfth century other documents with 'signs' attached to them, which the king's court would have probably rejected as irregular. There is a charter from the 1150's, for example, with a seal bearing the inscription *SIGNUM CLEMENTIE DEI* (Dean and Chapter Muniments: 4.2. Spec. 2). This is not the name of its owner but a 'SIGN OF GOD'S CLEMENCY', as the image on the seal makes clear. It displays the dove which brought the olive branch to Noah. In another charter associated with this one, the autograph cross of the donor, Ralph de Gaugy, has been deliberately concealed, when the ink was still wet, under a fold in the parchment (Dean and Chapter Muniments: 4.2. Spec. 1). I hope to discuss the significance of these mysterious 'signs' at Durham in a separate paper. What they suggest in general is that in the twelfth century the Durham monks were still experimenting with the use of writing for making title-deeds. They saw a different potentiality in writing from us modern literates and they were also aware of limitations in written record which we can no longer perceive. Because they retained their early title-deeds, even though some of them were unacceptable as evidence in the king's court, they have left a special record of how medieval writing was incorporated into a larger system of signs.

God's Writers

It is misleading to think of medieval laymen, like Adam son of Ilbert or Stephen of Bulmer, as living in some primitive world of signs, while monks and clergy operated in the proto-modern world of literacy. Obviously enough, they all lived in the same world, although it is true that medieval society created contrasting ideals, most notably in the knight with his sword and the clerk with his letters. The monks of Durham in the twelfth century were not functional literates using writing for their daily business. Some of them, like Prior Laurence (1149-54) who composed Latin verse, were highly literate in the medieval sense of mastering Latin, but their literacy did not stem from utilitarian needs. Although medieval scribal tradition used Latin letters, it had not derived directly from Roman imperial practice but from the British Isles, where the first great illuminated books of scripture had most probably been produced in the seventh century. Durham stood directly in this tradition because, through its possession of the body of Saint Cuthbert, it was the heir of the Celtic monks of the Holy Island of Lindisfarne. Among many of the earliest illuminated manuscripts, Durham possessed the magnificent Lindisfarne Gospels, which had probably been made in honour of Saint Cuthbert in 698 A. D. Such manuscripts were sacred relics as well as models of what books should be like. For example, at the dedication of the present Cathedral in 1104, the bishop of Durham exhibited from the pulpit the commentary on St. John's Gospel which Cuthbert himself had allegedly written (Arnold 1882: 361).

The Durham monks of the twelfth century were steeped in the tradition which the abbot of Sponheim described in his *De Laude Scriptorum*. Surrounded by the oldest and finest illuminated manuscripts, they directed their skills in writing not to ephemeral needs but to producing works of holy scripture which would last for a thousand years. Writings were signs of salvation. Even a business document, like Adam son of Ilbert's charter, was seen in this light, as it displayed his sign of the cross and showed his reverence for Saint Cuthbert. On the high altar in Durham cathedral stood the *Liber Vitae*, the 'Book of Life', in which the names of Cuthbert's benefactors were inscribed in letters of gold (Hamilton Thompson 1923). The difference in attitude between monastic scribes and modern literates is made clear in a sermon recorded in a Durham manuscript of the twelfth century (Mynors 1939: 9). The monks are exhorted to seem 'decorated' with the most beautiful ornament of sanctity as they strive to be 'God's writers' *(dei scriptores)*. The preacher then takes each implement which the scribe uses as a metaphor or sign of his state of mind. Thus 'the parchment on which we write for God is a pure conscience', our good works are made commendable to God through being noted by the pens of memory, the knife which scrapes the parchment is the fear of God which removes the hardness of sin through penance, and so on.

The Durham monks did not necessarily live up to such exhortations and these extended metaphors are typical of monastic sermons of the twelfth century. Nevertheless this sermon is significant, not only because it describes the writing process, but also because its extended images in words are comparable with the visual images in medieval manuscripts. In illuminated initials the letters merge into images, of twisting foliage and exotic creatures, so that the distinction between writing and pictorial art is sometimes impossible to make. Durham's books from the twelfth century, as much as their earlier books from Lindisfarne, display these characteristics. They are typical of medieval writings in these respects and this is not the place to describe manuscript art as such.

The relevant point in the present context is that the illumination of texts, which persisted as long as the medieval tradition itself, shows how lettering was seen as something more than a bare record of words. 'The various colours with which the book is illuminated', says the Durham sermon, 'not unworthily designate (*designant*) the multiform grace of heavenly wisdom, which is the light of every good' (Dean and Chapter MS. B. iv. 12, fo. 38). The colours overflow around the lettering and they weave such complex geometric and pictorial patterns because they mark out (*designant*) the courses of heavenly wisdom. The book becomes 'illuminated' through this process (Camille 1985: 29).

This is not to say that all medieval writings were illuminated (indeed the text of the Durham sermon itself is entirely plain), and neither does all medieval illumination designate the grace of heavenly wisdom. Nevertheless, even the humblest medieval writer differed in his ideals from a modern literate. The best medieval writing was intended to transcend reality and to stand for a thousand years because the holy scripture itself transcended human experience and stood for eternity. The commonest image of a scribe in medieval manuscripts is that of an evangelist writing the New Testament from divine inspiration. The Durham sermon is appropriately on the text 'I heard a voice from heaven saying unto me: Write!' (*Revelation*, ch. 14, verse 13).

The command to write in the Middle Ages came initially from the heavens above and not as a directive from the state. The principal function of writing was to reinforce and glorify the word of God. When writing came to be used for more mundane purposes, such as recording conveyances of property to the monks of Durham in the twelfth century, it was not immediately divorced from its sacred associations. Charters were signs of salvation for their lay donors because they were records of their gifts to the saints. They were therefore corroborated by signs of the cross or seals (or by Stephen of Bulmer's knife), in much the same way as texts of the scripture were embellished with illuminated letters and gold-encrusted bindings. Durham cathedral's unusual charters from the twelfth century are not antiquarian oddities or insignificant sidetracks on the march of progress towards modern literacy. On the contrary, they are precious survivals of a stage in medieval culture when monks and laymen, writers and non-writers, participated in the formation of signs which transcended the functional ability to read and write. I would associate this transcendence of writing's limitations with the 'take-off' of literacy and education in the medieval West, but that is an argument for another day.

Knife Handle and Label of Stephen of Bulmer. Durham cathedral: 3.1. Spec. 72. Text printed in Raine (1852), appendix, p. 135. Date: 1150 x 1200. Reduced.

Charter and Seal of Adam Son of Ilbert. Durham cathedral: 4.7. Spec. 9a. Text printed in Greenwell (1872), pp. 126-127. Date: 1150 x 1200. Reduced.

Bibliography

Note: This paper derives from my lecture given in Edinburgh in January 1984 in 'The Antiquary' Visiting Scholars Programme. The documents are reproduced by permission of the Dean and Chapter of Durham cathedral.

Arnold, Thomas (1882) editor *Symeonis Monachi Opera Omnia,* Rerum Britannicarum Medii Aevi Scriptores, volume 75, part 2.

Camille, Michael (1985) Seeing and Reading, *Art History* 8.

Clanchy, Michael T. (1979) *From Memory to Written Record: England 1066-1307* Edward Arnold and Harvard University Press, London and Cambridge, Mass.

Clanchy, Michael T. (1983) Looking Back from the Invention of Printing. In Daniel P. Resnick (editor) *Literacy in Historical Perspective*, Library of Congress, Washington.

Coldstream, Nicola and Draper, Peter (1980) editors *Medieval Art and Architecture at Durham Cathedral,* The British Archaeological Association Conference Transactions, volume 3, W. S. Maney, Leeds LS9 7DL.

Dean and Chapter Muniments, the Prior's Kitchen, Durham DH1 3EQ.

Greenwell, William (1872) editor *Feodarium Prioratus Dunelmensis* Surtees Society, volume 58.

Hamilton Thompson, A. (1923) *Liber Vitae Ecclesiae Dunelmensis* Surtees Society, volume 136.

Mynors, Roger A. B. (1939) *Durham Cathedral Manuscripts to the End of the Twelfth Century*, Oxford.

Ong, Walter J. (1982) *Orality and Literacy: The Technologizing of the Word*, Methuen, London and New York.

Raine, James (1835) ed. *Reginaldi Monachi Dunelmensis Libellus* Surtees Society, volume 1.

Raine, James (1852) *The History and Antiquities of North Durham*, London.

Webb, Clement C. J. (1909) *Ioannis Saresberiensis Policraticus* volume 2, Oxford.

What the Illiterate Think of Writing

Bengt Holbek

The question of literacy is usually seen from the point of view of the literate, but it is a fact that for as long as literacy has existed, the vast majority has been illiterate. My purpose is to focus on the views of this majority who knew *of* writing without having mastered the art themselves. Their understanding of the phenomenon is known to us mainly through records of folklore and related sources, but it has not, as far as I am aware, been made the subject of any study, at least in Europe. In my exposition, which will have to be rather condensed because of the amounts of material at disposal, I shall refer primarily to Danish folklore because that is what I know best, but the folklore of other European regions might have served the purpose equally well - as for other parts of the world, my knowledge is insufficient.

1. Runes

I shall begin with the runes, which were the first letters known in these parts. It was assumed at one time that they had been regarded as instruments of magic already at the time when they were in common use, i. e., down to the 13th or 14th century, but more recent investigations indicate that that was an unwarranted assumption. I am not qualified to take a stand on that issue, but it is evident that they had acquired this reputation by the 16th century, i. e., at a time when they had already for centuries been an arcane art. A theme known from numerous ballads recorded from then on tells of the use of runes as love magic. A woman is given something to eat or touch upon which runes have been written, or a stick inscribed with runes is secretly placed in her mantle, or runes are written on a bridge she has to cross. She is thus compelled to seek the bower of her admirer the following night, completely forgetful of propriety and virtue. This "casting of runes" is usually regarded as evil and the sorcerer as disreputable, but the spell does lead to a happy union in some ballads.

There is a characteristic change from the actual use of runes in earlier times to this poetic theme: the emphasis has shifted to the *act of writing* and to the *letters* themselves, whereas nothing is ever said about the *texts* of the spells. What we find here is the viewpoint of outsiders, people to whom the writing with runes is a mystery in itself.

There are parallel phenomena in later times. In our handwritten and printed collections of charms and spells, which date from the 17th century onwards, one finds runes as well as Greek and Hebraic letters here and there. The underlying idea seems to be that ordinary letters are too profane, not powerful enough for the special needs of magic. The use of incomprehensible words and strings of letters, of German and Latin phrases, of red ink, of special ways of writing, of rituals associated with the writing etc. undoubtedly serve similar purposes. This seems to reflect a transitional attitude towards writing: on the one hand, the belief of the illiterate in the power of the written word is retained; on the other, profane writing is well known - the belief therefore has to be associated with a *special* sort of writing. My knowledge of learned magic is negligible, but my impression is that it is based on the same attitude.

2. Charms and spells

Also the letters regarded as ordinary have, however, frequently been used for magical purposes. There are many inscriptions from Antiquity and later of the entire alphabet in Greek, Latin and runic letters, and these inscriptions are generally assumed to be magical. The underlying idea would then be that the alphabet in its entirety potentially contains all conceivable words, including the secret names of celestial and infernal entities. The expression in the Book of Revelations 1,8 and 22,13, "I am Alpha and Omega" (i. e., the beginning and the end, the first and last letters of the Greek alphabet), may be taken to mean "the sum total of knowledge"; these two letters are still used in Roman Catholic liturgy as a sign for God. But the alphabet may also be used for more mundane purposes. Thus, one may write all the letters of the alphabet on a piece of paper which is cut into small bits, mixed with a chopped-up hard boiled egg laid on Good Friday and given to a child just before he begins school. This practice, which has been recorded in Southern Germany, will help the child acquire learning. A more common practice, known since Antiquity, is to give children cakes formed as letters or cakes in which letters have been inscribed.

The number of magical formulas known from folklore is vast. Most of them have to be recited, or chanted in certain cases, but several, particularly those containing incomprehensible words or strings of letters or exotic signs, have to be written down to be effective. Some of them, e. g. those used for love magic, are written with blood. These formulas may be used to "bind" fevers or diseases, to protect against enemies, thieves, dangerous animals, venomous snakes, bees or conflagrations, to blunt the enemy's weapons, to make one "hard", i. e. proof against bullets, etc. Written formulas are carried somewhere about the body or they are cut to pieces and eaten; some formulas are to be burned, buried or destroyed in other ways, on the theory that what happens to the formula also happens to the danger against which it is directed. An example: diseases and fevers are often conceived of as demons. One cure is to write a word like ABRACADABRA or KALAMARIS on a piece of paper which is hung around the patient's neck. Day by day, one letter is cut off and given the patient to eat, or it is thrown into the fire or burned or given to a black hen to eat. When all letters are gone, the fever is gone. The assumption clearly is that the demon is somehow bound to or embodied in the formula, which is turned into a physical object capable of being handled when it is written down. The process of writing then becomes an act of binding. As for the formula in question, also another principle is at work, that of performing an act backwards or counter-clockwise. This principle counteracts or dissipates the force associated with the normal procedure. Thus, the act of reading the Lord's Prayer backwards is an invocation of the Devil; the same is naturally true of the black mass.

3. Reading as a means of controlling supernatural powers

The techniques for mastering the demons of fevers and diseases, which are undoubtedly of pre-Christian origin, were analogically transferred to the sphere of Christianity many centuries ago.

Numerous charms and spells contain more or less well preserved fragments of medieval benedictions (usually in questionable Latin), and even if they have no such element they often end with the three crosses indicating the formula, "In the name of the Father and of the Son and of the Holy Ghost". The liturgy of the Roman Catholic church includes a number of benedictions, not only of human beings and their activities, but also of domestic animals, food, crops, buildings and other objects. The theology behind this may have been respectable enough, but the finer points of theology have a tendency to get lost in folk religion. Benedictions are rather conceived of as acts of power in which divine protection is not merely invoked, but *forced* into service; the distinction between religion and magic is not always as clear as a good Christian would prefer it to be. It is assumed that most of the benedictions which have been preserved in our collections of charms and spells represent the handicraft of monks and priests who lost their jobs at the Reformation. Their activity may have been a deplorable development from the point of view of the Reformers, but it was a strengthening of the arsenal of the folk healers. They made collections of powerful benedictions and prayers to be read against this or that, a practice that has continued almost down to the present.

Blessing was not the only prerogative of the clergymen. Exorcism is part of the old ritual of baptism and besides, there are special rituals of exorcism to be used for the salvation of people possessed by demons. Both benedictions and exorcisms are *read*, recited from books, a fact which has occupied the imagination of laymen for centuries. Benedictions might be found in the common prayer books, but where could the really powerful exorcisms be found and how did one learn to use them? Our folklore has it that this art was taught at the Black School at Wittenberg. In other parts of Europe, Salamanca is mentioned as the seat of this sinister school; the Freemasons, who were believed to be sorcerers, had theirs at Venice. Some clergymen went to such schools to study the arts of laying ghosts, of banning devils and of making infernal powers work for them, but at the peril of losing their souls. The Devil would take them in the end unless they were very holy or clever, or both. There are numerous legends about this.

The books containing the secret formulas of the black art have several names in popular tradition, e. g. the Sixth and Seventh Books of Moses or the Book of Solomon, but the most common name by far is that of Cyprianus, who was a sorcerer according to an early Christian legend. Once he tried to get the holy Justina into his power, but failed; his demons told him that she was protected by Christ, whose power was greater than theirs. When he heard this he burned his books of sorcery and was baptized, later to become a bishop of great holiness himself. Despite the fact that he burned his books, a great many collections of magical formulas carry his name. It is said that they are written with blood, that the owner of such a book goes to Hell at death unless he gets rid of it first, that it is useless to throw it away or burn it because it always returns unmolested to its owner, and that the only recourse is to sell it at a lower price than that for which it was bought. It furnishes its owner with great power, but if an unauthorized person reads it, unmanageable devils appear and all kinds of calamities happen unless the rightful owner returns in time to read the formulas backwards - a theme known from the tale of *The Magician and his Pupil*, but also from numerous legends.

The reading of exorcisms is a common motif in popular legends. It is thought of as a physical act. In one legend, e. g., the clergyman is called to the inn because one of those present discovers that a stranger with whom his comrades are playing cards is really the Devil - his left foot is a hoof. The clergyman arrives with his book, bores a tiny hole in the came surrounding the window pane and *reads* the Devil through that hole; naturally, there is a terrible stench of sulphur afterwards and the local people give up the sin of cardplaying. In another legend, a farm or manor-house is haunted by a ghost. A clergyman is called and begins to read, but the ghost "strikes the book from him". The same happens to the second clergyman and finally there is nothing for it but to call an old, strange priest. When he starts reading, the ghost cries, "You once stole a loaf", but the priest answers, "I was poor then" and throws a penny to the ghost. His debt is thus paid and his sin atoned for, so that he is without guilt and therefore able to "read the ghost down", i. e., into the ground. It is said in other versions of the legend that the ghost strikes the first two books from him, but that the third book is too strong for it. This quantification of the power of reading is a characteristic feature of folklore. It is said in a tale about a man who went to the University to be a student of divinity that he passed the first examination and the second one too, but the third one was too much for him, as if it had been a stone too big to lift.

4. The pact with the Devil

Mortal men have consorted with beings of the nether world since time immemorial. We saw how Cyprianus the sorcerer conjured them in his attempt to ensnare the Christian virgin. In the Middle Ages, the notion of a compact with the Devil developed; but it seems to be to the Renaissance that we must turn for the belief that the contract had to be *in writing*. This testifies to an increase in the use of writing and a corresponding loss of confidence in the given word. The theme is developed in the chapbook of *Doctor Faustus*, which appeared in German in 1587, in Danish the following year and in English a few years later. We know his story principally from Goethe's treatment, but numerous other writers have been attracted by the theme both before and after him and even a few imitations have also appeared. One of them relates of the Duke of Luxemburg who became the marshal of France but was thrown into the Bastille in 1659. Soon after a booklet appeared in which it was said that he had signed a compact with the Devil to get out of his prison; this book also appeared in Danish. Tales about such compacts are well known in the folklore of later centuries, but it is perhaps less well known that several people, usually men driven to despair by their poverty, actually tried to imitate Faustus and the Duke by drawing up contracts in which they promised their souls to the Devil in return for money. Unfortunately, their contracts were found in some cases and the culprits were easy to apprehend since their names had to be in the text. The first known Danish case of this kind is from 1634, but there was a veritable craze in the 1720's. A few decades later, however, the attitude had changed completely. Where the University - which was the court in such cases - recommended execution of the sinner in 1634 and some still recommended this course in the 1720's, the very notion of a pact with the Devil had come to be regarded as ridiculous in the higher academic and clerical circles a generation later. In folklore, however, the idea persisted, undoubtedly because it fitted in with the common belief in the power of the written word as a means of establishing contact with supernatural beings. Naturally, the pact had to be written with the writer's own blood. This created a bond between the writer and the paper on which the contract was written. It is probably of significance that blood was believed to be the seat of the soul, which was the merchandise the Devil was after.

5. Writing in Heaven

After having explored the relations between writing and the nether world we must turn to the higher world as well. Here we find two ancient themes, both of which are reflected in folklore in various forms. One concerns the writing *in* Heaven, the other the messages sent *from* Heaven in written form. In both themes, writing expresses the power and permanency of the divine will.

In the Book of Revelations, the *Book of Life* is mentioned (3,5). It seems to be identical with the book sealed with seven seals which is described further on (ch. 5). The contents of that book are not mentioned there, but it may be inferred that it contains the names of those who have consigned themselves to God. It is further implied that the names of sinners are struck from the list. In Christian tradition, this theme takes the form that Michael the Archangel, who is otherwise in charge of the scales on which the souls of the dead are weighed, enters our names in this book. A curious shift in emphasis may then be observed. The book belongs to Eternity and this is taken to mean "forever" or "since the dawn of time". What is written in Eternity is itself eternal: it has always existed and will always exist; but this means that our fate is always already determined. Nothing happens but that which is "written". In this conception, which gives rise to a sort of fatalism (the agreement of which with Christian doctrine may be open to question), writing is not merely recording, but determining and shaping.

This celestial bookkeeping has its infernal counterpart, but naturally a ridiculous counterpart, since the Devil is God's ape: devils record our sins as assiduously as angels record our good deeds. A medieval legend tells of a man who had become so holy that he could see the devils wherever they were at work. They were particularly busy in churches during mass because many sinners paid too little attention to the Sacrament or even thought unholy thoughts. One devil registered so many sins on a piece of parchment that it was completely filled. He then took it between his teeth to stretch it - a situation known from many fresco paintings - but it slipped so that he banged his head against the beam behind him. The holy man laughed at this, but laughing in church is a sin and he lost his faculty of seeing devils right away.

It is an ancient belief in the Near East that gods send us their messages in the form of writing. One well-known example is that of the writing on the wall mentioned in the Book of Daniel (ch.

5), but a far more important one is that of the Ten Commandments which were written on the two stone tablets God handed to Moses on Mount Sinai. In Hellenistic times, the belief that divine messages might take the form of letters fallen from Heaven spread throughout the Roman empire. Such letters are also mentioned in the Middle Ages. They were copied and when printing was invented they were also printed and sold by the thousands. In letters of this kind, God enjoins the reader to obey the Ten Commandments, to go to Church every Sunday etc. In return, the reader is promised protection against wounds, nose-bleeding, inflammation and other ailments. Copies of such letters were carried by soldiers, by women in childbirth and by others in dangerous situations. Some of the copies still extant carry the marks of prolonged use.

6. The Bible

No kind of writing is holier than the Holy Writ itself in European folklore. The Church teaches that it is "inspired by God", but, as was said, the finer points of theology do not survive in oral tradition: the Bible was *written* by God, which means that it is a repository of useful power. Quotations from the Bible may be written on slips of paper which are then carried as amulets to make the carrier proof against wounds in the same way as letters fallen from Heaven, or they are eaten as remedies against diseases, immured in houses as protection against fire etc. Quotations from the Book of Psalms and the Book of Revelations have been most frequently used. The same practice has been analogically transferred to hymn books and other religious literature. To mention but one example: in former times, people feared that unbaptized children might be taken by the elves, since they were heathen, i. e., not members of the Christian community. But holy letters were a strong protection against the elves and consequently a leaf from the hymn book might be put in the cradle.

Even well educated people have retained the belief in the special power of the Holy Writ down to the present. Two examples may illustrate this: it has been a common practice in fundamentalistic circles always to have a bowl filled with slips of paper containing scriptural quotations. One would take a slip at random or offer the bowl to a visitor with the same purpose. Or the Bible itself may be used as an oracle: the seeker of divine guidance will open the Book at random and place a finger on the page without looking. The verse one's finger has chosen will then be God's finger pointing at one's own self in the same way as the slip of paper taken at random from the bowl. These practices still testify to the age-old belief that the writing is identical with the writer. Again, we are faced with the problem of distinguishing religious practice from magic: what is the difference between the use of the Bible as an oracle and the use of an Ouija board to receive messages from the dead? In both cases, writing is a means of receiving a message from the Beyond.

7. Discussion

So much for the evidence. The presenting of that was the easy part in spite of the amount of material; but I feel that I also have an obligation to make at least a stab at the problem of interpretation.

The examples have been taken from different places and different periods. One must reckon with the possibility that they do not constitute a uniform picture. Still, I have tried to arrange my examples so as to illustrate a line of development in the following way:

The use of magical runes as a ballad theme testifies to a situation in which a certain form of writing is known to exist, but the poets do not know it at first hand. Their attitude reflects the viewpoint of the illiterate - or so I think. The writing itself, the very letters, are seen as magical. The effect is not associated with the text of the writing, but with the writing as such.

At a later stage, the phenomenon of writing is more widely known. The old belief in the magical power of writing is retained, but it has had to be transferred to some *special* writing because ordinary writing has lost its nimbus; it is used by too many. Those who retain this old belief are on a constant search for ways of imbuing it with the magical power they still associate with writing. This situation, which I should like to characterize as "half-literacy", also seems to be the background of learned magic.

At a still later stage, most of the belief in the magic of writing has been lost, but traces still linger on within the framework of a recognized form of religion. The ancient belief, that God speaks to those who are ready to listen, assumes an oracular form which must still be characterized as magical. It is of course associated with the sort of games in which the random element of chance is read as an expression of divine will.

What appears to me to be the most characteristic feature of the folklore about writing is that writing is interpreted as a physical act of power. Why should this be so? Let me hazard a guess: we all reason by analogy when confronted with unknown phenomena. The illiterate do the same thing. When we hear speech, we see the speaker at the same time or we have other means of knowing that he or she is physically present. If a text is read aloud, analogical reasoning leads to the conclusion that the speaker must somehow be present in the text, be it recorded on paper, a coin, a stone tablet or some other material object. It is well known that people have reacted strongly in our time to voices recorded on grammophone records and tapes. The speaker has been entrapped in these mechanical devices.

Techniques of an analogous kind have been known since the dawn of history and probably much longer. They are known as magic and there are two principal forms (which often function together): one may produce a likeness, an effigy, of the being one wishes to influence, or one may base one's magic on something that belongs to that being, such as blood, nail parings or bits of clothing. As far as I can see, the illiterate or half-literate interpret the technique of writing in analogy with this.

Here the power of the *name* plays a special role. It is a property in the same way as the blood, nail parings, bits of clothing etc. used in sympathetic magic. If I know the name of a person, an animal or a supernatural entity, I possess a certain power over that being. This is where we may profit from what we heard yesterday about the power of rhetoric. Writing is - I submit - interpreted by the illiterate as a particularly powerful version of speaking, a form of rhetoric in which the being one wants to influence becomes physically bound to the medium one writes upon.

Such a belief in the power of rhetoric is hardly possible in modern societies and we find it difficult to understand that it has ever existed. I should like to offer some comments on that as well. Let me suggest that speaking is an act of creating. When we speak, we shape our own conception of the world, and that of others, too. At least we try. It is a constant struggle to obtain and retain this power of defining the world. But if my conception of the world is fixed by some agency beyond my control, my speaking has no power. To mention a single example: I might want to give you an impression of myself to suit me, but I cannot. All kinds of facts about me are on record already: when and where I was born, who my parents were, what my given name is, where I went to school, my military, criminal and academic career, if any, my wife/wives and children, the state of my bank account etc. I have no control of these date which set very strict limits to how I can present myself. This explains, I think, why we find it difficult to understand the attitude of the illiterate towards the phenomena of speaking and writing. We do not ourselves experience the power invested in these acts and we consistently fail to see how the past has to be a reflection of the present in illiterate cultures (it still is to some extent even in our own culture, a fact rarely recognized).

What I am driving at is this: it would be a mistake to think of the illiterate in negative terms, as people who have *not* received a certain kind of training - all negative definitions are inherently bad. They should be thought of in positive terms instead, as people who interpret this technique, which is familiar to us, in analogy with other techniques which are familiar to them.

MAGICAL FORMULAS from F. Ohrt: *Danmarks Trylleformler II*, Cph. 1921.

1. *A b a d e p g p y̵t † 2 A t p t ß x*
(write this in your hand and touch a girl; she will love you)

2. *abbaraspaa   abburapaa   abburapua*
(against toothache. Write and carry on your head 1 day; then burn it)

3.

Abracadabra	or Abracadabra
Abracadabr	bracadabra
Abracadab	racadabra
Abracada	acadabra
Abracad	cadabra
Abraca	adabra
Abrac	dabra
Abra	abra
Abr	bra
Ab	ra
A	a

(several procedures, as explained in the text; used against several diseases and fevers, not least the local form of malaria, "kolden")

4. *Agata x Sagata x Amen*
(against "worms" in your teeth; write on butter and bread)

5. *Ara havardur vigga disa*
(write your name with blood and put the paper under his pillow while saying this three times; he will love you)

6. *4 antus et alaus refartus Imini fartris Triliot Spieritus*
    sanctus Knal † artus knal fartris colatris amen †††
(found in cowshed on the island of Funen, placed in a beam so that all cows had to pass under it. Prevents them from losing their calves)

7. *† dufa † fadia † aba † franest † pene † pliata †*
    i Navn nominem
(write and carry; no one can shoot you)

8. *HEBER † NABI † QAVL † HASE †*
(write on strip of new parchment which is wound round the patient's right arm on the first Sunday of a new moon before sunrise; the parchment is sewn with a strip of leather; the letters must turn inwards and must be protected from water. To be carried a year and a day, afterwards to be cut off and burnt. Useful against epilepsy if done while praying to God for mercy and giving alms to the poor in the name of Jesus)

9. *Inri Rufi*
(binds a shotgun if you look fixedly at it while saying *Inri Rufi hold*
- you may free it again by saying *Inri Rufi løs*)

10. *Omigion Argion Tara Gramaton*

11.   SATOR
       AREPO
       TENET
       OPERA
       ROTAS
(write on a piece of cheese and give to those you suspect of theft; the thief cannot eat it. The formula, which contains the letters of the words PATER NOSTER, is a so-called magical quadrangle, it contains the same elements whichever way it is read)

12. *Rojse, sampis, Rabie*
(write in your left hand with blood taken from the left ear of a black cat; you will win at all games).

Bibliography

Bächtold-Stäubli, Hanns (1927-1942) (ed.) *Handwörterbuch des deutschen Aberglaubens*, I-X. Berlin.

Bæksted, Anders (1952) *Målruner og troldruner. Runemagiske studier.* Copenhagen.

Grundtvig, Svend & al (1853-1976) *Danmarks gamle Folkeviser*, I-XII. Copenhagen.

Henningsen, Gustav (1969) Trolddom og hemmelige kunster. In Axel Steensberg (ed.) *Dagligliv i Danmark 1620-1720.* Copenhagen, 161-196.

Ohrt, Ferdinand (1917-1921) *Danmarks Trylleformler*, I-II. Copenhagen & Kristiania.

Wildhaber, Robert (1955) *Das Sündenregister auf der Kuhhaut* (FF Communications No. 163). Helsinki.

Writing and the Other: Travellers' Literacy, or Towards an Archaeology of Orality

Michael Harbsmeier

Much has been said and written on the effects of writing and literacy on the perception of the past. Much less is known about how writing has shaped the ways in which other, contemporary cultures have been perceived by those relying on this means of communication. In this paper I want to discuss the when and the how of the process through which writing and literacy themselves came to be perceived in early modern Europe as a most important distinctive feature of our own as opposed to some other cultures and societies. Of course most writers of travel accounts have been aware of the fact that some of the societies they visited and described did get along without the written word. But it was only from early modern times onwards that some European travellers discovered and perceived the consequences and implications of this distinction in their descriptions of what then came to be known as savage, primitive, preliterate or oral societies.

I. Travellers' Literacy

652 years ago Ibn Khaldun was born in Tunis.[1] But there are other reasons than this for recalling what he thought about the sociological significance of writing and books. Khaldun had no doubts about the intimate relationship between writing and power.

---

[1] This paper was originally given on Khaldun's birthday, May 27th 1984. Without a grant from the Danish Council for the Humanities as well as many discussions with colleagues at the Centre for Comparative Cultural Research of the University of Copenhagen, it would never have seen the light of day.

It should be known - he writes in his *Muqaddimah* or Introduction to History - that both 'the sword' and 'the pen' are instruments for the ruler to use in his affairs. However, at the
beginning of a dynasty, so long as its people are occupied in establishing power, the need for 'the sword' is greater than for
'the pen'. In that situation, 'the pen' is merely a servant and
agent of the ruler's authority, whereas 'the sword' contributes
active assistance. The same is the case at the end of a dynasty
when its group feeling weakens and its people decrease in
number under the influence of senility. The dynasty then
needs the support of the military. The dynasty's need of the
military for the purpose of protection and defence is as strong
then as it was at the beginning of (the dynasty) for the purpose
of getting established. In these two situations, 'the sword' thus
has the advantage over 'the pen'. At that time, the military
have the higher rank. They enjoy more benefits and more
splendid fiefs. In mid-term of the dynasty, the ruler can to
some degree dispense with 'the sword'. His power is firmly established. His only remaining desire is to obtain the fruits of
royal authority, such as collecting taxes, holding (property), ex-
celling other dynasties, and enforcing the law. The pen is
helpful in all that. Therefore the need for using it increases.
The swords stay unused in their scabbards, unless something
happens and they are called upon to repair a breach. In this
situation, the men of the pen have more authority. They oc-
cupy a higher rank. They enjoy more benefits and greater
wealth and have a closer and more frequent and intimate contact with the ruler. At such a time, the wazirs and the military
can be dispensed with. They are kept away from the intimate
circle of the ruler and have to beware of his moods. (1967: 213)

Ibn Khaldun's theory of the functional interrelationships between the pen and the sword is of course an integral part of his
general sociology of the dynamic interaction between towns,
tribes and dynasties in the Muslim world. Like other crafts, writing is linked to urban civilization, and only develops along with
"the social organization, civilization and competition for luxu-
ries" generally characteristic of the urban islands in a tribal sea.

Claude Lévi-Strauss, in his better-known 'Leçon d'Écriture' in
Tristes Tropiques, is no less interested in the relationship between writing and power. But whereas Ibn Khaldun considered
the pen and the sword as essentially alternative instruments for

the exercise of power under changing conditions, Lévi-Strauss tries to show that the very institution of writing itself is inextricably linked to power, inequality and exploitation:

> If we want to correlate the appearance of writing with certain other characteristics of civilisation, we must look elsewhere. The one phenomenon which has invariably accompanied it is the formation of cities and empires: the integration into a political system, that is to say, of a considerable number of individuals, and the distribution of those individuals into a hierarchy of castes and classes. Such is, at any rate, the type of development which we find, from Egypt right across to China, at the moments when writing makes its debuts; it seems to favor rather the exploitation than the enlightenment of mankind... If my hypothesis is correct, the primary function of writing, as a means of communication, is to facilitate the enslavement of other human beings. The use of writing for disinterested ends, and with view to satisfactions of the mind in the fields either of science or of the arts, is a secondary result of its invention - and may even be no more than a way of reinforcing, justifying or dissimulating its primary function. (Lévi-Strauss 1976: 292)

Ibn Khaldun was sure that the sword came first, and was different from the pen. Lévi-Strauss seems to be arguing, on the contrary, that the pen itself is a kind of sword, that writing in other words is at the very basis of exploitation, inequality and repression, of caste and class. For this reason, Jacques Derrida has entitled his justly famous critical comments on Lévi-Strauss' "Leçon d'écriture" in his *De la Grammatologie* "La violence de la lettre" (1967: 149 ff). Ibn Khaldun was well aware of the fact that the tribal Bedouin people were illiterate: "They are not able to read and write" (1967: 327). But he also claimed that the "group feeling" and "social cohesion" which he saw as the foundation of the leadership and superiority of the tribal dynasties and thereby of power were themselves in no way dependent on literacy and writing: on the contrary, literacy and writing tended to deprive people of the very basis of their strength and superiority (Gellner 1981: 26). For Lévi-Strauss the exact opposite seems to be true: for him it is the weakness, fragility and prepolitical nature of the power of the Nambikwara chief which is threatened by the introduction of paper and pen. Writing, according to Lévi-Strauss, brings with it power, hierarchy and exploitation. The Nambikwara neither read nor write: they are preliterate, as are the tribes of the deserts. But what appears to be a reason for strength and superiority in the deserts emerges as weakness and vulnerability in the Amazonas. Pen and sword arrive hand in hand in the New World, where they confront preliterate societies lacking both. In the Maghreb they alternate, the one entering the towns only when the other has temporarily left.

For Lévi-Strauss the relationship between societies with and without writing is an external one. Writing and violence come, as does history in general according to Lévi-Strauss, from the outside. Ibn Khaldun, on the contrary, describes the shifting internal relationships of pen to sword in a world where desert and town, tribes and civilizations interact with one another according to the regular pattern of the rise and fall of succeeding tribal dynasties. Ibn Khaldun describes one world and the interaction of modes of communication within this one world. Lévi-Strauss describes two worlds, two radically different modes of communication: one from which violence, power and writing are absent and where the spoken word, orality and authenticity alone are present. Between Ibn Khaldun and Lévi-Strauss a New World has been discovered: the world of orality, preliteracy, non-violence and authenticity. Ibn Khaldun has no conception of such a world, and indeed according to Jacques Derrida it is nothing but an imaginary product of the ethnocentrism of alphabetical writing and logocentric metaphysics.

In the search for the historical origins, if such there are, of this New World of orality and authenticity, Derrida and others often go back as far as Plato and his theory of writing (e.g. Ong 1982: 79 ff). But if we restrict ourselves to those texts which not only discuss modes of communication theoretically, but in which the distinction between literacy and orality itself determines the way in which another culture and society is both perceived and described, we might perhaps more profitably look at another French traveller to the New World of America: at Jean de Léry and his *Histoire d'un voyage fait en la Terre du Brésil*, first published in 1578 (Léry 1580), which has directly influenced Claude Lévi-Strauss. According to Jean de Léry writing was widespread throughout the Old World of Europe, Asia and Africa, and the absence of writing was for him one of the distinctive features which marked off the otherness of the fourth continent, of the American savages. His "Writing Lesson" deserves to be quoted in full:

As for writing, be it sacred or profane, not only do they not know what it is; but what is more, since they have no characters to signify anything, when at first I was in their country to learn their language and I wrote down a few sentences and then read them out to them afterwards, they, thinking this was some form of sorcery, said to one another: "Is it not a marvel that this man, who yesterday could not say a word in our language, by virtue of this paper he has, and which causes him to speak so, is now understood by us?" This is the same opinion as the savages of the Spanish Isle entertained of the Spaniards who were there first: for he who has written the history of that time says this: "The Indians, knowing that the Spaniards, without seeing or speaking to one another, but merely by sending letters from one place to another, by this means could hear one another, believed that they either had the spirit of prophecy, or that the letters spoke. With the result," he tells us, "that the savages, fearing to be discovered and surprised in wrongdoing, were by this means held so strictly to the path of duty that they no longer dared lie to nor rob the Spaniards." For which reason I say that, for whosoever cares to expand on this matter, a fine subject presents itself to him, allowing him as much to praise and exalt the art of writing, as to show how the peoples who inhabit these three corners of the world, Europe, Asia and Africa, have more reason to praise God than the savages of this fourth corner called America: for while they can communicate in no way amongst themselves except by word of mouth, we on the contrary have this advantage, that without moving from one spot, by means of writing and the letters we send, we can declare our secrets to whomsoever we please, be they as far distant as the other end of the world. Thus, apart from the knowledge we gain from books, in which the savages appear to be completely lacking, this invention of writing that we have, of which they are also entirely deprived, must also be numbered among the ranks of the singular gifts that the men of these parts have received from God. (Léry 1580: 231-232)

Jean de Léry thus not only acknowledges, as many earlier writers had done, the fact that these American savages could neither read nor write, but takes this fact to be one of the most distinctive features of the Otherness of the Indians, setting them apart not only from the people of Europe, but also from those of Asia and

Africa. According to Michel de Certeau's analysis of de Léry's text (Certeau 1975; see also Certeau 1980), de Léry was thus among the first to develop the idea of orality as part of the definition of the object of what was later to become anthropology. De Léry is far from being in agreement with Lévi-Strauss' view of the disingenuous conspiracy of power and writing. But like his famous follower and compatriot de Léry tries to describe a new world, the essential otherness of which results from the absence of literacy and writing as instruments of communication. For both de Léry and Lévi-Strauss this absence is tantamount to the presence of the very object of their anthropological discourse. For both of them the absence of writing among the savages is one of the very reasons for their writing about them. This, incidentally, also seems to apply to Sir Edward Evans-Pritchard, who, in his famous book on *Witchcraft, Oracles and Magic among the Azande,* writes as follows:

> Azande often say: 'The poison oracle does not err, it is our paper. What your paper is to you, the poison oracle is to us,' for they see in the art of writing the source of a European's knowledge, accuracy, memory of events, and predictions of the future. The oracle tells a Zande what to do at every crisis of life. It reveals his enemies, tells him where he may seek safety from danger, shows him hidden mystic forces, and discloses past and future. Truly a Zande cannot live without his *benge.* To deprive him of that would be to deprive him of life itself. (Evans-Pritchard 1937: 263)

Herodotus has often been claimed as the father of ethnology. But as François Hartog has shown in a comparison of Herodotus with precisely Lévi-Strauss and Jean de Léry, Herodotus never distinguishes between his own and other cultures in terms of a distinction between literacy and orality:

> Whether writing is valorized as a 'singular gift' (de Léry) or depreciated as 'perfidy' (Lévi-Strauss) the writing lesson will in either case play for ethnology something of the role of the primal scene. Herodotus, on his side, escapes this configuration and, from this point of view, he is therefore not the father of ethnology. In the last analysis the writing of de Léry 'invents' the savage, as the account of Herodotus 'invents' the barbarian; and the barbarian is not the savage, since the barbarian, unlike the savage, can write. The Persian can write, and

has made of writing, even to the extent of bodily mutilation, a writing of power; now, the Persian is the very type of the barbarian. The Egyptian can write, and yet he is a barbarian. If savagery and writing, then, are in opposition to one another, barbarism and writing go very well together. Writing, then, is for the ethnologist the true measure of savage speech, yet at the same time there is something of this speech which always eludes him: Michel de Certeau demonstrates this very well in his discussion of Tupi speech, which 'figures as a missing jewel in the casket of narrative'. Now, this speech, intangible as it is, precisely in so far as it is a lost object, is what perpetuates writing indefinitely, what produces the ethnological text. Such is not the case with Herodotus, for whom the speech of the other is not at once the object of discourse and the profound moving force behind the same discourse: it is not that which makes him write. (Hartog 1980: 246-247)

Living in a world "between literacy and orality" (Hartog), neither Herodotus nor Ibn Khaldun made literacy and writing part of the definition of his own society as against some other. Oral and written modes of communication existed for them side by side without excluding each other; on the contrary they constantly interacted and came into conflict with one another. With Jean de Léry and Lévi-Strauss, the situation has changed. Literacy has become a mode of excommunication, a distinctive mark of a civilization that has become conscious of literacy as one of its most important achievements, conscious too of the price it has had to pay for this achievement: the loss of the authenticity, presence and indivisibility of the spoken word. This difference between Herodotus and Ibn Khaldun on the one hand and de Léry and Lévi-Strauss on the other can also be seen as a difference between *restricted* and *universal literacy*. With restricted literacy other criteria than the use of writing as a means of communication are primary in differentiating "us" from "the others". Literacy is here subordinated to criteria of language, kinship or religion ("people of the Book", for example), geography or whatever. Only a closed world of universal literacy, a world, that is, which can think of itself as a literate world as opposed to other preliterate ones - only such a world was able to discover and invent new worlds in terms of preliteracy and orality. The transition from restricted to universal literacy in this sense thus has as a symptom, as it were, the production and proliferation of texts describing other cultures and societies in terms of other modes of communication. It can be claimed to some extent that universal literacy depends on the production and reproduction of such images of the other.

To summarize: Herodotus and Ibn Khaldun saw the pen and the sword, the oral and the written, as distinct but interdependent. Following Jean de Léry, Lévi-Strauss discovered the sword in the pen by postulating a new world characterized by the absence of both. My contention is, then, that the transition from the first to the second kind of literacy, from restricted to universal literacy considered as modes of communication and excommunication, can be reconstructed through an analysis of one of its written, or, in the present case, printed symptoms: the texts in which other cultures are seen as other, as oral or preliterate modes of communication. The remaining part of this paper is devoted to precisely this end. By means of a series of examples taken from early modern German travellers' accounts and descriptions of what would be described today as preliterate societies in Africa, Asia and America, I will attempt to describe a change in the travellers' perceptions and representations of their modes of communication.

II Towards an Archaeology of Orality

The German soldier Hans Staden, afterwards a powdermaker, was held captive for more than nine months by the same Tupinamba Indians visited by Jean de Léry at about the same time and described so elaborately in the book that he published twenty years later. Staden's account of his dramatic adventures among the "naked, man-eating, savage and ugly people of the New World", which was published in Marburg in 1557 with the active assistance of Professor Johannes Dryander, mentions only incidentally the absence of writing and books among the Indian cannibals. One day, preparations were being made to kill one of the Indian war captives, who, like Staden himself, had been a slave in the village for some time. The night before the cannibalistic celebration a storm tore off the roof of the captive's hut:

> Then the savages began to be angry with me, and said in their language *"Appo meiren geuppawy wittu wasu Imman* - the bad man, the wizard now makes the wind to come, for during the day he looked into the thunder-skins (*Donnerheude)"*, meaning the book which I had. And they said that I did it be-

cause the slave was our (the Portuguese) friend, and that I, perhaps, intended thereby to hinder the feast through bad weather. (1884: 85; Ch. XXXVI)

The "thunder-skins" was a book which the Indians had themselves taken from a Portuguese ship they had captured along with some French allies, and which they had given to Staden the day before.

Apart from this incident - yet another example of the magical power that oral man is so often said to attribute to books and letters - Staden never mentions the absence of books and writing. In fact he has no difficulty or hesitation whatsoever in rendering dialogues and conversations between himself and his savage hosts or among the Indians themselves. Often he even gives a transcription of the native words, as in the above example, or when he quotes their almost proverbial joking with the captives and slaves they are about to kill and eat:

It was night when we arrived...and they drew the canoes ashore, had made a fire, and then led me to it. There I had to sleep in a net which in their language they call *Inni*, which are their beds...The ropes which I had round my neck, they lashed to a tree above, and they lay during the night round about me, mocking me and calling me in their language *Schere inau ende* -'Thou art my bound Beast'. (1884: 57; Ch. XX)

Then, when he was taken into the Indians' fortified village:

...all the women ran to me, and struck me with their fists and pulled my beard, and spoke in their language: '*Sche innamme pepicke a e* '. That is as much as to say 'With this blow I revenge my friend, him whom those among whom thou hast been have killed'. (1884: 60; XXI)

On another occasion a huge cloud threatens the Indians in their boat, and they are afraid that they might not reach the coast before the storm breaks. So they ask Hans Staden:

'*Ne mungitta dee. Tuppan do Quabe, amanasu y an dee Imme Ranni me sis se*'. That is as much as to say 'speak with thy God, so that the great rain and wind may do us no harm'. I remained silent and made my prayer to God, as they demanded it from me, and said 'O thou almighty God, thou heavenly and earthly Lord, who from the beginning hast helped and hast heard those who among the godless call upon thy name, vouchsafe me thy mercy, so that I may perceive that Thou art still with me, and that the savage heathens may see, that Thou my God hast heard my prayer!' I lay bound in the canoe so that I could not turn round to see the weather, but they looked constantly behind them, beginning to say, '*Oque moa amanasu'*. That is, 'The great Tempest passeth away'. Then I raised myself a little and looking back, saw that the cloud had passed off, upon which I thanked God. (1884: 57-58; XX)

Elsewhere Staden is for the most part content with rendering the conversations, which were always in the Tupinamba tongue in his German translation. Most of the talk he reports is about cannibalistic issues, as when the chief Carima-cui tells him about a dream he has had and which has scared him much:

...and he called me to his hut and gave me to eat and then complained of it to me, and said, he had once been to war, and had captured a Portuguese, and had killed him with his own hands, and had eaten of him so plentifully, that his chest had ever since been delicate. And he declared that he would eat of no other. So now he had dreamt of me such a terrible dream that he thought he was also to die. Him also I bade be of good cheer, but he was to take care never to eat human flesh again. (1884: 80; XXXIV)

The distribution of the passages directly transcribed in the Tupinamba language throughout Staden's narrative is not random. In fact they only occur in Chapters 20 and 21, at that point of Staden's narrative when he has just been captured and is led to one of the native villages where he has to stay for nearly a year. The only exception is the passage we quoted to begin with, the episode with the magical book. Apart from this, only Staden's capture and entry into the cannibals' own village have moved him to express himself directly in the cannibals' own language. The linguistic exoticism of these passages thus has a simple psychological explanation: it is an expression of the dramatic character of Hans Staden's confrontation with the possibility of death at the hands of the naked, man-eating savages. This confrontation is of course the main theme of the book, which Staden only wrote, on his own as well as his editors' testimony, for the greater glory of Him who miraculously saved him from this terrible destiny:

> Kind reader! This, my navigation and travel, I have purposely described with brevity only to recount how I first fell into the hands of the barbarous people. Therewith to shew how mightily against all hope, the Helper in need, our Lord and God, has delivered me from out of their power....Now, many might say: 'Yes; were I to print all that during my life I have attempted and seen, it would make a big book.' It is true; in such manner, I should also be able to describe much more. But the case here is different. I have sufficiently, here and there, pointed out the object which induced me to write this little book, and thus we all owe to God praise and thanksgivings, that he has preserved us from the hours of our births to the present hours of our lives. (1884: 166-7)

Hans Staden's little book tells the story of how the Tupinamba treat their enemies twice. First, there is the narrative of his own dramatic adventure from which we have quoted so far. The second version is to be found in the other part of his book, which gives, in thirty-eight numbered chapters, a more systematic description of the country he visited and the customs of its inhabitants. The chapter headings take the form of questions, and there is good reason to believe that it was Professor Johannes Dryander who particularly urged Staden to provide this description and perhaps even formulated some of the questions himself. In this second part questions of language and communication are not mentioned at all. The longest chapter by far, and the one that is most lavishly illustrated with woodcuts, is the one on "How they blow their enemies to death and how they treat them", which renders the Indians' statements and proclamations in the context of their ritual cannibalism in plain German. The "static-descriptive" account of the naked and savage other is thus almost completely without linguistic exoticism.[2] Only the dramatic events leading to the hero's captivity, not the strange customs of the

---

[2] The only exception proves the rule: Chapter XXV of the second part deals with the fundamental question: "Why one enemy eats the other". My distinction between 'dynamic-narrative' and 'static-descriptive' passages, as well as my concern with linguistic exoticism are heavily indebted to Troubetzkoy 1980. See also Harbsmeier 1982.

other, give rise to any fascination with the other's mode of communication.

The same chapter of the second part of Staden's book, the one dealing with "how they treat their enemies" ends rather strangely. After concluding "All this I have seen and I have been there" (1884: 159; XXIX), Staden continues:

> They also cannot count any certain number beyond five; when they would count more, they point to their fingers and toes. If they desire to speak of any greater number, they point to four or five persons, as many fingers or toes as they want to express. (1884: 159)

It is surely not their mode of communication that made the Tupinamba appear strange and exotic to Hans Staden, Johannes Dryander, or the contemporary readers of this book.

I hope it has become clear by now that Hans Staden had no idea of orality whatsoever. But if we compare his rendering of native communication and communication with the natives with that of Jean de Léry, the contrast becomes even more striking. De Léry too describes what the Tupinamba used to say to their captives before putting them to death:

> 'Are you not of the people named *Margaias*, who are our foes? And have you not yourself killed and eaten some of our family and friends?' He, more composed than ever, answers in his own language (for the *Margaias* and the *Toupinenquins* understand one another) *'Pa, che tan tan, aiouca atoupaué* ': that is to say, 'Yes, I am very strong, and have indeed slaughtered and eaten several of them.' Then, to show more contempt for his enemies, putting his hands on his head, he exclaims: 'Oh, it is not something I have made up! Oh, how bold I have been in attacking and capturing your people, whom I have eaten so many many times!" - and other similar statements that he adds. For this reason too, the other will say to him that he has in mind there and then to slaughter him: 'Since you are now in our power, you will soon be killed by me, then *smoked* and eaten by all of us'. 'Very well,' he answers back (as resolved to be killed for his people as Regulus was constant in enduring death for his Roman republic), 'my family will also avenge me.' Further, in order to demonstrate that, although these barbarous peoples greatly fear natural death, nevertheless such prisoners, considering themselves happy to die thus publicly

in the midst of their enemies, care not in the least about doing so, I will adduce this example. (1580: 215-16)

This last comment clearly shows that the savage words and their meaning are just as much at the centre of de Léry's and his readers' attention as their actions and practices.

In the same vein, the dialogue between Jean de Léry and one of the Indians, which was later to become famous through Montaigne's development of the same theme, and in which the Indian wonders greatly about what makes these Europeans travel to places so far away from home, ends with the following remark:

That, briefly and truthfully, is the discourse which I heard from the very mouth of a poor American savage. (1580: 177)

One doesn't even have to refer to the entire chapter, in which de Léry gives his readers what almost amounts to a dictionary of the Tupinamba and Tupinquin language in the form of a systematic interrogation printed both in French and the native language, to see that linguistic exoticism and the otherness of the savage modes of expression and communication are a very central concern of de Léry's account.

Hans Staden knew their language just as well, to say the least. But he did not confront the savage way of life of the naked man-eaters of the New World of America in terms of meaning, expression and communication so much as in terms of action, practice, confrontation with death and miraculous salvation.

To judge from the number of editions and translations of his work, (Fouquet 1944) Hans Staden is by far the most widely read of all early modern German travellers. But a considerable number of lesser-known soldiers, doctors, sailors, adventurers and, as we shall see, priests and missionaries have also written about their experiences with faraway cultures and societies that we would describe today as preliterate. Few of these travellers, however, mastered the native languages as well as Hans Staden. This might explain much of how they perceived such other modes of communication and expression. But the very fact that knowledge of the native language was first felt to be a problem to be dealt with by just those travellers who, also for a number of other reasons, can be claimed to have developed a new sensitivity to modes of expression and communication confirms our argument concerning a change in the sensibility and perceptiveness of German travellers around the turn of the 17th/18th centuries.

Looking, as I have done, at the representations of modes of communication that can be found scattered through these travellers' texts, one can clearly see that until the end of the seventeenth century the literacy of all the German travellers was more like that of Hans Staden than that of Jean de Léry. Communication was mainly perceived as action, not as meaning. Almost all the travellers were impressed by the noisiness of the savages. If they quote them at all *verbatim*, it is mostly cases of the savages speaking directly to the traveller. Very often, however, the only words quoted directly in the native tongue are addressed to a figure that haunted contemporary consciousness, and in particular the texts of our travellers, to a surprising extent: the Devil. Often his name - Vitzli - Putzli or whatever - is the only native term mentioned at all. For the rest, the noisy savage utterances, which for the most part do not appear to have been perceived as articulate speech at all, are addressed to the dead, as in mourning or mortuary ritual, descriptions of which figure astonishingly frequently throughout our texts. In fact, I have not found a single instance before the end of the 17th century where a savage is simply reported as speaking to one of his fellow savages.

The exception proves the rule. Ulrich Schmiedel, whose report of his military expedition among some other South American Indian tribes was first published in 1567, actually goes so far as to mention a contract among some Indian tribes. But this contract had only one objective: to create an alliance so that together they were in a better position to kill the Christians in a surprise attack. Samuel Braun, to take another of the exceptions, in his account of his travels to Africa and America from 1624, relates that the people in Loango in West Africa engage in conversations while eating, despite the fact that they do not have proper chairs to sit on. He also directly quotes oral customs in connection with the audience regularly given by the king to all his people:

> The king comes out of his court only three or four times a year. He then gives anyone an audience and sits like the others, with only his *Manna Magiischy*, who, as soon as he pours out for the king, calls out to the people and says that all those who see the king drink shall die. Immediately they hear this, they fall down on their faces until he has drunk. Then they rise again and clap their hands together, saying in their lan-

guage *'Sackarella Sackarella Manna Loanga'*, which means 'the King of Loanga pleases us'. This lasts until it is night, when the king's warriors come with drums and horns, causing a great noise and tumult. If, however, someone inadvertently sees the king drink, he must die immediately. With this person's blood the king is anointed, as if thereby the king's honour, which would have been taken from him by those watching, were redeemed. I myself saw how the king's own nine-year-old child got up from the ground, fell on the arm of its father the king, perhaps out of love, and saw him drinking, whereupon *Manna Magiischy* said: 'This child must die.' This indeed happened: in the father's presence, the child's brain was beaten in and the *Manna Magiischy* anointed the king's arm with the blood of the slain child. (quoted from Jones 1983: 56-57)

Thus Samuel Braun, like Ulrich Schmiedel and Hans Staden, could only hear and understand the voices of savages when they meant death.

The same is true of Adam Brand, also called Isbrand, who wrote about his voyage overland to China in 1698. In his long description of some shamanistic Siberian tribes, all sorts of strange sounds and gestures, dance, trance and music, noise and movement figure very prominently. In only one instance does he quote what these people say. When they have killed a bear, an animal which they hold very much in esteem, they whisper into the dead bear's ears: "It was the Russians who did it". (Brand 1698: 73).

The best example of all to illustrate the tendency among 16th and 17th-century German travellers to describe savage communication as inarticulate noise addressed mainly to the Devil, the dead and those to be killed and eaten, is to be found in the manuscript of Josua Ultzheimer, written in 1610, but only published in printed form in this century (1971). Many different savage peoples from Africa, Asia and the New World are mentioned and described in this text; but common to them all is their apparent aversion to plain talk. Religious worship, according to Ultzheimer, is accompanied by "singing, bells, jumping and leaping" (1971: 78); they "weep for three months when mourning" (79); "man and wife sing to each other while giving birth to a child" (79); they will not even talk, "but make their wishes known to each other by whistling" (100); the cannibals' wives "sing and dance to tease their husbands' victims" (136). When political decisions are made, "they shriek and beat themselves on their breasts" (149). They behave "like the papists at mass, singing, ringing bells and clapping their hands all the time" (145) instead of uttering meaningful words. One thing is quoted directly in the native tongue. In connection with human sacrifice some African savages "first cut off the head" of their victim, "and then they cut him into pieces. These they leave on the ground saying: 'In the same way do we want to cut all the enemies of our king into pieces.' Then the people scream with loud voices *Sarramena ba oba Sarramena ba oba Sarramena ba oba*' while at the same time stamping on the ground. This means as much as: 'Might the king cut off the head of all enemies.'" (160-61)

For Ultzheimer communication among the savages is apparently nothing but noise and action. Even their sexual intercourse cannot do without it:

> The people bear nice, golden, neat, but thick bells - roughly as big as the egg of a dove - grown fixed to their manhood. They sound very lovely and are made very artfully. Of these they may have three, four or five between the flesh and the skin of their private member. (195-96)

Like almost all of the numerous Germans who sailed with the ships of the Dutch East India Company round the Cape of Good Hope to India and the Far East throughout the 17th century, Ultzheimer also tells us on several occasions how the savage idolaters talk directly to the Devil himself through their oracles:

> To conclude this description of Guinea, I cannot omit to say that, just as the Papists annually on Corpus Christi Day go around their fields and bless them against storms, so the Guineans annually gather together in each and every village on a certain day in April and make their *füttisse* or devil-images to honour their *füttisse* or false god, the Devil. These images are nothing but a heap of dirt squeezed together. In doing this, as stated above, they use almost the same kind of ceremonies as the Papists at their mass. When such *füttisse* are ready, they ask the Devil how the corn and other fruits will fare that year, what kind of foreign ships will arrive, what illnesses will occur, how their pregnant wives will give birth, and what sort of wars will arise. If there happens to be present a Christian who mocks the Devil or calls him a liar, or merely

contradicts the Blacks by ridiculing him, then the Devil is dead silent and says nothing more as long as the Christian is present. When they again ask and want to have an answer, he orders that the marked people (by whom he means the Christians, perhaps on account of Holy Baptism) should first be turned away and got rid of, or else he is not willing to say anything. If, however, the Christian is silent from the start or goes away, the Devil answers their questions through the heap of dirt. Sometimes things turn out as he has said, sometimes very differently. Afterwards they place such a *füttisse* here and there on their possessions in the fields. The fields are supposed to be protected by it, and none of them go and touch it; for whoever does so (apart from the Christians) dies immediately. (1971: 55; Jones 1983: 36)

The Devil's medium, the heap of dirt is mentioned in Ultzheimer alone, as are some other details, but the story of the Devil's oracle and its silence in the presence of Christians is told time and again by almost all of our travellers, as if to confirm that only the Devil himself can have any knowledge of the meaning of the savage word, which is thus forever inaccessible for good Christians.

But this was to change towards the end of the century, when we can trace the emergence of a new mode of perception of the other.

The priest and missionary, Wilhelm Johann Mueller, who published his account, *Die Africanische/ Auf der Guineischen Gold-Cust gelegene Landschafft Fetu*, in 1676, was rather uneasy about the secrecy surrounding the idolatrous savages' devil-oracles. For Mueller it is not the Devil alone, but also the heathen priests who try to hide the truth from their people as well as from Christian observers. Mueller tries in vain to attend one of their secret nightly encounters with Satan:

I have often asked the heathen priests - not out of idle curiosity, but solely in order to investigate the truth thoroughly - to take me with them when the false god was to be questioned; but I was not able to obtain permission, as they always refused, alleging that if they did so they would suddenly be killed and strangled. From this I drew the conclusion that these priests of Satan deal in nothing but lies and drag the poor common people around by the nose as they choose. (Mueller 1676: 58; Jones 1983: 164)

These heathen priests not only speak to the Devil; they also deceive their own people, lying to them and thus communicating with them. Mueller thus discovered an act of human communication behind the idolaters' interaction with the Devil. Thus he can compare the idolaters' ridiculous way of coping with the future through oracles with what everyone reading his book is familiar with from home:

> These and similar heathen customs used by the Fetu people in enquiring about future matters seem crazy, indeed ridiculous to us Christians, although they are no different from when, in the public market-place or in a conjuror's booth here in Europe, a comic entertainer performs, or when children play odds and evens in the streets. (1676: 63; Jones 1983: 166)

No wonder, then, that Mueller is also the first to develop his own 'writing lesson', which I will quote in full:

> They have a powerful memory. Although they can neither read nor write, they are able to retain fresh in their memory for a long time things which have happened. This memory turns out to be accurate, when one talks to them about the arrival of the Dutch at Moree, the conquest of the castle St. George D'El Mina, the building of this or that fort on the Guinea coast, and of native wars. Many of the old people are able to give a good account of these stories. They strengthen their memories by zealously repeating old stories; for since they often sit around idly all day, they talk to one another of past times. Young people and children listen to such discourse with avid ears, and absorb it in their hearts. In this way knowledge of past matters is always propagated. Many of them boast of their good memory. A distinguished merchant once told me: if we Christians were not able to read or write, they, the Blacks, would far surpass us; for although they had no books or writings, they knew how to work out in their head their trading account, which often ran into several thousands, and to retain it. (1676: 32-33; Jones 1983: 153-4)

Thus it is no accident that Mueller at the beginning of his description gives a list of the Fetu terms of insult, and concludes his book with a vocabulary of the Fetu language divided into twenty chapters ranging from 'On God and the Heathen Services' to 'Numeralia' from one to a thousand (1676: 288ff; Jones 1983: 269ff).

Our story of a change in the perception of the other can perhaps be most appropriately traced through the long series of descriptions of the Hottentots which are to be found as either the first or the last of the ethnographic, 'static-descriptive' passages in all the early modern German travel accounts of journeys to East India.

The very first accounts, by Balthasar Springer (1506) and Hans Mayr (1506), who sailed round the Cape with Portuguese ships in 1505-6, agree in mentioning a people without a language. In fact, that is the only thing they have to say about the Hottentots. For the next 150 years an increasing number of writing travellers merely confirm that the Hottentots indeed have neither language nor religion. With steadily increasing detail the travellers describe how the Hottentots sing and dance on the beaches at night, crying out 'Ho, ho, ho, he, he, he' to the moon, from which behaviour they reportedly have their name. Along with the stories of how they eat almost-raw intestines, only squeezing them clean with their fingers, how they use these same intestines as stinking decorations and also as a kind of wedding ring, reports on the extirpation of testicles and of their strange physical appearance, these descriptions consolidated into one of the most persistent and widespread ethnographic stereotypes of early modern Europe.

Towards the end of the 17th century, however, this stereotyped image gradually began to lose its hold on the travellers' minds. The image of the Hottentot began to change into something quite different. Processes of acculturation and other developments had changed both the Hottentot way of life and in particular the relationships of the (mainly Dutch) settlers with them so much that the old, often-quoted stories were increasingly felt to contradict actual practice and experience. And as more and more travellers could hardly avoid seeing some of the books written by their predecessors, a demand for more detailed, accurate descriptions based more on documented personal experience than on hearsay began to arise. It was thus gradually acknowledged that the Hottentots did in fact have a language. Johann Schreyer, for example, who was prevented by an accident from continuing his voyage from the Cape to the East Indies, and therefore gives a much more extensive and detailed account than usual, no longer denies that the utterances of the Hottentots, which must have seemed extremely strange to European ears, were nevertheless acts of speech.

> They have no books, they know nothing of reading and writing, nothing of God and his Holy words: there is no church, no baptism, no communion, no priest or absolution, no law nor gospel. Therefore they are the most miserable people under the sun; they can also learn no language apart from that which they have heard from their mothers, nor is there anybody who can understand them. (Schreyer 1679: 20)

Johan Petri Cortemünde, a Danish captain who stayed at the Cape in 1672, can only compare their language to the clucking of hens, and already shows some concern that it "cannot be broken up into letters, and therefore", interestingly enough, "is strange to listen to" (1675: 88).

Olfert Dapperts's paragraph on the Hottentot language, published as part of his famous and influential *Accurate Description of the African Regions...* , originally published in Dutch in 1668, is in the same vein:

> Their speech is full of clucks like those of the turkey-cocks; they clap or clack each word in the mouth, as if a man were snapping his thumb, so that their mouth goes almost like a rattle, continuously clapping aloud with the tongue, each word with a different clap. Some words they can only utter with considerable difficulty, seeming to fetch them up from the back of the throat like a turkey-cock, or like the people on the German Alps do, who through drinking ice-water get swellings at the neck. Because of this our countrymen, observing this impediment and extraordinary stuttering in speech, have given them the name of Hottentots, in the same way as that word is commonly used here at home as a taunt against anybody who stutters and stammers in uttering his words. (Dappert 1668: 71)

Dappert's theory of the origins of the name of the Hottentots is interestingly different from the theories of earlier travellers: according to them it was derived from the use of some such word in their dancing songs and later found its way into the Dutch and other European languages. Once more, perceptions of the other have proved to have changed.

With Peter Kolb and his *Caput Bonae Spei Hodiernum. Das ist: Vollständige Beschreibung des Afrikanischen Vorgebürges der Guten Hoffnung...*, first published in 1719, we come finally to what could easily be misunderstood as the positive hero of our story. Kolb explicitly discusses various opinions on the question of the Hottentot language at the beginning of his book.

> It will not be without some use, he states, also to relate something of the Hottentot language. The more so because opinions on this issue vary so much. Those who have written hitherto on this subject can be divided into three groups: some people think that the language cannot be learned at all; others assert that it can easily be learned and therefore also written and reduced to certain rules; the third group, finally, believes that one can learn the language, but that it is difficult to write and even more difficult to bring into any order. (1719: 29)

From his own experience Kolb knows that a lot of Europeans do in fact master the Hottentot language. But these are people who have been living among the Hottentots since childhood. But, Kolb continues, even if we could imagine an adult foreigner becoming as fluent as a native speaker,

> then again he soon faces the problem that he cannot translate it. The reason is that his teacher has no command of German. But even if one speaks it more or less perfectly, how is he to go about teaching it to anyone else, when he himself cannot tell him that he must form his tongue thus or thus when he wants to make this or that sound? Yet even when he teaches him this, still he is only over the first hurdle, when the next immediately follows: namely to take care once more to distinguish for oneself between all the smacks with the tongue and the mouth as exactly as possible, in order to communicate them to the other person. He who overcomes these difficulties and many others, and has no other resources than those he can get from the Hottentots, will certainly not claim any more that the Hottentot language is easy; on the contrary it is more probable that a woeful lament would be heard. For the Hottentots have no letters or anything of the sort, but one must learn everything from their mouth. (1719: 30-31)

It is no exaggeration to say that Peter Kolb is literally obsessed by the idea of orality. Estimating that it will take at least half a century "before we will see a printed sheet in their language"[3], Kolb has an almost Gargantuan vision of the future exploration of what goes on inside the mouths of the Hottentots:

> If at last one knew how they move their tongues and bend them, and knew the place in the mouth where they make one or the other smack with the tongue, then perhaps it could happen sooner that one could gain a better knowledge of their language, and in time, if not actually write it down, at least more easily be able to teach it to others. (1719: 31)

As was the case with Jean de Léry, orality constitutes for Peter Kolb both what he is writing about and his reason for writing about it. The final proof of this is to be found in the last chapter of his book, which contains a detailed description of mortuary ritual among the Hottentots. About one hour after coming back from the burial, the gathering suddenly stops talking and weeping:

> Thereupon the very oldest man of the whole Kraal stands up, steps into the circle of men and women, takes off the little piece of hide that they wear over their member and which, as is well known, they call a *kulkross,* and pisses with his own water on all those sitting around. I was astonished, when I saw this the first time, over such an immodest deed and was minded to run off, so as not to see still greater irregularities. Yet my desire to know everything well prevented me from my intention. Therefore I stayed and watched the whole proce-dure, until they broke up. (300)

Kolb thus does not leave; on the contrary he tries to find out about the meaning of these strange customs:

---

[3] In fact, it took almost twice as long for the first book to appear in a Khoi lan-guage: J. P. Vanderkemp's *A Hottentot Catechism* appeared in 1806 (Cole 1971: 15). Besides, Cole's study of the history of African linguictics seems to confirm Auroux's lament: "One of the fundamental weaknesses of the history of linguis-tics is that no one has ever really dreamt of ransacking accounts of voyages...and the archives of missionaries." (Auroux 1984: 294)
Voltaire himself, in the eighteenth century, had his own peculiar vision of the place of the Hottentot language in evolution: "To these various stages corre-sponds a language formed to a greater or lesser degree: inasmuch as families still wandering in the woods only understand one another by means of cries and ges-tures, and the Hottentots have a kind of 'stammering' or 'clucking'". (quoted in Duchet 1971: 303)

All these ceremonies are strange and remarkable and noteworthy, and so I was very anxious also to know the reasons for them. The wetting with urine, they say, means to say that the oldest man, who does this, thanks all the others for the last respects that they have paid the deceased. But when I objected, asking why he did not do it orally, which would have been more seemly, since he so shamefully exhibited his own member to all and sundry, great and small, young and old, I could however get no other answer from him than that it was an old custom that no Hottentot could have the heart to change, if he did not want to become weary of his life. (301)

Innumerable further examples could be quoted from later German travellers to show that Johann Wilhelm Mueller and Peter Kolb were no exceptions, on the contrary only the earliest examples of what became throughout the eighteenth century not only a norm, but a rule without exceptions. Since then, the savage, who at about the same time changed his spots from 'savage' to 'primitive', has been an object of observation and interpretation, his modes and means of communication, his orality, becoming the very foundation of the otherwise constantly changing distinction between us and the other.

With Pastorius' moralizing description of the attitudes of the native Pennsylvanian Indians from 1700, the world had already been turned upside down:

They are otherwise serious and men of few words, and are astonished when they observe in the Christians so much superfluous prattle besides other frivolous behaviour (1700: 29).

Of course, the change in the perception of oral modes of communication which we have observed has much to do with changes in the relationship between oral and written performance in the travellers themselves. Staden and most of his early successors at first related their adventures orally, and only later, by chance or mostly at the request of somebody in their audience with better access to the printing press, wrote them down for publication. Johann Wilhelm Mueller and Peter Kolb, as well as an increasing number of the later writer-travellers, took notes from the very beginning of their voyages, and clearly set out with the intention of writing and publishing accounts of their experiences out there.

This change is also evident from the way in which publication of the more or less incredible stories was justified in the prefaces, which also grew more and more voluminous. In the case of Hans Staden, Johannes Dryander, the previously mentioned editor and professor, refers in his preface to his personal acquaintance with Hans Staden, and especially with his father and family, whom he had known to be honest people, since he himself was from the same village not far from Marburg. When Jürgen Andersen from Tondern (South Jutland) had his account of an East Indian voyage published in 1656, his editor, the learned and cosmopolitan Adam Olearius, did not refer to any such external evidence. On the contrary he was content with describing the checking procedures he had made use of in order to make sure that Andersen was telling the truth. When Andersen, on coming home, gave his first, oral version of his story, Olearius hid himself in a closet so that he could take notes of all that Andersen was about to relate. Later he compared this transcription of Andersen's oral account with what the poor Dane had written himself. And since both versions proved to be almost identical, Olearius had no doubts about the truth of his incredible stories (Andersen 1669).

In a recent article on 'Protestantism and Literacy in Early Modern Germany' Richard Gawthrop and Gerald Strauss (1984) have argued convincingly, on the basis of purely 'internal' evidence, that it is first from the 'Second Reformation' and Pietism, not, as is often assumed, from Luther and the Reformation proper that one can trace the beginnings of a transition from restricted to universal literacy in Germany. The 'external' evidence presented in this paper clearly confirms their chronology and conclusions.[4]

The case for a mutual dependence between Protestantism (and the Second Reformation) and the transition from restricted to universal literacy as defined in this paper can also be made negatively. Following a most useful suggestion made by François Hartog, I have looked at two of the most outstanding early Jesuit writers on West Indian culture and society. There writing lessons prove to be of quite a different kind. Acosta, in fact, seems to refuse to entertain any idea of orality, stressing instead the difference between letters (alphabetic writing), ciphers and pictures as a

---

[4] Despite writing and quoting fairly extensively on the question of literacy in early Spanish ethnography, Anthony Pagden (1982: 129 ff., 163 ff.) gives an extremely muddled analysis, distorted by his 'modernist' assumptions and his anachronistic attempt to make Las Casas and Acosta in particular into 'three-stages theorists' *avant la lettre*.

dividing line between 'us' and 'the other'. Coming to the Indians of Peru, he seems to admit that

> Before the Spaniards came to the Indies, they of Peru had no kinds of writing, either letters, characters, ciphers or figures, like to those of China and Mexico: yet preserved they the memory of their antiquities, and maintained an order in all their affairs of peace, warre and policie, for that they were careful observers of traditions from one to another, and the young ones learned, and carefully kept, as a holy thing, what their superiors had told them, and taught it with the like care to their posteritie. (Acosta 1604: 405)

Thus far it seems as if Acosta is about to tell of the same writing lesson as for example Jean de Léry. But he continues:

> Besides this diligence, they supplied the want of letters and writings, partly by painting, as those of Mexico (although they of Peru were very gross and blockish) and partly, and most commonly by *Qippos*. The Qippos are memorialls or registers, made of bows, in which there are divers knots and colours, which doe signifie diverse things, and it is strange to see what they have expressed and represented by this means: for their Quippos serve them instead of books of histories, of laws, ceremonies and accounts of their affairs. (1604: 405-6)

Father Joseph François Lafitau, at the beginning of the 18th century, writes not only about the Indians of Peru, but of Indians in general. He also denies the possibility of orality:

> The Indians annals are not very long since they (the Indians) are hampered by the lack of alphabetical letters. Their chronology does not show the errors which can be found in their computations and follows the revolution of many centuries. It is not that they have not marked epochs and a way of conserving the memory of historical events and things which most merit recording. For, besides the fact that the Iroquois, Huron and others treat matters by wampum belts, as I have said, and the Mexicans by hieroglyphic writing and the paintings of which we have spoken, all the Indians have annals of a sort marked by certain knots, but among all the barbarians, these chronicles are very limited and imperfect. (Lafitau II: 134)

Michael Harbsmeier

This is indeed a far cry from the writing lesson of the radical Calvinist Roger Williams, contained in the introduction to his *A Key into the Language of America: or, an help to the language of the Natives in that part of America, called New-England,* which was first published in London in 1643:

> They have no Clothes, Bookes or Letters, and conceive their Fathers never had; and therefore they are easily persuaded that the God that made English men is a greater God, because Hee hath so richly endowed the English above themselves: But when they heare that about sixteen hundred yeeres agoe England and the Inhabitants thereof were like unto themselves, and since they have received from God, Clothes, Bookes, &c. they are greatly affected with a secret hope concerning themselves. (Williams 1643: 23; see also Peacock 1984)

III Conclusions

The story I have tried to tell so far is apparently that of a discovery: the discovery of orality and spoken language as a mode of communication at once radically different from, but also reducible to, writing. Hans Staden and the other early German travellers had no perception of such a difference. They lived in a world between orality and literacy. They moved freely from spoken to written expression; their world was one of action and noise, in which man-eating, devil-worship, death and all sorts of terrible dangers determined the way in which the other, the savage, the tyrannical, barbarian heathen was both perceived and described. With Johann Wilhelm Mueller and Peter Kolb we have come much closer to the world of Jean de Léry and Claude Lévi-Strauss, which is also much closer to the world in which we live today.

What has changed is the mode of coordination between the travellers' eyes and ears: the traveller's eye has learnt to hear the words and meanings behind the savages' noisy actions and practices; the traveller's ear has become eager to see the letters, rules and grammars behind what earlier travellers had heard as the loud and shrieking voices of savages in action.

Following Walter J. Ong (1982), Justin Stagl (1980), Johannes Fabian (1983) and others, this transformation could also be described as a move towards visualism as a mode of distanciation,

222

which to some extent could be explained in turn as a consequence of the proliferation of the printing press, which was in fact instrumental in the production of all our texts. The influence of Peter Ramus and of Ramism, which actually played a major role in the emergence of another genre, the so-called apodemic literature, with its detailed instructions on what the eyes and ears of people traveling ought to see and hear, was perhaps also important. However, the reduction of the change in modes of perception and description to the effect of changes in the modes and means of communication is itself an integral part of the very problem at issue in our analysis. This procedure, tempting as it is, particularly for people participating in conferences on literacy, only repeats the act by means of which our tragi-comic heroes Mueller and Kolb transformed the other into an object of description, observation and investigation in terms of their proper but strange modes and means of communication.

The rise of what we have called universal literacy clearly depended on violence and the sword to establish the economic, political and material conditions for travellers like Jean de Léry, Johann Wilhelm Mueller and Peter Kolb, not to mention Claude Lévi-Strauss and all the rest.

The sword came first, enforcing that degree of peace and mutual respect which is always a necessary condition for any potential observer to have a chance to see and hear the others as communicating beings. Thus far Ibn Khaldun was perfectly right in his sociology of literacy and his neat distinction between the pen and the sword as well as in his holistic view of the dynamic interaction between societies and modes of communication.

However literacy, once established and developed from a restricted to a universal stage, gains a momentum of its own. Through the use of literacy and writing as a means of discrimination and excommunication in its own right, literacy itself becomes power and repression, the pen a substitute for the sword.

Apparently only images of death, cannibalism and the Devil were able to do the kind of job that literacy alone is sometimes dreamt to be capable of by its professional addicts, once the sword has done its work and thus falls silent for a while. Compared with other known means of discrimination and excommunication, however, literacy, even in its universal form, may prove the least harmful, especially if it can be made instrumental in the discovery, invention and development of less unsatisfactory modes of discrimination.

Bibliography

Acosta, Father Joseph de (1604) The Natural History of the Indies. Reprinted from the English Translated Edition of Edward Grimston. Editor Clements R. Markham, 2 volumes (= Works Issued by the Hakluyt Society LX, LXI, London 1880).

Andersen, Jürgen and Iversen, Volquard (1669) Orientalische Reise-Beschreibungen. In der Bearbeitung von Adam Olearius, Schleswig 1669. Facs. edition, editet by Dieter Dieter Lohmeyer. Tübingen 1980. (=*Deutsche Neudrucke*, Reihe Barock, vol. 27)

Aouroux, Sylvain (1984) Linguistique et anthropologie (1600-1900). Britta Rupp-Eisenreich (ed.), *Histoires de l'antrhopologie: XVIe - XIXe siècles*, Klincksieck, Paris.

Brand, Adam (1698) Beschreibung der chinesischen Reise/welche vermittelst einer Zaars. Gesandtschaft Durch Deren Ambassadeur Herrn Isbrand Anno 1693, 1694 und 1695 von Moscau über Gross-Ushiga/Sibirien/Dauren/ und durch die Mongolische Tartarey verrichtet worden..... Hamburg.

Brun, Samuel (1624) des Wundartses und Burgers zu Basel/Schiffarten welche er in etliche newe Länder und Insulen/zu fünff unterschiedlichen Malen/ mit Gottes hülff/gethan, Basel 1624. Facs. edition, edited by Walter Hirschberg, Graz 1969.

Certeau, Michel de (1975) Ethno-graphie. L'oralité, ou l'espace de l'autre: Lery. In:*L'écriture de l'histoire*, Paris, pp. 215-48.

Certeau, Michel de (1975) Writing vs. Time: History and Anthropology in the Work of Lafitau, *Yale French Studies*, 1980.

Cole, Desmond T. (1971) The History of African Linguistics to 1945. In: Thomas A. Sebeok (ed.),*Current Trends in Linguistics,*, vol. 7, The Hague, Paris, pp. 1-29.

Cortemünde, J. P. (1675) Dagbog fra en Ostindiensfart 1672-75. *Søhistoriske Skrifter*, editor Henning Henningsen, vol. V, København 1953.

Dappert, Olfert (1668) An Accurate Description of the African Regions... Amsterdam. Reprinted in part in I. Schapera (ed.),*The Early Hottentotts*. Cape Town 1933.

Derrida, Jacques (1967) *De la grammatologie*, Paris.

Duchet, Michel (1971) *Anthropologie et Histoires au siècle des lumières*, Paris.

Michael Harbsmeier

Evans-Pritchard, E. E. (1937) *Witchcraft, Oracles and Magic among the Azande*, Oxford.

Fabian, Johannes (1983) *Time and the other. How Anthropology Makes its Object*, Columbia.

Fouquet, C. (1944) Bibliografia da "Verdadeira Historia" de Hans Staden, *Boletim Bibliografico*, vol. IV, pp. 7-31, Sao Paulo.

Gellner, Ernest (1981) *Muslim Society*, Cambridge.

Harbsmeier, Michael (1982) Reisebeschreibungen als mentalitäts-geschichtliche Quellen, In: Antoni Maczak and Hans-Jürgen Teuteberg (eds.), *Reiseberichte als Quellen europäischer Kulturgeschichte*, (=Wolfenbütteler Forschungen 21) Wolfenbüttel.

Hartog, François (1980) *Le miroir d'Hérodote. Essai sur la representation de l'autre*, Paris.

Jones, Adam (1983) German Sources for West African History 1559-1669. (=*Studien zur Kulturkunde* 66) Wiesbaden.

Khaldun, Ibn (1967) *The Muqaddimah. An Introduction to History*, transl. Franz Rosenthal, abridged and edited by N. J. Dawood, London.

Kolb, Peter (1719) Caput Boni Spei Hodiernum. Das ist vollständige Beschreibung des Africanischen Vorgebürgers der Guten Hoffnung, Nürnberg. I quote from: *Unter Hottentotten 1705-1713*, editor Werner Jopp, Tübingen 1979.

Lafitau, Father Joseph François (1724) *Customs of the American Indians Compared with the Customs of the First Times* , edited and translated by William N. Fenton and Elizabeth L. Moore, 2 vol., Toronto 1977.

Léry, Jean de (1580) *Histoire d'un voyage fait en la terre du Bresil*, Geneve. Facs. ed. by Jean Claude Morisot, Geneve 1975.

Levi-Strauss, Claude (1976) *Tristes Tropiques*, Harmondsworth.

Mayr, Hans (1506) Reisebericht. In: Franz Hümmerich, *Quellen und Untersuchungen zur Fahrt der ersten Deutschen nach dem portugesischen Indien 1505-6*. München 1918 (=Abhandlungen der Königlich Bayerischen Akademie der Wissenschaften, Philosophisch-philologische und historische Klasse, XXX. band, 3. Abhandlung).

Mueller, Wilhelm Johann (1676) *Die Africanische Landschafft Fetu*, Hamburg. Facs. ed. by Walter Hirschberg, Graz 1968. Partly translated in Jones 1983.

Ong, Walter J. (1982) *Orality and Literacy. The Technologizing of the Word*, London, New York.

Pagden, Anthony (1982) *The Fall of Natural Man. The American Indian and the Origins of Comparative Ethnology,* Cambridge.

Pastorius, Franciscus Danielus (1700) *Umständige Geographische Beschreibung der zu allerletzt erfundenen Provintz Pensylvaniae* .... Franckfurt und Leipzig.

Peacock, John (1984) Writing and Spreech after Derrida. In: Francis Barker et al. (eds.), *Europe and its others.* Colchester. Vol. 2: 78-90)

Schmidel, Ulrich (1602) *Warhafftige Historien Einer Wunderbaren Schiffart....1534-1554,* Nürnberg. Facs. ed. by Hans Plischke, Graz 1962.

Schreyer, Joahann (1679) *Neue Ost-Indianische Reisebeschreibung von Anno 1669 bis 1677 handelnde von den unterschiedlichen Africanischen und Barbarischen Völkern sonderlich derer an dem Vorgebürge Caput bonae Spei sich enthaltenden sogenennten Hottentotten....* Leipzig. Reprinted in S. P. Naber (ed.), Reisebeschreibungen von deutschen Beamten und Kriegleuten im Dienste der Niederländischen West- und Ostindischen Kompanien 1602-1797, vol. VIII, The Hague 1931.

Springer, Balthasar (1506) *Merfart,* In: Hümmerich 1918 (see Mayr 1506).

Staden, Hans (1557) *Warhaftig Historie und Beschreibung einer Landschafft der Wilden/Nacketen/Grimmigen Menschfresser Leuthen/ in der Newen-welt America gelegen....* Marburg. (I have used the following translation: The Captivity of Hans Stade of Hesse in 1547-1555 A.D. Transl. Albert Tootal, editor Richard F. Burton, (= Works issued for the Hakluyt Society LI.))

Stagl, Justin (1980) Die Apodemik oder "Reisekunst" als Methodik der Sozialforschung vom Humanismus bis zur Aufklärung. In Stagl, Justin and Rassem, Mohammed (eds), *Statistik und Staatsbeschreibung in der Neuzeit,* Paderborn

Strauss, Gerald and Gawthrop, Richard (1984) Protestantism and Literacy in Early Modern Germany, *Past and Present,* nr. 104: 31-55.

Troubetzkoy, Nicolas (1980) Une Oeuvre littéraire: le "Voyage au-dela des trois mers". *L'Ethnographie,* tome LXXVI, nr. 80-81.

Ultzheimer, Josua (1610) *Warhafte Beschreibung ettlicher Reisen in Europa, Africa, Asien und America 1596-1610.* Edited by Sabine Werg, Tübingen 1971. Partly translated in Jones 1983.

Michael Harbsmeier

Williams, Roger (1643) *A Key into the Language of America: or a Help to the language of the Natives in that Part of America called New England.*. London. Reprinted in: The Complete Writings of Roger Williams, vol. 1, New York 1963.

Phrasikleia - An Archaic Greek Theory of Writing

Jesper Svenbro

Among the legends dealing with the origin of the Greek alphabet, there is one that seems less frequently quoted than the others,[1] probably because of its overtly ethnocentric character: with one stroke, it wipes out the Phoenician origin of writing, so important for those who wish to consider myth an allegorical staging of History. The legend I am thinking of is to be found in the fragments of the historian Skamon of Mytilene, author of a work entitled *On inventions* in several books. According to Skamon - who lived in the fourth century B.C. and who was the son of the historian Hellanikos[2]-, the letters of the alphabet were named "Phoenician" after Phoinike, the daughter of the Attic king Aktaion, the inventor of writing. To quote our historian, Aktaion "is told to have been without male offspring, but to have had the daughters Aglauros, Herse and Pandrosos: [a fourth one,] Phoinike [,] is told to have died when still a young girl (*parthénos*). For this reason, Aktaion named the letters 'Phoenician' (*Phoinikêïa tà grámmata*), wanting to bestow some kind of honor (*timê*) on his daughter".[3]

If this legend at first sight seems a mediocre mishmash of elements known from the traditions on Athenian autochthony, where Aglauros, Pandrosos and Herse are the daughters of Kekrops and not of Aktaion, it largely compensates for this

---

1 The scholia to Dionysius Thrax list a dozen of inventors, in particular Kadmos and Palamedes (*Anecdota graeca* II.774, 781-786 Bekker). Cf. in general Jeffery 1967; for Kadmos, see Edwards 1979: 22-23 etc.; for Palamedes, Detienne 1984.
2 For the date of Skamon, see Jacoby 1927, who quotes the *Souda* (s.v. *Hellánikos*) where Skamon is given as the son of Hellanikos of Mytilene.
3 *FGrHist* 476 F 3 = Photius and *Souda*, s.v. *Phoinikêïa grámmata*. Aktaion seems to be an Attic counterpart of Kadmos, the Theban inventor of writing, who had four daughters (no son: Euripides, *Bacchae* 1305) and, curiously enough, a grandson named Aktaion, the famous hunter.

"mediocrity" by connecting alphabetic writing with the commemoration of the dead.[4] The earliest Greek alphabetic documents that have come down to us do not concern - as one might have expected - economic activities in the strict sense (inventories, book-keeping and the like). Our earliest alphabetic documents are of a different kind: inscriptions on various objects dedicated to the gods or belonging to human beings, be it a statue, a drinking vessel or a tombstone.[5] In fact, alphabetic writing found one of its first applications in the commemoration of the dead.

From the archaic period we have a great number of sepulchral inscriptions. But it happens very rarely that we are able to study an inscription together with the sepulchral monument to which it belongs, as the inscribed base often is all that remains of a monument, the statue being lost. For this reason, the discovery of Phrasikleia's *sêma* (or memorial) in 1972 at present-day Merenda, in the ancient Attic deme of Myrrhinous - south of Marathon - becomes singularly important. "For the first time in the history of archaic Greek sepulchral sculpture", writes a French archaeologist, "we are in possession of a statue and an epigram, assuredly belonging together, which are both almost intact" (Daux 1973: 383). In fact, the base of the statue was found separately already in the eighteenth century and was published more than a century ago.[6] Nevertheless, it is important to underline that the conditions of its interpretation have changed radically after the discovery of the statue to which it belongs. On one hand, scholars have made the mistake of obstinately clinging to interpretations prior to the discovery of the statue, as if the statue could not shed any light on the epigram;[7] on the other hand, the mistake of considering the epigram as a "simple text without pretension nor

---

[4] According to Tacitus, Kekrops is also believed to have invented the alphabet (*Annals* XI.14); a tradition reported by Cicero gives him as the originator of Attic funeral customs (*Laws* II.63).

[5] See Jeffery 1961, Guarducci 1967-1973, Pfohl 1967 and Lazzarini 1976. For an overview, cf. Pfohl 1969.

[6] By Boeckh 1828: 46-47, from the manuscript of Michel Fourmont who visited Greece in 1729-1730 and saw the inscribed base in the wall of the Panaghia church, some 200 meters from the spot where the statue was found in 1972.

[7] This is the case with N.M. Kontoleon who, in an article published in 1975 (Kontoleon 1974), defends the interpretation he proposed in his Collège de France lectures in 1967 (Kontoleon 1970: 53ff.).

implication" (Daux 1973: 388), in spite of the - admittedly - high quality of the statue. What is a "simple text"?

Here is a description of the statue: "It is the life-size representation of a young woman; her right arm is held along the body, her hand pinching the folds of her khiton without really making them disappear; her left forearm is placed horizontally before her chest, her left hand holding a flower, vertically, between her breasts. Thick sandals; a long khiton, tightened around the waist by a belt, bestrewed with rosettes and delimited by ribbons decorated with meanders (e. g. the middle vertical ribbon) or with tongue-and-groove patterns; all these motifs are incised and painted. The young woman wears a necklace and earrings, and a bracelet around both wrists. On her head: a diadem (crown, *stephánē*) decorated with a row of pearls and, above, with a row of lotus flowers alternating with flower-cups of the same type as the one she holds in her left hand.[8] On both sides of her head, three plaits fall down over her chest. The state of preservation is exceptional and the traces of color are numerous. The statue is the work of Aristion from Paros, whose name and origin are inscribed on the base; this sculptor, already known from other dedications (one complete, two restored) was active during the third quarter of the sixth century" (Daux 1973: 383-384).

The almost perfect state of preservation of this statue, which has been dated to around 540 B.C. (Jeffery 1962: 139), calls for a commentary. Most probably it was buried shortly after being completed. As Carl Nylander has pointed out to me, the fact that the statue shows no sign of mutilation indicates that it was buried by people who wanted to protect it from destruction. Destruction by whom? Not by the Persian invaders, in this case: the fragments of pottery found around the statue exclude such a low date (Mastrokostas 1972:324). But the year 540 is suggestive. It is most probably the year when the tyrant Peisistratos returns to Athens, expelling the Alkmeonid family (Schachermeyr 1937: 171-172). According to Isocrates, the followers of Peisistratos "not only demolished the houses of the Alkmeonids but they even opened their graves" (*The team of horses* 26). This suggests that the statue of Phrasikleia was buried by the Alkmeonids on the return of Peisistratos. The artistic quality of the statue is a further confirmation of this hypothesis, as it agrees with what we know of the Alkmeonids' interest in art (Lévêque and Vidal-Naquet

---

[8] Lotus flower-cups, according to Mastrokostas 1972: 317.

1964: 83-89). But there is another fact worth taking into account: the name of the young girl. She is called Phrasikleia. The second element of this name is derived from the word *kléos*, "fame", a word central not only to archaic Greek culture in general[9] but to the Alkmeonid family in particular: among the names given to its members, *Megaklês*, approximately "Great-fame", is repeated in an almost obsessional manner from generation to generation, and *Kleisthénēs*, "Fame-strong", as well as *Periklês*, "Wide-fame", are other examples showing the obsession with *kléos* typical of the Alkmeonids.[10] Consequently, it would not be unreasonable to assume that the young girl called Phrasikleia belonged to the Alkmeonid family.

If Phrasikleia's memorial thus may have a value as a *document* for the history of sixth century Athens, it is also a *monument* in its own right, to use Michel Foucault's distinction (Foucault 1969: 182). And it is precisely as a monument, obeying rules of its own, that the Phrasikleia ensemble - statue and epigram - will be subject to investigation in the following pages.

I have already touched upon the name of the girl, Phrasikleia. If we follow Pierre Chantraine's *Dictionnaire étymologique*, this proper name should be taken to mean "Famous-for-her-thoughts" or something of the kind.[11] The element *Phrasi-* is said to be an old dative plural of *phrēn* (which is very approximately rendered by "thought"), whereas the element *-kleia* is derived from *kléos*, "fame", as I have already pointed out. The name Phrasikleia would thus be constructed in the same way as e.g. *Nausí-thoos*, "Swift-by-means-of-his-ships", where the element *Nausi-* is the dative plural of *naûs*, "ship".

But things become complicated. Chantraine mentions another proper name where the element *Phrasi-* has assuredly nothing to do with *phrēn* or *phrénes*. This name is *Phrasí-dēmos* (Chantraine 1968-1980:1225). Like the analogous name *Blepsídemos*, this proper name means "He-who-cares-for-the-people". Here the element *Phrasi-* is derived from *phrásai/phrásasthai*, aorist infinitives of the verb *phrázein/phrázesthai*, "show/care for". Now if we consider the name Phrasikleia within its proper frame, i.e. the Attic onomastic system, it is clear that it belongs to

---

[9] Cf. Detienne 1967: 20, Nagy 1974: 231-255 and Nagy 1979: 15-18, etc.

[10] See the genealogical table in Lévêque and Vidal-Naquet 1964: 56.

[11] Chantraine 1968-1980: 1225 and 1228 on *Phrasi-klês*, the masculine counterpart of *Phrasí-kleia*. Cf. *Iliad* 24.201-202.

the following series of women's proper names (Bechtel 1902:21): *Daxí-kleia* (cf. the adjective *dexí-melos*, "sheep-receiving", *Erasí-kleia* (cf. *erasi-khrématos*, "money-loving"), *Mnesi-kleia* (cf. *mnesí-theos*, "god-remembering"; cf. also *Mnesi-épes*, a man's proper name meaning "Epos-remembering"), *Sosí-kleia* (cf. *sosí-polis*, "city-rescuing"). Of these four women, the first one "receives" *kléos*, the second one "loves" it, the third one "remembers" it, the last one "rescues" it. Each one of them, in her own manner, "cares for" the audible fame called *kléos*.

This excursion into the field of onomastic studies compels us to understand the proper name Phrasikleia in a new manner.[12] It means "She-who-indicates-*kléos*" or "She-who-cares-for-*kléos*", depending on whether we derive its first element from the active form *phrásai*, "indicate", or medium *phrásasthai*, "care for", an ambiguity that should not trouble us, on the contrary.[13] To anyone whose profession it is to make *kléos* resound and who receives the command to write the epigram for the dead girl, this meaning of Phrasikleia constitutes a formidable challenge to his entire poetic skill.

In fact, "fame" is not a very accurate translation of *kléos*. In the first place, because *kléos* is the technical term for what the poet bestows on individuals who have accomplished something remarkable, as we know from the studies of Marcel Detienne and Gregory Nagy (Detienne 1967: 20, Nagy 1974: 261 and 1979: 16). Secondly, because *kléos* belongs entirely to the world of sounds: "HAU we hear is a *kléos*", says Homer in the *Iliad* (2.486), and the verb used for "hear" is *akoúein* (cf. Nagy 1974: 244-246). *Kléos* is acoustic, or it is not *kléos*. This sonority of *kléos* is confirmed by etymology: in the Germanic languages, we find the following cognates of the word: Icelandic *hljóð*, Swedish *ljud*, Danish *lyd*, German *Laut*, all meaning "sound" (Hellquist 1980: 581). In English, the adjective *loud* is another significant relative of *kléos*.

This much for *kléos*. But what does the verb *phrázein* mean? Contrary to what we are liable to think - probably because of modern derivatives like "phrase" or "phraseology" -, *phrázein* does not denote the act of speaking in its sonority. It does not cover the acoustic manifestation of the linguistic performance.

---

[12] Cf. already Fick 1894: 281-282 on *Phrasi-klês* etc.

[13] For the convenience of the reader not familiar with Greek grammar, one may translate "draw attention to/pay attention to". The notion of attention - objective or subjective - is, in fact, fundamental to the verb (cf. its etymological relation to *phrḗn*, "thought": Chantraine 1968-1980: 1228).

As Aristarchus, the great Alexandrian scholar, says: *phrázein* is never the synonym of *eipeîn*, "speak", in Homer (Lehrs 1865: 84-86). Nor is it the equivalent of *légein*, "say", in later Greek (Schmidt 1876: 89-90). The etymology of *phrázein*, related to *phrḗn*, "thought", seems to preclude such a meaning, incongruous with the silent character of mental activity.[14] That is why the *Souda*, the ancient lexicon, can give it as a synonym of *sē-maínein*, "signify", and *dēloûn*, "show" (*phrázousi: sēmaínousi, dēloûsi*). It is of course possible to *phrázein*, "show", something in an oral statement, but the accent is then not on the acoustic character of the message. We may think of a passage in the *Odyssey* where Ulysses, disguised as a beggar, provides Penelope with the "signs" (*sḗmata*) which she is supposed to recognize: her eyes are filled with tears "when she recognizes the *sḗmata* that Ulysses has clearly presented, *péphrade*" (Od. 19.250; cf. 23.206, 24.346). The non-acoustic character of *phrázein* is evident in the expression *antì phōnês kheirì phrázein*, "show something with one's hand instead of the voice" or rather "show with gestures when the voice cannot be used". This expression is found in Aeschylus' *Agamemnon*, where Klytaimestra tells Kassandra - who does not speak Greek - to use the language of gestures: "Show it with Barbaric hand if you cannot use language", *antì phōnês phráze karbánōi kheirí* (1061). The same expression is found in Herodotus, where an Amazon uses the language of gestures in order to communicate with a Scythian: "Then she bode him by means of gesture, *têi dè kheirì éphraze*, (for they did not understand each other's language) to bring a friend the next day" (IV. 113). Again, *phrázein* is used in a context marked by linguistic alterity: it designates the act of transmitting a message by means of silent signs. That is why *phrázein* is as appropriate as *sēmaínein* (Plato *Phaedrus* 275d) for designating what written signs actually do: in Euripides' *Iphigenia in Tauris*, the heroine of the play says to Orestes: "If you save my *graphḗ*, my written message or writing, it will silently indicate, *phrásei sigôsa*, what I have written" (762-763). Writing "indicates" or "shows", it does not speak by itself (except metaphorically, as in Herodotus I. 124 etc.). Nor does the stone on which it may be engraved speak in the strict sense of the word: stone is *áphthongos* "voiceless".

---

[14] Fournier 1946: 50-51 seems less convinced by this etymology than Chantraine 1968-1980: 1228, but points out that it is implicitly accepted by Homer in a line like *Il.* 9.423 (or by Hesiod, *Works and Days* 688, one may add), which provides us with an obvious example of *figura etymologica*.

However, inscribed or not, it may *provoke* speech, in the same way as the sepulchral monument (*sêma*) imagined by Hektor in the seventh Book of the *Iliad* : "'Here the *sêma* of a brave man who died long ago, killed by brilliant Hektor.' Many a man will once speak (*eréei*) like that; and my *kléos* will never perish" (*Il.* 7.89-91). Inscribed or not, the *sêma* is in itself silent, but whoever recognizes it when passing by will speak. The stone will trigger speech.[15]

Reminding us that Indic *dhyâma*, "thought", is the cousin of Greek *sêma*, Gregory Nagy has tried to resolve what seems to be a semantic problem at first sight (Nagy 1983): how are we to understand the semantic relation between "thought" and "sign"? The answer given is that Greek *sêma*, "coded message" (to use Nagy's own translation), cannot be mentioned without bringing to mind the idea of a *nóēsis*, of an *anágnōsis* or of an *anagnôrisis*, keywords for the decoding of signs, for reading and for recognition, which are found *in presentia* in the neighborhood of the word *sêma*. There is no *sêma* without *nóēsis*, "decoding": this would be something like a linguistic reflex in ancient Greek. The *sêma* remains incomplete without the "thought" implied by its decoding.

If, on the other hand - as when Penelope recognizes the signs that Ulysses *shows* her -, *sêma* is the natural object of *phrázein*, "show", "indicate", the same word also means "sepulchral sign", "memorial", "tomb", as we have already seen. In this sense, which of course does not exclude the other meanings of the word here, *sêma* is placed at the very beginning of the Phrasikleia epigram, immediately before the element *Phrasi-* of the girl's name:

---

15 Theognis 568-569. The fact that an object designates itself as "I" in archaic Greek inscriptions does not make it a "speaking object" - an *oggetto parlante* (Burzachechi 1962) - even in a metaphorical sense: only to logocentric ideology the connexion between the first person and the voice appears necessary. I develop this theme in a forthcoming study (Svenbro 1984).

> *Sêma Phrasikleías: koúrē keklēsomai aieí,*
> *antì gámou parà theôn toûto lakhoûs' ónoma.*

Sêma Phrasikleías: *koúrē*   *keklēsomai*   *aieí,*

(I am)   Phrasikleía's ....
sêma ....
....I shall........................always
....be called...................
....*koúrē*.......................................

antì   *gámou*   *parà* *theôn* *toûto* *lakhoûs'*   *ónoma*
....having received............
....this....................name
....from the gods.......................................
in exchange of marriage...

By means of the word *sêma*, the inscription starts by confirming what we are already doing: the word is in fact an invitation to the kind of "recognition" called "reading", *anágnōsis* in Greek. But to the Greeks, reading is *reading aloud*. Not that they were incapable of silent reading, as one extreme position wants it, but the normal way of reading a text in ancient Greece was without any doubt reading it out aloud (Knox 1968: 421 and 435). Their relation to the written word might perhaps be compared to our relation to musical notation: not that it is impossible to read music in silence, but the most common way of doing it is playing it on an instrument or singing it out aloud in order to know what it sounds like.

Now, whoever "recognizes" or "reads" Phrasikleia's *sêma* in the Greek way will therefore read it aloud. And in doing so, the reader will immediately notice the emphatic alliteration in the first line of the epigram where four kappas are heard, the first and the last one followed by a lambda: [kl] [k] [k] [kl]. Four sigmas are equally present. This "clicking" character of the line gives us an important key to its interpretation, as it gives weight to the *kléos* contained in the name Phrasikleia, the semantics of which is thus reactivated.[16] The *kléos* to which *Phrasí-kleia* "pays attention" receives the attention of the reader too. The semantic content of the words concerned with the alliteration confirms this hypothesis: Phrasikleia's *kléos* will precisely consist in the fact that she "will be called" - *keklẽsomai,* she says[17] - *koúrẽ,* "girl", "daughter", "virgin", "kore".[18] When people will speak of Phrasikleia in the future, they will refer to her as a *koúrẽ.* That is the word one will hear whenever she is talked about, for she has received this designation from the gods in exchange of, or instead of, marriage *(antì gámou).* The designation *koúrẽ* is the "lot" assigned to her by the gods in exchange of the "lot" of marriage. This *koúrẽ* will thus remain unmarried for ever *(aieí),* a fact which excludes her identification with the goddess Kore, who becomes the wife of Hades and as such bears another name.[19]

If there is an allusion here, and I think there is one, it is not to Kore but to another goddess, whose status and function are defined in the *Homeric Hymn to Aphrodite.* Of the three goddesses capable of resisting Aphrodite's powers, says the *Hymn,* one is Hestia, who, explicitly, is called *koúré* (20). In fact, Hestia swears "to remain a *parthénos* for ever", *parthénos éssesthai pánt' émata* (27). But, continues the *Hymn,* "in exchange of marriage, *antì gàmoio,* Zeus the Father grants her a beautiful *géras,* honorific portion or lot" (28; cf. Vernant 1965: 103). This expression presents a perfect analogy with the second line of the Phrasikleia epigram. Like the verb *lankhánein,* "receive (as one's lot)", of which *lakhoûs (a)* is an aorist participle, the noun *géras* belongs to the vocabulary of division and distribution (Borecky 1965,

---

[16] The last point should be stressed, in order not to give the impression that the Greeks always paid this kind of attention to proper names. Of course, they did not. But *when* they did, the nature of their onomastic system facilitated interpretation and reinterpretation, as most Greek proper names make use of semantically recognizable elements.

[17] Without being etymologically related to *kléos,* the verb *kaleîn,* "call", is often associated with it: see Chantraine 1968-1980: 485, 540-541.

[18] For the formula occupying the second half of the first line, cf. *Il.* 2.260, *Od.* 6.244, *Homeric Hymn to Aphrodite* 242, *Homeric Hymn to Apollo* 324. In these four cases, it is used to define family relations (father, husband, wife), which strongly suggest the translation "daughter" for *koúrẽ* in the Phrasikleia epigram.

[19] The identification of Phrasikleia with Kore is one of the issues in the controversy between Kontoleon and Daux (Kontoleon 1970: 54, Daux 1973: 386-388, Kontoleon 1974: 3-12), the ambiguities of which cannot be disentangled here.

Jesper Svenbro

Nagy 1979: 132, Benveniste 1969: 43-50). A *géras* may be an honorific portion of food or of booty or, as here, an honorific status.[20] Hestia's *géras* will be her place in the middle of the house, at the hearth. She is the goddess of domestic fire. Another *koúrē*, Antigone in Sophocles's tragedy, uses the same vocabulary when she calls herself *álektron, anuménaion, oúte toû gámou méros lakhoûsan*, "unmarried, not having heard the nuptial song, not having received the portion of marriage" (917-918; 889; cf. Borecký 1965: 47). Having lost her brothers, Antigone is going to die without having given birth to a grandson to her dead father (918), which is what she is supposed to do as an "heiress" (*epíklēros*) if the paternal hearth is to survive (Vernant 1965: 117-121). This is her sad "portion", *méros*. The participle *lakhoûsan* (918), "having received", is identical with the one used in the Phrasikleia epigram.

Like Antigone, Phrasikleia has not received the "portion" of marriage. Her "portion" is the designation *koúrē*, received in exchange of marriage, which also may mean that this designation is equal in value to marriage. Normally, the young girl, similar to a young plant (*neázon*), will be called *gunḗ*, "woman", "wife", later in life. Thus, in Sophocles, Deianeira says that the young woman is free from cares "till the moment when she will be called wife instead of girl", *héōs tis antì parthénou gunḗ klēthêi*.[21] The expression used by Deianeira is in fact symmetrically opposed to the one we have encountered in the Phrasikleia epigram. In Phrasikleia's case, the normal course of life has been "frozen" by death, which has crystallized her status as a *koúrē* for all time to come. This means that she will remain attached to her father's hearth for ever, without any possibility of her being carried away by a marriage that would have brought her to another man's house, the house of a husband. She will never become the wife of a stranger, she will always remain the *koúrē* or daughter of her father,[22] for whom she keeps the metaphorical fire of *kléos* like a no less metaphorical Hestia.

For the sculptor has represented her as holding a lotus flower-cup in her left hand, before her chest. She shows forth this lotus,

---

[20] Cf. above p. 1 the honor "bestowed on" Phoinike by Aktaion: verb *aponémein*, which belongs to the same vocabulary.

[21] Sophocles, *Trachinian Women* 148-149; cf. 144.

[22] With the genitive of the father's name, *koúrē* naturally takes the meaning "daughter"; sometimes, as I believe is the case in the Phrasikleia epigram, the mere context suggests it (see Liddell-Scott-Jones, s.v. *kóre*, 3). Cf. above note 18.

238

she takes care of it: in Greek, *éphrase* or *ephrásato*. But as we have already seen, *Phrasí-kleia* means "She-who-indicates-*kléos* "or "She-who-takes-care-of-*kléos*". To venture a Greek expression: *kléos éphrase*, "she shows forth *kléos*". That is what her name says that she does. Thus, the lotus which she shows forth (a visual sign) has taken the place of *kléos* (an acoustic sign). According to her name, Phrasikleia shows forth something which cannot be seen, only heard: *kléos*. As a statue, she shows forth something which cannot be heard, only seen: a flower. In this transgressive interplay between image and word, the Phrasikleia ensemble accomplishes a remarkable metaphorical operation, the principal implications of which I shall now try and define.

Like the fire of the hearth, the fire of the house, the fire of Hestia, the lotus flower is believed to open or "rekindle" in the morning and to close or "lower" at nightfall. Theophrastus writes: "The flower is white, resembling in the narrowness of its petals those of the lily, but there are many petals growing close upon another. When the sun sets, these close and cover up the 'head', but with sunrise they open and appear above the water."[23] This flower behaves then like a domestic fire, it *is* in fact the metaphorical sign of fire, in short: a stylized fire, familiar from art (Cook 1925: 771ff.). Does not Homer speak of the "flower of fire", of the *puròs ánthos*? He does - in a well-attested variant of *Iliad* 9.212, quoted by Plutarch: *autàr epeì puròs ánthos apéptato*, "but when the flower of fire had flown".[24]

This vegetal metaphor has a suggestive parallel in the expression *puròs spérma*, "seed of fire".[25] The "seed of fire" is the precious and precarious seed which must not die during the night in order to avoid the borrowing of fire from another household in the morning. The continuity of the fire of the hearth symbolizes the autonomy and continuity of the house: for this reason, the domestic fire has to be carefully looked after. If she has no broth-

---

[23] Theophrastus, *Enquiry into Plants* IV.8.9; cf. Cook 1925: 772. On the lotus, cf. also Guarducci 1981.

[24] *Moralia* 934b; the line was known to Aristarchus, who rejected it. For other instances of *puròs ánthos*, notably in Aeschylus (*Prometheus Bound* 7), cf. Cook 1925: 771-772.

[25] *Od.* 5.490. The whole formula runs *spérma puròs sõzon*, "preserving the seed of fire"; cf. the proper name *Sōsí-kleia*, quoted above p. 5; cf. also Vernant 1979: 64. The Greek word for "spark (used to kindle a fire)" is *zõpuron*, composed by *zõ(o)* -, "living", and *pûr*, "fire". Plato speaks of the survivors of the Flood as the "small sparks, *zõpura*, of mankind" (*Laws* III.677b).

ers and if her father dies, the girl who is in charge of the paternal fire must not marry into the house of another family. She becomes the "heiress" (*epíklēros*) of the house (Vernant 1965: 117-121). She must marry the next-of-kin of her dead father. No stranger's seed is admitted to keep the domestic fire alive. In fact, the son of the "heiress" will be considered not the grandson but the *son* of his biological maternal grandfather.[26]

We do not know whether Phrasikleia had any brothers capable of securing the continuation of their father's domestic cult. What we do know is that her relation to her father (dead or alive) is more close than ever by the fact that she has died a young girl, *koúrē* or *parthénos*. She will remain his daughter for ever. But as she is dead, she cannot of course look after the real paternal hearth. The fire she is in charge of is a metaphorical fire - a flower. However, as she is called Phrasikleia, this fire is at the same time a *kléos*, a "renown", her own renown as much as that of one or several ancestors, in short: the renown of her family. According to Proclus, "the names given to children by their fathers have the purpose of commemorating [something or somebody] or of expressing a hope or the like".[27] One illustration may suffice. Achilles' son Neoptolemos is named after the circumstance that his father was "young" (*néos*) when he first went to "war" (*pólemos*). At the same time, Neoptolemos is a suitable name for the boy who, like his father, was very young when he fought his first battle, thus coming up to the expectations attached to him, in a culture of mimesis, as the son of Achilles.[28]

---

[26] I cannot develop this theme here: let me just say that the constellation father/daughter/son-in-law/grandson (where the grandson is often named after his maternal grandfather) functions as a model for writing and reading, the daughter being the written word (*graphē*) of her father and his grandson being the *lógos* read out aloud by the son-in-law, identical with the reader (*entunkhánein* in fact means "read" and "have intercourse with", as in Plutarch, *Solonn*20.4, according to whom the husband of an "heiress" is supposed to have intercourse with her thrice a month). This legitimate grandson should be contrasted with the illegitimate children that a Greek is thought to beget if he dreams that he writes from right to left (Artemidorus, *Interpretation of dreams* III.25).

[27] Proclus, *Scholia to the Cratylus* 47.1xxxviii Pasquali, quoted by Sulzberger 1926:429.

[28] Sulzberger 1926: 389-390 quoting Pausanias X.26.4. The relation father/son is normally one of resemblance in ancient Greece: see *Od.* 4.141-144, Hesiod, *Works and Days* 182, etc.

Phrasikleia, then, "shows forth" a lotus flower, identical with the domestic fire, identical in its turn with her own and her family's *kléos*. This series of homologies is less arbitrary than it may appear. In Greek, one of the epithets of *kléos* is precisely *ásbeston*, "unquenchable" (*Od.* 4.584, 7.333), which means that *kléos* is considered to be a fire. But again the fire metaphor coexists with a vegetal metaphor: to the Greeks, *kléos* is also, and most significantly, defined as *áphthiton*, "unfading" (*Il* 9.413, etc.). It is like a plant that does not fade (Nagy 1974: 243). Phrasikleia's *kléos* is an unfading flower that no stranger will pluck.

Holding a flower in her hand, a flower unceasingly reborn, the flower of fire, the young girl thus enacts her *kléos* with a silent gesture. In fact, the gesture of her hand *mimes* her own name Phrasikleia. The entire *sêma* may be seen as the staging or figuration of her name. Phrasikleia shows forth her *kléos*, she looks after it lest - *ephrásato mě*, as one would say in Greek - it should go out; and the element *Phrasi-* in her name suggests that she succeeds in doing so, as it derives more directly from the aorist *phrásai* than from the present *phrázein*. Phrasikleia sees to it that her family remains alive in collective memory. She attracts the reader, triggers a reading aloud of the epigram, and in doing so she may well be said to give birth to a son called *Lógos*, the sonorous, eagerly longed-for descendant of her father. Hers is a marvellously efficacious writing, which produces a resounding *kléos* whenever it is read aloud.

The flower Phrasikleia holds in her hand is closed, not open. This is a significant distinction, as it suggests the mode of existence of the *sêma* itself, its double mode of existence:[29] through the Night of Oblivion, Phrasikleia's *kléos* waits patiently like a closed lotus flower for the Day of Recognition - the day of reading (*anágnōsis*), of thruth (*a-lĕtheia*) - when its meaning will be realized in the reading aloud of the epigram. Every reading aloud thus becomes an audible blossoming of meaning, in other words: true *kléos*. In fact, Homer uses the "blooming" of the voice as a recurrent metaphor, and it is worth noticing that it is used in contexts where a person is suddenly bereft of speech: "and her (his) blooming voice was held back", goes the formula (*thalerě dé hoi éskheto phōně*).[30] In Phrasikleia's case, the blooming of *kléos*

---

[29] A re-reading of Wellek & Warren 1962: 142-157 ("The mode of existence of the literary work of art") would not be uninteresting from this point of view.
[30] *Il* 17.696, 23.397, *Od.* 4.705, 19.472.

is also held back, as long as the epigram remains without a reader. In fact, every period that the *sêma* must endure in darkness, without readers and without spectators, is a state of waiting, where meaning is hardly more than a spark, a faint gleam - *nur zurückgeschraubt*, to use Rilke's very precise formula -, a seed of fire or a flower-cup ready to blossom. This veritable theory of the sign and its double mode of existence is "already" in the name *Phrasí-kleia*, where the first element refers to the world of silent signs, whereas the second one refers to the world of living sounds, of *kléos*, of reading aloud.

The contradiction contained in the name Phrasikleia was the challenge that the epigram writer and the sculptor accepted. They did it with such a zeal that even the categories of grammar are summoned to enact the passage from silent sign to vocal realization: the *sêma*, which designates itself as a first person,[31] shifts imperceptibly from the neuter to the feminine gender (*sêma* is neuter, *lakhoûsa* is feminine),[32] thus anticipating its own "return to life" in the act of reading. If we take this subtle movement into account, as well as the movement from silence to sound in the name Phrasikleia, we may finally venture the following interpretation of the girl's crown, where closed and open lotus flowers alternate in an "eternal" circle:[33] it is the *mise en scène* of the very functioning of the sepulchral *sêma*, whose meaning blooms or rekindles whenever its inscription is read out aloud.

---

[31] The signature of the *sêma* defines it as a first person: *Aristíõn Pári* [*ós m' ep*] *ó* [*ẽ*]*se*, "Aristíõn from Paros made me", where the restitution is guarantied by epigraphical as well as metrical factors. The regularity of the lettering does not admit for Jeffery's restitution without *m'* and with [*ie*] instead of [*e*] (Jeffery 1962:138) but suits perfectly the restitution quoted, first proposed by Lolling (Lolling 1876 and 1879) and adopted by Mastrokostas 1972:320. In fact, a second signature by Aristion reads *Aristíõn m' epóẽsen* (Pfohl 1967: 12 number 35). This forms an enhoplian (∪ - ∪ - ∪∪ - ∪) whereas *Aristíõn Páriós m' epóẽse* forms a reizianum preceded by an iambic metron (∪ - ∪ - | ∪ ∪ - ∪ ∪ - ∪); without the *m'* , the meter collapses (∪ - ∪ - | ∪ ∪ ∪ ∪ ∪ - ∪). See Moranti 1972.

[32] For an analogous movement, see Richter 1961: 165: "I am [the stele] of Phanodikos, son of Hermokrates, of Prokonnesos; and I gave a mixing bowl [...]." Cf. also Pfohl 1967: 8 (number 23), and (in the opposite direction) Pfohl 1967: 45 (number 128), 49 (number 139) and Lazzarini 1976: 315 (number 952).

[33] For the "eternity" of circular movement in Presocratic philosophy, see Alkmaion, fr. B 2 Diels-Kranz, and Parmenides, fr. B 5 Diels-Kranz.

Bibliography

Bechtel, Friedrich (1902) *Die attischen Frauennamen nach ihrem System dargestellt*, Göttingen.

Benveniste, Emile (1969) *Le vocabulaire des institutions indo-européennes*, volume 2, Paris.

Boeckh, August (1828) *Corpus Inscriptionum Graecarum*, volume 1, Berlin.

Borecky, Borivoj (1965) *Survivals of Some Tribal Ideas in Classical Greek* (Acta Universitatis Carolinae. Philosophica et historica, volume 10), Prague.

Burzachechi, Mario (1962) Oggetti parlanti nelle epigrafi greche, *Epigraphica*, volume 24, 3-54.

Chantraine, Paul (1968-1980) *Dictionnaire étymologique de la langue grecque*, Paris.

Cook, Arthur Bernard (1925) *Zeus. A Study in Greek Religion*, volume 2, Cambridge.

Daux, Georges (1973) Les ambiguïtés de grec κόρη, *Comptes rendus de l'Académie des Inscriptions et des Belles-Lettres*, 382-393.

Detienne, Marcel (1967) *Les Maîtres de vérité dans la Grèce archaïque*, Paris.

Detienne, Marcel (1984) Les lettres inventives de Palamède, *L'écriture, son autonomie, ses nouveaux objets intellectuels en Grèce ancienne* (to be published), symposion held in Paris, September 19-22, 1984.

Edwards, Ruth (1979) *Kadmos the Phoenician*, Amsterdam.

Fick, August (1894) *Die griechischen Personennamen nach ihrer Bildung erklärt*, 2nd edition, Göttingen.

Foucault, Michel (1969) *L'archéologie du savoir*, Paris.

Fournier, Henri (1946) *Les verbes "dire" en grec ancien*, doctoral dissertation, Paris.

Guarducci, Margherita (1967-1975) *Epigrafia greca*, volumes 1-3, Rome.

Guarducci, Margherita (1981) Dioniso e il loto, *Quaderni ticinesi di numismatica e antichità classica*, volume 10, 53-69.

Hellquist, Elof (1980) *Svensk etymologisk ordbok*, volume 1, 3rd edition, Lund.

Jacoby, Felix (1927) Skamon, *Paulys Real-Encyclopädie der classischen Altertumswissenschaft*, 2nd series, volume 3, 437, Stuttgart.

Jesper Svenbro

Jeffery, Lilian (1961) *The Local Scripts of Archaic Greece*, Oxford.
Jeffery, Lilian (1962) The Inscribed Gravestones of Archaic Attica, *Annals of the British School at Athens*, volume 57, 115-153.
Jeffery, Lilian (1967) Ἀρχαῖα γράμματα: Some Ancient Greek Views, *Europa. Festschrift für Ernst Grumach*, William C. Brice ed., 152-166, Berlin.
Knox, Bernard M. W. (1968) Silent Reading in Antiquity, *Greek, Roman and Byzantine Studies*, volume 9, 421-435.
Kontoleon, Nikolaos M. (1970) *Aspects de la Grèce préclassique*, Paris.
Kontoleon, Nikolaos M. (1974) Περὶ τὸ σῆμα τῆς φρασικλείας (Ἀπολογία μιᾶς ἑρμηνείας), *Ἀρχηαιολοκὴ Ἐφημερίς*, 1-12.
Lazzarini, Marialetizia (1976) *Le formule delle dediche votive nella Grecia arcaica* (Atti della Accademia nazionale dei Lincei. Memorie. Classe di scienze morali, storiche e filologiche, 8th series, volume 19, fascicle 2), Rome.
Lehrs, Karl (1865) *De Aristarchi studiis homericis*, 2nd edition, Leipzig.
Lévêque, Pierre and Vidal-Naquet, Pierre (1964) *Clisthène l'Athénien* (Annales littéraires de l'Université de Besançon, volume 65), Paris.
Liddell, Henry George and Scott, Robert and Jones, Henry Stuart *A Greek-English Lexicon*, Oxford.
Lolling, H. G. (1876) Der Künstler Aristion. *Mitteilungen des deutschen archäologischen Instituts. Athenische Abteilung*, volume 1, 174-175.
Lolling, H. G. (1879) Zum Grabstein der Phrasikleia, *Mitteilungen des deutschen archäologischen Instituts. Athenische Abteilung*, volume 4, 10.
Mastrokostas, Euthymios I. (1972) Myrrhinous: la koré Phrasikleia, oeuvre d'Aristion de Paros et un kouros de marbre, *Athens Annals of Archaeology*, volume 5, number 2, 298-324.
Moranti, Maria (1972) Formule metriche nelle iscrizioni greche arcaiche, *Quaderni Urbinati di cultura classica*, number 13, 7-23.
Nagy, Gregory (1974) *Comparative Studies in Greek and Indic Meter*, Cambridge (Mass).
Nagy, Gregory (1979) *The Best of the Achaeans*, Baltimore (Ma.) and London.
Nagy, Gregory (1983) *Sêma* and *nóēsis:* some illustrations, *Arethusa*, volume 5, number 1-2, 35-55.

Pfohl, Gerard (1967) *Greek Poems on Stones. I. Epitaphs. From the Seventh to the Fifth Centuries B.C.* (Textus minores, volume 36), Leiden.

Pfohl, Gerard (1969) Die ältesten Inschriften der Griechen, *Quaderni Urbinati di cultura classica*, number 7, 1969, 7-25.

Richter, Gisela M. A. (1961) *The Archaic Gravestones of Attica* (with an epigraphical Appendix by Margherita Guarducci), London.

Schachermeyer, Fritz (1937) Peisistratos, *Paulys Real-Encyclopädie der classischen Altertumswissenschaft*, volume 19, 156-191, Stuttgart.

Schmidt, J. H. Heinrich (1876) *Synonymik der griechischen Sprache*, volume 1, Leipzig.

Sulzberger, Max (1926) *"Ονομα ἐπώνυμον*. Les noms propres chez Homère et dans la mythologie grecque, *Revue des Etudes grecques*, volume 37, 381-447.

Svenbro, Jesper (1984) J'écris, donc je m'efface. L'énonciation dans les premières inscriptions grecques, *L'écriture, son autonomie, ses nouveaux objets intellectuels en Grèce ancienne* (to be published), symposium held in Paris, September 19-22, 1984.

Vernant, Jean-Pierre (1965) *Mythe et pensée chez les Grecs. Etudes de psychologie historique*, Paris.

Vernant, Jean-Pierre (1979) A la table des hommes, *La cuisine du sacrifice en pays grec*, Eds.: Marcel Detienne, Jean Pierre Vernant, 37-132, Paris.

Wellek, René and Warren, Austin (1962) *Theory of Literature*, 3rd edition, New York (N. Y.).

Phrasikleia. From Mastrokostas 1972: 313.

List of illustrations

Page 181: (1) "Knife Handle and Label of Stephen of Bulmer". Durham cathedral: 3.1. Spec. 72. Text printed in Raine (1852), appendix, p. 135. Date: 1150 x 1200. Reduced. (2) "Charter and Seal of Adam Son of Ilbert". Durham cathedral: 4.7. Spec. 9a. Text printed in Greenwell (1872), pp. 126-127. Date: 1150 x 1200. Reduced.

Page 246: Phrasikleia. From Mastrokostas 1972: 313.